Visions of
Heaven
Hell
and
Purgatory

Then I saw an Angel standing on the sun.
He cried out in a loud voice
to all the birds flying high overhead,
"Come here! Gather for God's great feast..."
Rev 19:17

Scripture passage from which
the cover art was taken.

Journeys of Faith®
1-800-633-2484
Bob & Penny Lord

Other Books by Bob and Penny Lord

THIS IS MY BODY, THIS IS MY BLOOD
Miracles of the Eucharist - Book I
THIS IS MY BODY, THIS IS MY BLOOD
Miracles of the Eucharist - Book II
THE MANY FACES OF MARY
a Love Story
WE CAME BACK TO JESUS
SAINTS AND OTHER POWERFUL WOMEN
IN THE CHURCH
SAINTS AND OTHER POWERFUL MEN
IN THE CHURCH
HEAVENLY ARMY OF ANGELS
SCANDAL OF THE CROSS AND ITS TRIUMPH
MARTYRS - THEY DIED FOR CHRIST
THE ROSARY - THE LIFE OF JESUS AND MARY
VISIONARIES, MYSTICS AND STIGMATISTS
ESTE ES MI CUERPO, ESTA ES MI SANGRE
Milagros de la Eucaristía
LOS MUCHOS ROSTROS DE MARIA
una historia de amor

ISBN 0-926143-84-0

Cover Art   *"The Angel Standing in the Sun"* - J.M.W. Turner
from Revelations 19:17-18

Table of Contents

Above: *Bob and Penny Lord at an audience with Pope John Paul II*
Below: *Bob and Penny Lord appearing with Mother Angelica at Eternal Word Television Network*

Dedication

God is so good. He puts so many people in our path to affirm us, give us courage and inspire us to continue when everything seems so difficult. We have never seen such obstacles as in the writing of this book. That it has been accomplished is only through the goodness of God, and the Angels, Production and otherwise, He sent to help us.

Pope John Paul II - Our Holy Father has been our inspiration from the beginning. To us, he is truly our "*Sweet Christ on Earth*". His Catholic Catechism has been a gift from the Holy Spirit to traditional Catholics. We pray for his good health, and long Pontificate.

Mother Angelica and the Sisters of Our Lady of the Angels Monastery - Mother has always been a strong supporter of our Ministry. She is spreading EWTN and EWRN to the whole world in fulfillment of the Bible passage in Revelations 14:6 - "*Then I saw another Angel flying high overhead, with everlasting good news to announce to those who dwell on earth, to every nation, tribe, tongue and people.*" We thank God that Mother has included us in her Mission.

Luz Elena Sandoval and Brother Joseph - Truly willing servants of the Lord, nothing in our Ministry would happen if it were not for these two committed laborers in the Lord's Vineyard. They are an integral part of our Community, totally consecrated to serving the Lord through our Ministry. Each day, with one mind, one heart, one spirit and one vision, we work side by side to evangelize the Church and the world.

To all the brothers and sisters who have helped us by their support of our Ministry, buying books and videos, attending our lectures and Missions, and watching our television programs, we could have done none of this without you.

We thank Our Lord for the loving support of our family, especially our grandchildren, **Rob and Andrea Ziminsky.**

I Believe in Life Everlasting

We were so overcome by the introduction to Article 12 in the Catholic Catechism, regarding the section in the Nicene Creed beginning with "*I believe in life everlasting*" that we wanted to place it in its entirety here.

"The Christian who unites his own death to that of Jesus views it as a step towards Him and an entrance into everlasting life. When the Church for the last time speaks Christ's words of pardon and absolution over the dying Christian, seals him for the last time with a strengthening anointing, and gives him Christ in viaticum as nourishment for the journey, she speaks with gentle assurance:

> "Go forth, Christian soul, from this world
> in the name of God the almighty Father,
> Who created you,
> in the name of Jesus Christ, the Son of the living God,
> Who suffered for you,
> in the name of the Holy Spirit
> Who was poured out upon you.
> God forth, faithful Christian!
>
> "May you live in peace this day,
> may your home be with God in Zion,
> with Mary, the virgin Mother of God,
> with Joseph, and all the Angels and Saints....
>
> "May you return to [your Creator]
> Who formed you from the dust of the earth.
> May holy Mary, the Angels, and all the Saints
> come to meet you as you go forth from this life...
> May you see your Redeemer face to face..."[1]

---

[1]Section 1020, Page 266, taken from Prayer of Commendation

Introduction

There was a newspaper article, around the turn of the century, addressed to a little girl who was asking if there was a Santa Claus. It began with *"Yes, Dorothy, there is a Santa Claus."* We'd like to begin this book with a statement, truer and more encouraging than the one to Dorothy. ***"Yes, my brothers and sisters, there is a Heaven, Hell and Purgatory."***

A great deal of interest has come about in this last decade of the Twentieth Century about **Heaven, Hell and Purgatory.** The controversy has run hot and heavy, to the point of a certain theologian ridiculing one of our most prestigious Cardinal Archbishops, John Cardinal O'Connor, in a national newsmagazine. However, to the best of our knowledge, that dissident theologian is no longer teaching in his university, and Cardinal O'Connor is still going strong.

On the other end of the spectrum there have been prophetic statements made that we are in the *end times*. In one of his visions, St. Don Bosco saw the world in ruins, a lone column standing above the rubble of destruction. On it the date 199- was engraved; the last number was not legible. There are only a few years left to this decade. According to St. Don Bosco's prophecy, there is not much time! *Is it hopeless; are we helpless?* Don Bosco had another vision:[1]

"He saw a large ship, with the Pope at the helm. Also, in his words,

"'In the midst of this endless sea, two solid columns, a short distance apart, soar high into the sky. On the one side, a statue of Our Lady, the Blessed Virgin, stands high above the sea. At her feet is a large inscription, which reads 'Auxilium Christianorumae' (Help of Christians). On the other side, and much higher, is a Giant Host, at the base of which is written 'Salus Credentiumae

---

[1]For more about Don Bosco's visions and life, turn to the chapter in this book and the one in *"Saints and other Powerful Men in the Church"*

(Salvation of Believers). The two columns stand tall and strong, warding off the thrashing of raging winds.'

"*St. John Bosco describes smaller ships surrounding the large ship and the columns. Many of them attack the flagship, while others defend it. No sooner is the Pope killed than he is replaced by another Pope. The battle continues. The new Pope tries to steer his ship between the two columns, but is having an extremely difficult time of it because of the constant pummeling by the furious hurricane. Finally, he succeeds in bringing his ship between the columns. He ties it up at each column. The wind cries out a bloodcurdling shriek, heard round the world, and dies. The enemy ships scatter in great fear, their battle lost, while the defending ships sing out praises to Our Lord Jesus, as they, too, tie up at the posts. A peaceful calm blankets the sea.*"[2]

St. Louis Marie de Montfort prophesied about the apostles of the last days:

"*....towards the end of the world, ...Almighty God and His holy Mother are to raise up saints who will surpass in holiness most other saints as much as the cedars of Lebanon tower above little shrubs.*"

"*These great souls filled with grace and zeal will be chosen to oppose the enemies of God who are raging on all sides. They will be exceptionally devoted to the Blessed Virgin. Illumined by her light, strengthened by her spirit, supported by her arms, sheltered under her protection, they will fight with one hand and build with the other. With one hand they will give battle, overthrowing and crushing heretics and their heresies, schismatics and their schisms, idolaters and their idolatries, sinners and their wickedness. With the other hand they will build the temple of the true*

---

[2]From the chapter: "*Mary's Back, and She's Stronger Than Ever*"-the book: "*The Many Faces of Mary, a love story.*"

Solomon and the mystical city of God, namely, the Blessed Virgin... "

"They will be like thunder-clouds flying through the air at the slightest breath of the Holy Spirit. Attached to nothing, surprised at nothing, they will shower down the rain of God's word and of eternal life. They will thunder against sin; they will storm against the world; they will strike down the devil and his followers and for life and for death, they will pierce through and through with the two-edged sword of God's word all those against whom they are sent by Almighty God."

"They will be true apostles of the latter times to whom the Lord of Hosts will give eloquence and strength to work wonders and carry off glorious spoils from His enemies. They will sleep without gold or silver and, more important still, without concern in the midst of other priests, ecclesiastics and clerics. Yet they will have the silver wings of the dove enabling them to go wherever the Holy Spirit calls them, filled as they are, with the resolve to seek the glory of God and the salvation of souls. Wherever they preach, they will leave behind them nothing but the gold of love, which is the fulfillment of the whole law."

"They will have the two-edged sword of the Word of God in their mouths and the blood-stained standard of the Cross on their shoulders. They will carry the crucifix in their right hand and the rosary in their left, and the holy names of Jesus and Mary on their heart.

"Mary scarcely appeared in the first coming of Christ... But in the second coming of Jesus Christ, Mary must be known and openly revealed by the Holy Spirit so that Jesus may be known, loved and served through her."[3]

---

[3] an excerpt from Bob and Penny Lord's book:*"Visionaries, Mystics and Stigmatists"*

The days sound like *now*; the apostles sound like Mary's Army. The battle lines are clearly drawn. The Lord is gathering up an army of believers to defend the Church in this, the last great battle of the end of the Second Millennium. *When the Saints come marching in, will you be among their number?*

If we were to use the prophecies attributed to St. Malachy, the Irish saint of the Twelfth Century, his controversial predictions regarding the descendants of Peter- the Popes and the Papacy, we would have to believe we are truly in the last days. He prophesied:

"In the final persecution of the Holy Roman Church there will reign Peter the Roman, who will feed his flock among many tribulations; after which the seven-hilled city will be destroyed and the dreadful Judge will judge the people."[4]

[When we attended Holy Mass with his Holiness, at the beginning of his Papacy, he called himself a *Roman*! He had just returned from his first trip to his beloved Poland!]

Fr. Stephen Gobbi, founder of the Marian Movement of Priests, had an inner locution at Lourdes in 1989, in which he said Our Lady talked about these next eleven years, as times of difficulty, trial and tribulation. According to these figures, that would bring us to the year 2,000. While Our Lord Jesus tells us that no one knows the day or the time of the end of the world,[5] many of the prophecies in the Book of Revelations regarding the last days, in particular the prophesies of the seven plagues in Chapter 16, as well as Our Lord's description of the end of the world,[6] would give us reason to pause and reflect on the possibility that we're coming closer and closer to that time.

---

[4]Prophecies of St. Malachy
[5]Mark 13:32
[6]Luke 21:8-33

Because so many people believe that these are truly the last days, that all the occurrences we've mentioned above, plus much more that we haven't mentioned, are just around the corner, that we're approaching the angry Jesus that we see in the Last Judgment in the Sistine Chapel-the God of Judgment and not the Jesus of Divine Mercy, we should begin taking very seriously the way we're living our lives, and what we can expect for our final judgment - reward or punishment. In the final analysis, we have only three options: *Heaven, Hell or Purgatory.*

Not very many people have seen *Heaven, Hell or Purgatory.* We believe, it's extremely important that you know, as much as the *Church* can possibly tell you, about the place where you might spend eternity, so that you can protect yourself from any incorrect information you may receive from false locutionists, visionaries or prophets.

We have researched and want to share with you visions of *Heaven, Hell and Purgatory,* as dictated by the most reliable sources we have, the *Saints* and accepted *Visionaries* who have passed the test of time. We also want you to get the *Catholic perspective* on these most important subjects, which will have such an important effect on your eternity. For this, we've gone through Council documents as written in the Catholic Catechism and the Catholic Encyclopedia. We want to be sure that the information we give you is the authentic teaching-the Magisterium of the Church.

We really try not to write controversial books. What we write about are the *truths* of the Church. And sadly, for the last two thousand years, many have found the Truth controversial, as passed down by Jesus Christ, and have left the Catholic Church, founded their own Church with their own concepts, only to have others find *their* Church controversial and form *another* Church, and on and on. And so, the Lord Who died for all of us, still weeps, as He did over Jerusalem.

Why a book on *Heaven, Hell and Purgatory?* Again, it's because all three are either being doubted, disputed, denied or grossly distorted, with us the innocent lambs being led to the slaughter, as the controversy continues. Every time we felt that one of our Heavenly Family was being attacked, we wrote a book, thinking no one would buy it, but feeling the obligation, nevertheless, to defend one of our Heavenly Family. Did you prove us wrong!

You love the Eucharist and not only bought and keep on buying Book I of **"This is My body, This is My Blood,** *Miracles of the Eucharist*", but Book II as well.

Many told us that another book on Mary would not sell. Well, there again you showed us what a hunger you had to know more about Mother Mary and our personal relationship with her, as well as those to whom she appeared, as you ordered and reordered and continue to reorder **"The Many Faces of Mary,** *a love story*."

The existence of Angels was being denied altogether. They, who are mentioned in Scripture 320 times, were being passed off as myths. We wrote **"Heavenly Army of Angels."** We found that there were more Angel lovers than we would ever have thought possible. It was the same with the **Saints**, the **Martyrs** and the **Visionaries**. We are told that these books and television programs have filled the void that was left when the Supernatural was not taught in our churches, anymore. Always the same response, you had such a thirst, to know more.

We were amazed when you responded so overwhelmingly to our book on the Heresies that have attacked the Church up to and including today, **"Scandal of the Cross and It's Triumph"**.

Well, here we go again. The battle rages. There are those who are faithfully teaching the Magisterium of the Church, and others preaching a magisterium of their own, with every tenet of our Faith under attack. For some unknown reason, it is all-out war against the existence of Angels, *Heaven, Hell and Purgatory*. Are the dark lurking powers of evil trying to destroy all semblance of the Supernatural in our Church? We believe the Lord is calling us again to defend all that we believe in!

We pray that you will read this book and recommend that others read it, too. We must all have *someone* in Purgatory. When was the last time you asked for a Mass to be said for the Poor Souls in Purgatory? When was the last time you asked for prayers or Masses for members of your family, who are deceased? When was the last time you offered up a *Plenary Indulgence* for the deceased?

We do not want anyone to go to Hell. We all seek eternal life in Heaven with our Heavenly Family. We have a responsibility to reveal, to *everyone*, these important teachings that the Church has always taught and upheld. Confused over who and what to believe? Read ahead about the Saints who had *Visions of Heaven, Hell and Purgatory*.

Is there a place called Heaven? Is there really a place called Hell? And how about Purgatory, do we still teach that? These questions trouble us. But why would our families and friends not have doubts on the existence of *Heaven, Hell and Purgatory*? Some of our Twentieth Century heretics have made it their life's work disputing the existence of the Angels, the devil, God as a Father, Adam and Eve and the Fall, whether Jesus rose from the dead in Body and Spirit, is Jesus really Present in the Eucharist, and on and on, until they've picked us clean; there is nothing left for us to believe; we are truly dried up bones. And if they would dare strike at the heart of the Church and her teachings, then, why wouldn't they attack *Heaven, Hell and Purgatory!*

If there is no Hell, then is there a Heaven? Is this, our time on earth, all there is? Can you imagine the despair of a family who has lost a child, a husband, a wife, or a parent, if this were so? Can you feel the utter hopelessness of

someone suffering intense pain from a terminal illness, if he
or she could not look forward to a Heaven without pain and
suffering?   Can you comprehend the endless helplessness
and loneliness of a poor destitute soul with no home, no
family, no one to love or be loved by, no one who cares, all
alone, with very little on earth, if this is all there is? Can you
envision the sheer terror of a poor dying soul who has lost
his or her belief in life after death?

There are those who pridefully teach that there is no
Heaven, Hell and Purgatory, no personal devil; and then we
wonder why there is so much sin on earth, murder and
violence in our streets. If there is no reward or punishment,
why obey laws?   We look to Science to heal plagues
spreading throughout our world, when the real remedy is the
healing of the soul. We spend millions trying to keep people
alive, and ignore our life after death, our *eternal life*. Is it
because we are being taught, there is nothing after this life;
or is it because it is put in terms sounding like double-talk
that only the theologian speaking or writing can understand?

As we researched these Saints, who have had visions of
Heaven, Hell or the *Souls in Purgatory*, we read how they had
visions of the devil attacking them as they lay dying; we see
how their unending faith in the Lord and His Promise
sustained them at their last moments. We discovered how
many times the *Poor Souls*, of even people known for their
piety on earth, would appear to those on earth, pleading for
their prayers and for Masses to be said for them to alleviate
their pain in Purgatory.

Is there a Purgatory? To those who dispute the existence
of Purgatory, then what? Are they saying that everyone is
going to Heaven, that everyone is ready to be in the
presence of the Spotless Lamb? Suppose someone dies in
an accident? *Is everyone in a state of Grace?* Your parents
and grandparents, relatives and friends who have gone on
before you, were they ready to enter the Kingdom? Would

it be God's Will they be thrown into the pits of Hell, or receive that gift of Compassion from the God of Mercy, Purgatory? In this book, we will endeavor to include Mother Church's teachings, from the very beginning.

We believe that Purgatory is a gift of God's Love, a place where we can pay our debts, a place where we can be made presentable to greet our Bridegroom in Heaven. You will read how the Poor Souls *desire* to go to Purgatory, because they do not want to appear before the Lord in debt. In centuries past, a pilgrim had to get his house in order and pay all outstanding debts before he could leave for a pilgrimage, to be debt-free. Does it not stand to reason that we would do the same for our great pilgrimage to Heaven?

The Poor Souls do not want Jesus to see them with soil on their souls. Do you remember the day that you were married, how carefully you prepared for that moment when your spouse would see you at the altar? You were spotlessly clean, looking beautiful, innocent, pure, and virtuous in your long white gown. Do you remember your spouse's eyes when you reached his side? As the poor soul prepares to face her eternal Spouse Jesus, she too, desires to appear before the Lord in a white robe, cleansed of all her imperfections, no stain of venial sins or faults remaining.

Do you remember going to confession before the Nuptial Mass, so that there would be no sin left on your soul that could wound the other? You knew that sin does not content itself with only one soul but like a glutton devours the other and then another. You wanted to wipe the slate clean so that the two of you could begin your new life. You wanted nothing to stand between you and your spouse that could jeopardize a holy life together. How much more so, with our Heavenly Spouse, Jesus and *our* eternal life together!

Is there a Heaven? Jesus made a promise, and we believe Him! He rose from the dead that we might also look forward to our Resurrection. Think of what Saint Paul said:

"But if Christ is preached as raised from the dead, how can some among you say there is no Resurrection? If there is no Resurrection of the dead, then neither has Christ been raised. And if Christ has not been raised, then empty (too) is our preaching; empty, too, is your faith. Then we are also false witnesses to God, because we testified against God that He raised Christ, Whom He did not raise if in fact the dead are not raised. For if the dead are not raised, neither has Christ been raised...and if Christ has not been raised, your faith is in vain; you are still in your sins."[7]

Is there a Hell? It is referred to as the nether world in the Old Testament *sixty-nine* times!

In The Song of Moses, we hear God saying: *"For by My wrath a fire is enkindled that shall rage to the depths of the nether world, consuming the earth with its yield, and licking with flames the roots of the mountains."*[8]

Do we choose to ignore this warning? God was angry with His children. He gave them His Love, always the faithful God to an unfaithful people. He delivered them from slavery. How did they respond? They worshiped false idols! How many times has God forgiven us? How many times has He allowed His Mother to hold back His wrath?

If we say there is no Hell, we make Jesus a liar. In the New Testament we read *seven* times, Hell being referred to as the netherworld and *twelve* times as Gehenna.[9] In Revelation, we see Hell referred to as Hades, *three* times.[10] Why are some disputing the Word of God? Jesus said:

---

[7]1Cor 15:12-17
[8]Deut 32:22
[9]Matt 5:22,29,30 Matt 10:28 Matt 18:9 Matt 23:15,33
  Matt 9:43,45,47 Luke 12:5, James 3:6
[10]Rev 6:8, Rev 20:13,14

"And as for you, Caphernaum:
  "Will you go to Heaven?
  "You will go down to the netherworld (Hell).
  "For if the mighty deeds done in your midst
  had been done in Sodom,
  it would have remained till this day."[11]

Why do some insist there is no Hell? Are they fearful of Jesus' words to Caphernaum? Do His words convict them? Do they convict us? Is He speaking to us, as the sinful Sodom of today? Will we have to apologize to Sodom and Gomorrah? Are we the new Caphernaum that walked out on Him when He spoke what they judged, too hard to bear? The mighty deeds that Jesus speaks of were the miracles, He performed there. Do we not have the greatest Miracle in our midst during the Holy Mass? Are we not condemned? Is the whole world not condemned? For on some altar, somewhere in the four corners of the world, every minute of the day, the Sacrifice of the Mass is bringing Jesus to us, truly present in the Eucharist. Are we accepting Jesus as He comes to us *vulnerably* under the appearances of a piece of bread and a cup of wine? Are we taking seriously the words of Jesus at Caphernaum? *"Unless you eat the Flesh of the Son of Man and drink His Blood, you have no life in you."[12]* Read again His words to Caphernaum and allow Jesus to place this as a stamp on your heart.

Is Our Lord bringing us fair warning and true hope? Is He using this book and the visions that the Saints had of *Heaven, Hell and Purgatory* to reach out to you, to your family, to the Church, to the world? Does He want you to live with His Justice as well as His Mercy in the forefront of your mind? Is He calling you and me to change? Please read on. *We love you.*

---

[11]Matt 11:23
[12]John 6:53

Left:
**St. John the Evangelist's
vision of Heaven**
I heard a loud voice from
the throne cry out: *"This is
God's dwelling among men.
He shall dwell with them
and they shall be his people
and He shall be their God,
who is always with them.
He shall wipe every tear
from their eyes, and there
shall be no more death or
mourning, crying out or
pain, for the former world
has passed away."
The One who sat on the
throne said to me, "See, I
make all things new!"*
Rev 21:3-5

Below: *Vision of Heaven on
the ceiling of Chiesa Nuova
in Rome - The Church
where St. Philip Neri
preached*

Is there a Heaven?

The Church Triumphant

A rainbow is a promise. God our Father reaffirmed the promise He made about our Redemption in the Garden of Eden[1] when Noah landed on the rock after having spent forty days and forty nights in the ark during the flood. The Lord stopped the rain, and gave us a double rainbow.

"God said: *'Here is the sign of the Covenant I make between Myself and every living creature with you for all generations; I set My bow in the clouds and it shall be a sign of the Covenant between Myself and you and every living creature of every kind."*[2]

Our Lord Jesus fulfilled the promise that God the Father made. As he committed to St. Dismas, the good thief, from the Cross, He also pledges to us*:

"Indeed, I promise you, this day you will be with Me in Paradise."*[3]

We believe that when we die, when we *shake off this mortal coil,*[4] we go to the next step in our eternal existence, from a physical, bodily life, to a new life, a new beginning.

We read that in Heaven we will know perfect happiness. We will see God in His *Beatific Vision*, in the fullness of His Glory. St. Thomas Aquinas, after having a vision of Heaven, stopped writing his Summa Theologiae, and stated to one of the brothers, *"The end of my labors has come. All that I have written appears to be as so much straw after the things that have been revealed to me."*[5]

No wonder the Saints could hardly wait to die. We can experience this to some degree right here on earth. St.

---

[1]Gen 3:15
[2]Gen 9:12-15
[3]Luke 22:43
[4]William Shakespeare - Hamlet
[5]Butler's Lives of the Saints

Teresa of Avila would get impatient with those who cried *"Oh if I could have just walked with Jesus when He walked the earth."* She would ask them if they did not know that they carry Him within, after they receive Him in Holy Communion and are with Him after the Host turns into Jesus' Body, Blood, Soul and Divinity? Don't they know He is in the Blessed Sacrament exposed on the Altar?

At that moment in the Mass, when the priest raises the Host in consecration, the overpowering Truth envelops me: He has arrived! The Lord of my life will agree to enter this weak and humble abode that I call my body and He and I will be one, in a few minutes. We believe that this moment, that of the Consecration of the Mass, when Jesus comes down on the altar under the form of bread and wine, is also the time when the Communion of Saints are most closely bound together. We believe that we, the *Church Militant*, kneel on one side of the altar, and that our brothers and sisters, the Saints, and our cousins, the Angels, who together form the *Church Triumphant*, kneel on the other side of the curtain which separates Heaven and earth. We gaze at Jesus in the Blessed Sacrament, and they gaze at Jesus in the Beatific Vision. We are most in communion with each other, as we adore our God together. We are also strongest at that time. We truly live the words of St. Paul: *"Because there is one bread, we who are many are one body, for we all partake of the one bread."*[6] We can feel the oneness of the Body of Christ.

At other times, we can feel our hearts beat fast when we kneel before Our Lord in the Blessed Sacrament as He is so regally being processed. Tears come to our eyes when the priest or bishop raises the Monstrance and blesses us. All we can think is, *It is the Lord; It is the Lord!* This is the closest we can come to experiencing He Whom we will know in

---

[6]1Cor 10:17

Heaven. Our hearts could not stand it, were we to see Him as we will in Heaven. They would burst with joy and ecstasy. And so, our merciful and generous Lord gives us a glimpse of Himself to prepare us for that great and glorious day when we will stand Face to face.[7]

Some questions most asked are: "How close to the Lord will I be in Heaven? Will I know the Lord like the Saints know Him?" It reminds us of the time when the mother of James and John asked of Jesus:

"Command that these two sons of mine sit, one at Your right and the other at Your left, in Your kingdom."[8]

You recall He replied to James and John:

"...to sit at My right and My left, this is not Mine to give but it is for those for whom it has been prepared by My Father."[9]

How well do you know Jesus on earth? Is He your priority? Who is your God? Is it god with a small "g" or the One and true God with a capital "G" Whom you worship? In Paul's letters to the Romans, he answers this question most clearly:

"For those who live according to the flesh are concerned with the things of the flesh, but those who live according to the spirit with the things of the spirit. The concern of the flesh is death, but the concern of the spirit is life and peace."[10]

How much time do you spend on matters of the spirit, of eternal life, in preparation for life with the Lord in Heaven? And how much time do you spend on the preservation of the body, the flesh that is decaying and passing away? It is the spirit which remains with us, our soul.

---

[7]1Cor 13:12
[8]Matt 20:21
[9]Matt 20:23
[10]Romans 8:5-6

How much time do you spend getting to know Jesus? Do you spend any time visiting Him in the Tabernacle; or, if you are so blessed, adoring Him in the Blessed Sacrament exposed on the Altar? How do you answer His cry to His trusted Disciples to spend an hour with Him? Will He look at you when you meet and ask you the same question He asked of them: "*So you could not keep watch with Me for one hour?*"[11] Then, will you not want to go to Purgatory to wipe away the times that you have put things of the world before Him?

It's funny, we wouldn't ask one spouse if we had the same relationship with his (or her) spouse. We respect the time they have spent together, the many years they have known one another, how they have laughed and cried together, shared so many crosses and enjoyed so many resurrections. We know that no one could be as close as they are. Is it difficult to believe that it would come to pass that those who have loved the Lord more on earth will love Him more and have more of Him in Heaven? As you cannot love someone you do not know, the more you have gotten to know Him on earth, the greater capacity you will have to love Him in Heaven. It makes sense! A thimble full of liquid is as full as a gallon jug. One is not fuller than the other, but one takes in a greater capacity than the other. The Mercy of God in Heaven is that you will never know what you are missing. If you did, it would not be Heaven; it would not be perfect happiness. We believe you will have the fullness of His Love, but is it to the fullness of how much you have loved Him? No one really knows; but what do you think?

For me, I want to have the most of Him in Heaven and on earth that I, in my imperfections and weaknesses, can

---

[11]Matt 26:40

possibly have. I walk confident, with faith in my Lord Jesus and in St. Paul's words which reassure us,

"And the One who searches hearts knows what is the intention of the Spirit, because it intercedes for the holy ones according to God's Will."[12]

Whatever He deigns to give me, I know I will be ecstatic, for I know that the love that He has for me, and for you, far surpasses our hopes and dreams. He is the Cup of Love Which runs over. We can not drink enough to empty the cup of never-ending love which He pours out to us.

To me, Heaven must be like when we are about to go on a pilgrimage. Our pilgrimages have always been longer than just the weeks at the Shrines, because we are preparing months before, in anticipation of what is to come. Do we look upon Heaven in the same way? If we do, then we will be able to sample a little bit of Heaven right here on earth. When we instruct pilgrims to prepare for their pilgrimage, we always suggest they read background material on the Saints or the Apparitions or perhaps the Miracles of the Eucharist so that when they arrive at the Shrine, they will know and understand more what the Lord has in store for them; and in so doing, will get so much more out of their pilgrimage.

Our time on earth is a pilgrimage to our final Home, with Heaven in our sights. We need someone with experience to guide us on a pilgrimage to the Shrines. What makes us think we can find our way to Heaven without assistance? If you go on a pilgrimage which turns out instead to be a tour, with a guide who knows little about the Shrines and the Apparitions, the Saints and the Miracles, etc., then you will not receive all that the Lord, His Mother, the Angels and the Saints have prepared for you at the different Shrines. Heaven is the Shrine, we all long to go to, where we will be in the company of the Lord and His whole Heavenly

---

[12]Romans 8:27

Will we know Him and them? As most of us studied long and hard to learn professions, so that we could live more fully our time on earth, do we not think it worth it to spend the rest of our lives learning about our Faith, so that we will live more fully our eternal time in Heaven?

Heaven and Holy Scripture

Heaven is mentioned frequently in Holy Scripture.

Jesus spoke of Heaven when He was delivering the Sermon on the Mount, in one of the Beatitudes:

"Blessed are the poor in spirit, for theirs is the kingdom of heaven."[13]

Then in John's Gospel, Jesus refers to Heaven as His Father's house:

*"In **My Father's house** there are many dwelling places. If there were not, would I have told you that I am going to prepare a place for you?"*[14]

In St. Peter's epistle, we hear Heaven once again mentioned, as the crown of glory:

*"And when the chief Shepherd is revealed, you will receive the **unfading crown of glory**."*[15]

St. Paul mentions Heaven repeatedly, as he brings hope to us, for ourselves and our loved ones. He also teaches what will be required from us to achieve that *crown of glory*:

*"But if Christ is in you, although the body is dead because of sin, the **spirit is alive** because of righteousness."*

*"If the Spirit of the One Who raised Jesus from the dead dwells in you, the One Who raised Christ from the dead will give life to your mortal bodies also, through **His Spirit** that dwells in you."*[16]

---

[13]Matt 5:3
[14]John 14:2
[15]Peter 5:4
[16]Romans 8:10-11

*"The Spirit itself bears witness with our spirit that we are children of God, and if children, then heirs, heirs of God and joint heirs with Christ, if only we suffer with Him so that we may also be **glorified** with Him."*

*"I consider that the sufferings of this present time are as nothing compared with the **glory** to be revealed for us."*[17]

*"Those He predestined He likewise called; those He called He also justified; and those He justified He in turn **glorified**."* [18]

St. Paul speaks of the mission of God's children, to be pure of heart and purpose:

"Thus should one regard us: as servants of Christ and stewards of the mysteries of God. Now it is of course required that they be found trustworthy.

"It does not concern me in the least that I be judged by you or any human tribunal; I do not even pass judgment on myself; I am not conscious of anything against me, but I do not stand acquitted; the One Who judges me is the Lord.

"Therefore, do not make any judgment before the appointed time, until the Lord comes, for He will bring to light what is hidden in the darkness and will manifest the motives of our hearts, and then everyone will receive praise from God."[19]

St. Paul speaks of God's Love for us, and our response to that Love. He reiterates what we have been saying: The degree of that love which each of us will receive will correspond directly to the quality of our love for Him.

But what do we consider God's Love? We all want to go to Heaven but we do not want to die to the world and its allure, its demands, its false promises. We want to know Jesus in the good times but like the apostles we have a

---

[17]Romans 8:16-18
[18]Romans 8:30
[19]1Cor 4:1-5

tendency to run away from Him when He asks us to help carry His Cross. St. Paul's words are as vital today, as at that time. We know that Paul's time of evangelization was, like that of his Savior, one of suffering, rejection and persecution. He stressed that man could not go to Heaven on his own but solely through Jesus Christ interceding to the Father. As Jesus Crucified saved us on the Cross, so Paul preached we must all go through the Cross, our own cross. And so he preached:

"I determined that while I was with you, I would speak of nothing but Jesus Christ and Him crucified."[20]

St. Paul humbly tells the Corinthians that as he came to them, preaching in his weakness, full of fear and apprehension, lacking the eloquence and persuasiveness to win them over; it was not he, but *"the Spirit"* Who had convinced them. Therefore their faith lay not in the wisdom of men but in the *"power of God."* Clearly defining God's wisdom, he said:

"It is not a wisdom of this age, however, nor of the rulers of this age, who are men headed for destruction."[21]

He goes on:

"No, what we utter is God's wisdom: a mysterious, a hidden wisdom. God planned it before all ages for our glory.[22] None of the rulers of this age knew the mystery; if they had known it, they would never have crucified the Lord of Glory."[23]

How many crucify Jesus by crucifying His Church? Do they know the mystery? Do they believe?

St. Paul speaks of Heaven when he writes:

"Of this wisdom, it is written:

'Eye has not seen, ear has not heard,

---

[20]1Cor 2:2
[21]1Cor 2:6
[22]that we might be one day in Heaven with Him
[23]1Cor 2:7-8

nor has it so much as dawned on man
what God has prepared for those who love Him. "[24]

Heaven and the Catholic Catechism

The Doctrine of Heaven is distinctly spelled out in the Catholic Catechism. We read:

"By virtue of our Apostolic authority, we define the following:

According to the general disposition of God, the souls of all the saints...and other faithful who died after receiving Christ's holy Baptism (provided they were not in need of purification when they died,...or, if they then did need or will need some purification, when they have been purified after death,...) already before they take up their bodies again and before the general judgment - and this since the Ascension of our Lord and Savior Jesus Christ into Heaven - have been, are and will be in Heaven, in the Heavenly Kingdom and celestial Paradise with Christ, joined to the company of the Holy Angels. Since the Passion and death of our Lord Jesus Christ, these souls have seen and do see the divine essence with an intuitive vision, and even face to face, without the mediation of any creature."[25]

One of the references in the Catholic Catechism is from Vatican II, *Lumen Gentium 49*:

"*When the Lord will come in glory, and all His Angels with Him, death will be no more and all things will be subject to Him. But at the present time some of His disciples are pilgrims on earth. Others have died and are being purified, while still others are in glory, contemplating 'in full light, God Himself triune and one, exactly as He is.'...Once received into their Heavenly home and being present to the Lord, through Him and with Him and in*

---

[24]1Cor 2:9
[25]Pg 267 - 1023 - Pope Benedict XII - Benedictus Deus (1336)

*Him they do not cease to intercede with the Father for us,
as they proffer the merits which they acquired on earth
through the one mediator between God and men, Christ
Jesus..."*

Heaven and the New Catholic Encyclopedia

The New Catholic Encyclopedia, considered one of the
most valid and soundest sources of information on the
Church, breaks up their article on Heaven into two parts, (1)
Heaven as the culmination of Salvation History, and (2)
State of Heavenly Glory, or the Beatific Vision, which is
covered in the next section. So in this paragraph, we'll
confine ourselves to Heaven as the culmination of **Salvation
History**.

*"Heaven is the state of happiness of those who have died
in Christ. Although it is also a place, this is of secondary
importance...We understand Heaven as the final state of
those who die in Christ by reference to the final state of
Christ Himself, Who is the Savior and Head of His
Mystical Body. It is only as members of the Mystical Body
of Christ that we can die in Christ; hence it is only as such
that we can enter the state of Heavenly glory. Thus we
conceive Heaven as the state of happiness that brings full,
lasting satisfaction to the whole of our being through our
union with the Holy Trinity in Christ together with all the
members of the Mystical Body.*

*"Heaven is the fulfillment of the life of grace on this
earth, that life of union with the Blessed Trinity through
Christ that all His members have in common. It is the
fulfillment of God's salvific plan for the whole world;
hence Heaven exists in the fullest sense only after the
Parousia[26] of Christ at the end of the world. Thereafter*

---

[26]The fullness or completion of the salvation of man in the history of
the world whereby the humanity of Christ the Savior and Messiah
revealed in His glory and in His Church is now manifest and fulfilled in

there shall be the restoration of the body, now a glorified body, to each who is saved, and even the fabric of this world, likewise restored, will probably be part of Heaven."

The Beatific Vision

We are taught that in Heaven our happiness will come, first and foremost, from our complete union with God, our spirit overflowing with His Love, at last beholding Him as He is in His Beatific Vision.

Pope Benedict XII declared the Church's teaching concerning Heaven in his constitution, *"The Blessed God."* Using Holy Scripture, he declared that the blessed:

"see God's Essence directly, and face to face,[27] *and thus the souls of the departed enjoy the Divine nature, and are thereby rendered truly happy in the possession of eternal life and peace."*

The New Catholic Encyclopedia and the Beatific Vision

"Theologians all teach that the essential element in the state of Heavenly glory is the union with the Blessed Trinity in mind and heart, (called the Beatific Vision, the Beatific love) resulting in the Beatific joy; they further teach that other factors round off this bliss, notably the glorification of the body and the enjoyment of the renewed universe and the company of the blessed. Although essential glory is possessed by all who die in the state of grace as soon as their purification (purgatory) is completed, the fullness of glory is theirs only after Christ's Parousia, when they receive back their bodies in the reconstituted universe."

If you read carefully, you'll find writings from the Catholic Catechism and the New Catholic Encyclopedia which affirm beliefs you've had all your life, but have not lately been able to defend, because you didn't know where

---

the revelation of Christ as God and Ruler of Heaven - Catholic Encyclopedia - Broderick

[27]cf.1Cor 13:12

the writings could be found. We have always believed that we would be in Heaven, body and soul. We have always believed that Heaven was a place, but many of us were shot down when we could not prove it. We'd hear things like, *"Oh, where is Heaven? Can you take the interstate or freeway to get there? Do you make a left turn at Purgatory?"* Well, here it is, folks, right in the Catechism and New Catholic Encyclopedia. We've always known that Our Lord Jesus and Our Lady were taken up into Heaven, Body and Soul. But we could never figure out where they would be. As the New Catholic Encyclopedia stated,

> *"Because Christ and Our Lady are now glorified in Body and because a body requires a place in which to dwell, Church tradition, following the language of Scripture, has constantly taught that Heaven is a place."*

†

These are some very powerful teachings. You may say to yourself, *"This is not the kind of reading we expect from Bob and Penny."* And you would be right. Normally, we don't get into such heady matters as what we're quoting above. But this is such an important subject, we can't take a chance of mis-stating what the Church is teaching, or having you misunderstand what we're saying. When you have to defend your beliefs about *Heaven, Hell and Purgatory*, which are very explosive subjects in certain circles, we don't want your only line of defense to be, *"Well, we read about it in Bob and Penny's book."*

It's true; you did. And you can be sure we would never lead you astray. But we got it from these very reliable sources. And none of this can be considered old-fashioned beliefs, or that we're dating ourselves. [Author's note: Once Penny was sharing about our beliefs in the teachings of the

Magisterium[28] and she was told by a very sophisticated person in this really droll voice, "*Oh, Penny don't use that term. You're dating yourself.*" Well, we don't want you to be accused of dating yourself. But if the new Catholic Catechism can use references from the various Councils of the Church, in this instance the Council of Florence (1439) and the Council of Trent (1536), two powerful Councils in the Church; that's good enough for us, and it's good enough for you.]

We want you to know the experiences of the Saints who had *Visions of Heaven, Hell and Purgatory.* We want to share those beautiful gifts with you. But we also want you to have a solid foundation in the Faith of the Doctrines of *Heaven, Hell and Purgatory.* We've spent a year researching these dogmas of our Church, so that you can use them in defense of our beliefs. We've indexed them, and inserted footnotes showing where certain teachings came from. You don't have to stand by with egg on your face while someone tells you that you don't know what you're talking about because you don't have a degree in Theology. As Mother Angelica says, "*All you need is the Bible and the Catholic Catechism!*" and that's where our information comes from. Read on, brothers and sisters, the best is yet to come.

---

[28]Magisterium - The power given by Christ to the Church together with infallibility by which the Church teaches authoritatively the revealed truth of the Scripture and holds forth the truth of tradition for salvation. This fact is contained in the nature and extent of the mission given to the Church (Matt 28:19-20) and the recognized acceptance of that mission as recorded in the Acts of the Apostles - Catholic Encyclopedia - Broderick)

Above:
A vision of the seven levels of Hell by Fra Angelico

Is there a Hell?

Of the three categories we are writing about in this book, the most frightening, and the one we really don't want to hear about is *Hell!* And Satan has been working overtime in this century denying his existence, and more than that, the actuality of a *place* where the damned will go to be punished, for their sinful way of life on earth, by being thrown into raging fires with demons hosting them for eternity.

The concept of *Hell* is mentioned one hundred and forty-six times in the Bible. If we add *Gehenna* to the configuration, it's another twelve times. So, I think we are standing on good authority, when we speak of the existence of Hell. We hear Jesus Himself saying to Peter:

"And so I say to you, you are Peter, and upon this rock I will build my Church, and the gates of **Hell** *shall not prevail against it."*[1]

And if that is not enough, in Revelation I, in the first Vision, we again hear Jesus say:

"Once I was dead, but now I am alive forever and ever. I hold the keys of death and the nether world (**Hell**).*"*

To repeat what we said at the very beginning of the book, *"Yes, my brothers and sisters, there is a Hell!"* and it's not a place you want to visit. Hell has become a formidable term, so much so that it has been removed as a word from the modern Bibles. It has been replaced by the word "netherworld" in the New Testament, and "nether world" in the Old Testament. But no matter how anyone would like to remove it from sight, it's there, and will always be there.

In recent years, dissident theologians have dismissed the term Hell and its concept. But the Catholic Catechism has no problem addressing Hell, by its proper name, or by definition. It states:

---

[1]Matt 16:18

33

"To die in mortal sin without repenting and accepting God's merciful love means remaining separated from Him forever by our own free choice. This state of definitive self-exclusion from communion with God and the Blessed is called 'Hell.'"[2]

"The teaching of the Church affirms the existence of Hell and its eternity. Immediately after death the souls of those who die in a state of mortal sin descend into Hell, where they suffer the punishments of Hell, 'eternal fire'. The chief punishment of Hell is eternal separation from God, in Whom alone man can possess the life and happiness for which he was created and for which he longs."[3]

In another section, the Catholic Catechism teaches:

"God predestines no one to go to Hell; for this, a willful turning away from God (a mortal sin) is necessary, and persistence in it until the end. In the Eucharistic liturgy and in the daily prayers of her faithful, the Church implores the mercy of God, who does not want 'any to perish, but all to come to repentance.'"[4]

How did Hell begin?

We read in Scripture that the Angels were already created when God formed the Universe:

"In the dawn of that day the stars sang together, and the Heavenly beings shouted for joy."[5]

When God created the Angels, He created them with free will! He gave them an opportunity to choose *for* Him or *against* Him. However, that choice was instant and irrevocable. Does that sound harsh? We are sure that with all the gifts God gave to the Angels, He allowed them to see

---

[2]Catholic Catechism # 1033
[3]Catholic Catechism # 1035
[4]Catholic Catechism # 1037
[5]Job 38:7

the total picture at that time: what their *obedience* meant to Him and what their *disobedience* would mean. The decision by Michael and the Good Angels to follow the Lord, was immediate and forever, for all time in memoriam. For the fallen angels, their disobedience was the same.

Why would angels go against God? Why do we choose false gods, at times, over the One True God, Who we know will never betray us? It is said, that if you were to go to Hell and invite the fallen to come out, they would refuse. Sounds crazy, doesn't it? Who would choose suffering over joy? Lucifer was the fallen angels' choice, the anti-god they chose to worship and now they know no other.

When God put the Angels to the test, He allowed them to see Truth and deceit at that very moment of decision. The Angels were granted full understanding. God offered Himself, the Truth Who would *never* betray them. And the fallen angels chose Lucifer the great deceiver, and his lies which would *always* betray. Maybe, because of this there is no forgiveness for the fallen angels, as there is for us, right up to the last breath of our life.

Whatever they chose, there was no turning back. *"He commanded, and they were created; by His command they were fixed in their places forever, and they cannot disobey."*[6] In their pride, the followers of Lucifer had chosen to be instruments of pain and confusion, sin and destruction. In their poverty, no longer in the presence of God, these fallen angels would try to separate all God's children from Him and His unconditional Love for them, whenever they could.

Scripture says: *"He who commits sin is the slave of sin."* The fallen angels chose the sin of pride, and they not only became the slaves of pride, but of all the other sins which quickly accompany that (pride) which is the greatest of the seven deadly sins.

---

[6]Psalm 148:6

When Lucifer fell it was through *pride*. He couldn't stand it that God would choose, through Jesus, to become Man. Man who is below the angels! He would not bow down before a Man! And God chose to be born of a woman! Intolerable! Another human, who was beneath him! He would not allow her to be his queen, and so he refused to obey God, and not satisfied to disobey alone, he led weaker angels to follow him. I can just hear Lucifer's arguments, can't you? "What a slap in the face to us. Did He not make us, specially? Are we not the closest to Him? He betrayed us!" This is probably the first time Lucifer called God imperfect. When he turned away from God, all the evil that was possible took over and he called God by the names, he, Lucifer, would live by: Betrayer, Liar.

The account of the creation of Hell is given to us in two places in Scripture, once in the Old Testament, and then again in the New Testament. We will give you the account from the Book of Revelation, which is more descriptive than the vision of Daniel.

"*Then war broke out in Heaven; Michael and his Angels battled against the dragon. The dragon and its angels fought back, but they did not prevail and there was no longer any place for them in Heaven. The huge dragon, the ancient serpent, who is called the Devil and Satan, who deceived the whole world, was thrown down to earth, and its angels were thrown down with it.*

"*Then I heard a loud voice in Heaven say:*

'*Now have salvation and power come, and the reign of our God and the authority of His Anointed One. For the accuser[7] of our brothers is cast out, who night and day accused them before our God. They defeated him by the Blood of the Lamb and by the word of their testimony; love for life did not deter them from death.*'

---

[7]the Hebrew word for Satan

'So rejoice, you Heavens and you who dwell therein!
But woe to you, earth and sea, for the Devil has come
down upon you! His fury, knows no limits, for he knows
his time is short.'"

"When the dragon saw that he had been cast down to
the earth, he pursued the woman who had given birth to
the male Child. But the woman was given the wings of a
great eagle,[8] so that she could fly to her place in the desert,
where, far from the serpent, she could be taken care of for
a year, and for two and a half years more.

"The serpent,[9] however, spewed a torrent of water out of
his mouth to search out the woman and sweep her away.
The earth came to the woman's rescue by opening its
mouth and swallowing the flood which the dragon spewed
out of his mouth.

"Enraged at her rescue, the dragon went off to make war
on the rest of her offspring, on those who keep God's
commandments and give witness to Jesus."[10]

The Battle Rages

The footnote at the bottom of this last passage in the
New American Bible tells us "*Although the church is protected
by God's special providence, the individual Christian is to
expect persecution and suffering.*" It gives as a reference the
Fall of Adam and Eve in the Garden of Eden. In the garden
of Eden when he seduced Eve, it was with a *lie*. He, the
author of lies dared to call the *Author of Truth*, a Liar. When
Eve said that God told them not to eat from the tree, that
they would die, the serpent answered: "*You certainly will not
die! No. God knows well that the moment you eat of it your*

---

[8]symbol of the power and swiftness of Divine help
[9]in this account, the serpent is depicted as a sea monster
[10]Revelations 12:7-17

eyes will opened and you will be like gods who know what is good and what is bad."[11]

Eve saw that the fruit looked good to eat. Thinking of the *moment* and satisfying that moment, she forgot the kindness and generosity of God the Father and ate it; so in keeping with the philosophy and advertisement of today. *"You deserve it! You only go around once! You have a right to happiness! It's expensive, but I'm worth it!"*

Lucifer promised her they would know as much as God, be like gods themselves. Sounds familiar, doesn't it? There is an ancient deadly heresy that has risen from Hell and is spreading like a putrid disease throughout the world. It teaches we do not need God, that we are gods, the masters of our own fate. And what happens when, like Adam and Eve, we eat of that fruit and our eyes are opened to our nakedness, our weakness, the soft clay we are made of? What happens when we discover we are nothing outside of our Creator? Do we believe Lucifer's lies that God will never forgive us, and despair? I pray not; for our Guardian Angel, who we may have put aside, the way we do those who tell us what we are about to do will harm us, is there waiting to lead us home to the Arms of our Father in Heaven.

And so, the war began with Adam and Eve. Because of one act of pride and disobedience, the world would suffer until the Second Coming of Christ. Why wouldn't they listen to Christ when He came, the first time? Why do we continue to kill one another, lie to one another, speak out against one another, refuse to love one another? Because the old battle goes on, and the general in charge of that army of dissidents, Lucifer, is still spreading his lies. And we, children of Adam and Eve, instead of listening to our new Adam and Eve, our Lord Jesus and His Mother Mary, are listening to the evil one, and suffering.

---

[11]Gen 3:4-5

Scripture tells us in Genesis 3:16-17:

"To the woman, He (God) said:

> *'I shall give you intense pain in childbearing,*
> *you will give birth to your children in pain.*
> *Your yearning will be for your husband,*
> *and he will dominate you.'*

"To the man He said,

> *'Because you listened to the voice of your wife and ate*

from the tree of which I had forbidden you to eat,

> *Accursed be the soil because of you!*
> *Painfully will you get your food from it*
> *as long as you live.*
> *It will yield you brambles and thistles,*
> *as you eat the produce of the land.*
> *By the sweat of your face*
> *will you earn your food,*
> *until you return to the ground,*
> *as you were taken from it.*
> *For dust you are*
> *and to dust you shall return.'"[12]*

And so, because of the seduction of Satan, God's original plan for us, to live in complete happiness with Him, was thwarted. We became heirs to Hell, which had not been planned for us, because of the disobedience of our first parents. The battle for our souls began at this point in history. St. Paul warns us:

> *"Put on the armor of God, that you may be able to stand against the wiles of the devil. For our wrestling is not against flesh and blood, but against the Principalities and the Powers, against the world rulers of this present darkness, against the spiritual forces of wickedness on high."[13]*

---

[12]Gen 3:16-19
[13]Eph 6:11-12

We are innocent victims of a battle which took place at the beginning of time, first between Lucifer and St. Michael, and then Lucifer and the children of God. As St. Paul says, the battle is between the Angels, fallen and Holy; we are just the prize. And the only reason Satan wants to drag us down to the depths of Hell is to hurt God.

But Hell is a decision which we make. It's determined by our thoughts and actions. God does not punish us, so much as we punish ourselves. If we opt for Heaven, we will work all our lives towards that goal. However, being human beings, and heirs of Adam and Eve, we will fall. But its up to us; salvation is just a church away (through our priests and the Sacrament of Confession).

> *"If we say, 'We have no sin,'*
> *we are deceiving ourselves,*
> *and truth has no place in us;*
> *if we acknowledge our sins,*
> *He is trustworthy and upright,*
> *so that He will forgive our sins*
> *and will cleanse us from all evil.*
> *If we say, 'We have never sinned,'*
> *we make Him a liar,*
> *and His word has no place in us.*
> *My children, I am writing this to prevent you from sinning;*
> *but if anyone does sin,*
> *we have an advocate with the Father,*
> *Jesus Christ, the upright.*
> *He is the sacrifice to expiate our sins,*
> *and not only ours, but also those of the whole world."[14]*

St. Catherine of Genoa tells us:

"It is evident that the revolt of man's will from that of God constitutes sin, and while that revolt continues, man's

---

[14]1 John 1:8-10 & 1 John 2:1-2

guilt remains. Those, therefore, that are in Hell, having passed from this life with perverse wills, their guilt is not remitted. When this life is ended, the soul remains forever confirmed either in good or evil according as she has here determined. As it is written: Where I shall find thee, that is at the hour of death, with the will either fixed on sin or repenting of it, there I will judge thee. From this judgment there is no appeal."[15]

Therefore, we make the decision for *Heaven or Hell*.

But, St. Paul tells us that if we put on the armor of God, and listen to our Guardian Angel, we will be saved from the fierce fires of Hell. Listen to your Guardian Angel. He is with you to guard you, guide you, protect you, light your way to Our Lord. God has sent him as a messenger to bring His Word to you. You don't dare not listen! We have been given especially the gift of our Angel and St. Joseph at the hour of death. Take advantage of it. *Thank You Jesus.*

---

[15]The Spiritual Doctrine of St. Catherine of Genoa

Above: ***Purgatory***

Below: ***Detail from Michelangelo's Last Judgment - Note the one soul being lifted out of Purgatory by a Rosary***

Is There a Purgatory?

The Church Suffering

Holy Mother Church, the Mystical Body of Christ consists of three Churches: *The Church Militant* - we the faithful who dwell on earth, *The Church Triumphant* - the elect who are in the presence of the Beatific Vision in Heaven, and *The Church Suffering* - those who are no less members of the Body but who are in Purgatory.

In this chapter, we want to talk of Purgatory, *The Church Suffering*. Those souls who dwell in Purgatory are more privileged than those who dwell on earth, as they are assured of entering into the Kingdom of God one day; whereas, those who are part of the Church Militant are vulnerable and have to fight the wages of sin that are constantly ready to attack and drag them down to Hell. The *Church Suffering* plays a compassionate role in God's Plan to save His children for Himself. For God has always loved us; and as He is unchanging, His Love is unchanging; and part of that unchanging Love is Purgatory.

The three Churches commune together, praying for one another. We call that the Communion of Saints. *The Church Triumphant* prays for *The Church Militant*, who in turn prays for *The Church Suffering*. We, the faithful who comprise The Church Militant, pray to the Saints in Heaven, The Church Triumphant, for their intercession and they, in turn, plead with the Lord on our behalf. The Church Suffering cannot pray for themselves; therefore they cannot hope for the intercession of the Saints in Heaven without the faithful, The Church Militant, praying in their behalf. However, once the Church Suffering become the Church Triumphant, after they have entered into the Kingdom, they in turn pray for the Church Militant, that's us, especially those who prayed to get them out of Purgatory.

It is really awesome when you think of the integral part we play in God's Symphony for Salvation. When we think of the three parts of the Church as a grand philharmonic orchestra with God as the Conductor, we can better understand the Communion of Saints, and how each musician has to play his individual instrument in harmony with the rest, in order to achieve the perfect Symphony of Salvation that the Lord, the Perfect Composer has created from the beginning of the world.

When we die and enter into the doors of Purgatory, we have the assurance that we will enter Heaven. Our salvation is assured. We are saved by the Blood of Jesus. But we have time to spend in Purgatory. Our first reaction should be, "Thank You Jesus, I'm saved." Our next reaction might possibly be, "But Lord, do I have a long time to spend in Purgatory?"

Our loved ones will not know how long we're going to be in Purgatory. They may be assured that we're saved, if we have made a contrite confession and have been absolved, but they do not know how much prayer we need and for how long, how many Masses and other means of atonement are necessary for the restitution due the Father. In not knowing how much time we have to serve, they might have a tendency to forget about us. *Out of sight, out of mind.* They don't mean to forget the Poor Souls, but the world creeps in, and priorities change. Really important things have to be done, and before they know it, the friends or relatives they promised to pray for on a daily basis, go on the back burner. Not that they necessarily stop praying for the Poor Souls in Purgatory, but maybe they forget the friends who have died some time ago. These may be the ones who need prayers the most.

A very holy nun appeared to one of the Saints in this book, and asked for prayers, especially the Mass. He replied, he never would have thought to pray for her; he was sure she was in Heaven. She told him she was spending a great deal of time in Purgatory because she was not enthusiastic when she went to Eucharistic Adoration. Not that she didn't go, or didn't spend her hour in reverence before the Lord, but that she just wasn't excited about going.

Don't for a moment think that anyone *doesn't* need your prayers. That's why a Guardian Angel always comes to you and whispers a name in your ear. Those who died need Masses! When we die, if you're still on earth, be sure to pray for us. We need prayers, not only now, but when we're burning off all our past blemishes in Purgatory. Say a Mass of thanksgiving that we made it into Purgatory, and then many many Masses that we get out of Purgatory.

Purgatory and the Papal Authority of the Church

Let us begin by speaking with first, the authority of His Holiness Pope Paul III who, in company with his Bishops, declared on January 13, 1547, in the Council of Trent:[1]

"If anyone saith (says) that
after the grace of Justification has been received,
to every penitent the guilt is remitted[2]
and the debt of eternal punishment is blotted out
in such wise (a way) that there remains
not any debt of temporal punishment to be discharged,
either in this world, or in the next in Purgatory,
before the entrance to the Kingdom of Heaven
can be opened to him:
let him be anathema (condemned)."

And if that was not enough, sixteen years and four Popes later, Pope Pius IV gathered his Bishops and Prelates from the four corners of the world, commenced another

---

[1]Canon XXX - Session VI
[2]absolved, forgiven, pardoned

Council of Trent[3] on December 4, 1563, and made this Decree on Purgatory at an Ecumenical Council:[4]

"Whereas the Catholic Church,
instructed by the Holy Spirit,
has, from the sacred writings,
and the ancient tradition of the Fathers,
taught in sacred Councils
and very recently in this Ecumenical Synod,
that there is a Purgatory
and the souls retained there are helped
by the suffrages[5] of the Faithful,
but particularly by the acceptable Sacrifice of the Altar[6]
the Holy Synod enjoins on Bishops
that they diligently endeavor
that the sound doctrine concerning Purgatory,
transmitted by the holy Fathers and sacred Councils,
be believed, maintained, taught,
and everywhere proclaimed by the Faithful of Christ."

So much for those within and without our Church who say there is no Purgatory. It sounds pretty simple to me: We are *required* to believe in Purgatory. And for those who might say that these are *old* pronouncements in *old* Councils, let us reiterate that no proclamation ever made by any Vatican Council has been nullified by a succeeding Council.

---

[3]Session XXV

[4]An Ecumenical Council is one to which all the bishops of the Catholic world and all other prelates or dignitaries entitled to vote, are invited to gather under the Presidency of the Pope or his representative. The decrees of an Ecumenical Council, when ratified by the Pope, are binding on all Christians. It is now sometimes called 'general council'. (The Catholic Encyclopedia - Broderick)

[5]additional prayers of the Divine Office for particular intentions, such as for the Church. (The Catholic Encyclopedia - Broderick)

[6]The Sacrifice of the Mass which is the ongoing Sacrifice of the Cross

Purgatory and Vatican Council II

"Until the Lord shall come in His majesty,
and all the Angels with Him and death being destroyed,
all things are subject to Him,
some of His disciples are exiles on earth,
some having died are purified,
and others are in glory beholding
'clearly God Himself Triune and One, as He is'
but all in various ways and degrees
are in communion in the same charity of God and neighbor
and all sing the same hymn of glory to our God.
For all who are in Christ, having His Spirit,
form one church and cleave together in Him.
Therefore the union of the wayfarers
with the brethren who have gone to sleep
in the peace of Christ
is not in the least weakened or interrupted,
but on the contrary,
according to the perpetual faith of the Church,
is strengthened by communication of spiritual goods."[7]

Fully conscious of this communion of the whole Mystical Body of Jesus Christ, the pilgrim Church from the very first ages of the Christian Religion, has cultivated with great piety, the memory of the dead, and *"'because it is a holy and wholesome thought to pray for the dead that they may be loosed from their sins', also offers suffrages for them."*[8]

Purgatory and the Catholic Catechism

The Church of the Twentieth Century has this to say about Purgatory. We quote from the Catholic Catechism:[9]

"All who die in God's grace and friendship,
but still imperfectly purified,

---

[7]Lumen Gentium # 49
[8]Lumen Gentium # 50
[9]Section III of the Profession of Faith, # 1030-1031-1032

are indeed assured of their eternal salvation;
but after death they undergo purification,
so as to achieve the holiness necessary
to enter the joy of Heaven."

The Church gives the name *Purgatory* to this final purification of the elect, which is entirely different from the punishment of the damned. The Church formulated her doctrine of faith on Purgatory, especially at the *Councils of Florence and Trent.* The traditions of the Church, through Holy Scripture, speak of a cleansing fire.[10]

Also, St. Gregory the Great tells us:

"As for certain lesser faults, we must believe that,
before the Final Judgment, there is a purifying fire.
He who is Truth says that whoever utters blasphemy
against the Holy Spirit will be pardoned
neither in this age nor in the age to come.
From this sentence, we understand that certain offenses
can be forgiven in this age, but certain others in the age to
come."

All this section, while written in language for today, comes from the two Councils, Trent and Florence, and from one edict by Pope Benedict XII, who preceded both Councils:

"...the souls of all the saints...and other faithful who died after receiving Christ's holy Baptism (provided they were not in need of purification when they died,....or, if they then did need or will need some purification, when they have been purified after death),...have been, are and will be in Heaven, in the Heavenly Kingdom and celestial paradise with Christ, joined to the company of the Holy Angels..."[11]

Even the renowned pagan philosophers, **Plato** and **Virgil** spoke of Purgatory. *Plato* taught that souls who had

---

[10]1Cor 3:15 - 1Pet 1:7
[11]Catholic Catechism #1023

lived a fairly good life, who had walked the middle road, were enclosed in a place where they were purified of their sins. *Virgil* maintained that souls couldn't free themselves of the sins they had committed while they were alive, and therefore had to go to a place where there was pain and where they suffered to atone for the sins of their past life.

†

What we have believed from the very beginning, right from the Old Testament till today, holds true for all time:
(1) Souls who are in Purgatory are those who have died in a state of Grace but have not been purged (cleansed), have not paid unresolved debts owed for offenses committed during the soul's time on earth.
(2) Purgatory is the place where Poor Souls are washed clean of all remaining blemishes, all imperfections, venial sins and faults. We say imperfections! When we think of God the Potter and the great care and hope He had for us at the moment of Creation, the image He saw of us, of what we could be, we then can look at ourselves and understand the imperfections the Church is speaking about, and the Divine Mercy of God to allow the slate of our soul to be wiped clean, while still on earth or after death in Purgatory.

How can we help those Poor Souls in Purgatory

This brings us to Indulgences, in particular *Plenary Indulgences*. Our dear Church makes it possible for us to wipe away all temporal punishment from our sins by the use of *Indulgences*. Indulgences are defined by the Catholic Encyclopedia as follows:
† The remission of the temporal punishment due for sins and hence, the satisfaction owed to God for one's sins.
† The Church grants such indulgences after the guilt of sin and its eternal punishment have been remitted by Sacramental absolution or by perfect contrition.

There are two kinds of indulgences: *Plenary and Partial*. **Plenary** wipes out all the temporal punishment resulting from sin. **Partial** is when only part of the temporal punishment is remitted.

An important requirement for a Plenary indulgence is that one must be *free from all sin*, mortal and venial. In other words, you must have gone to Confession or made a perfect act of contrition for a Plenary Indulgence to take effect.

As an example, we just came back from a Pilgrimage. In various shrines, there were Plenary Indulgences available. The requirements were:
(1) Confession within eight days of visiting the shrine.
(2) Reception of Communion.
(3) Praying for the Pope's intention. This consists of reciting the Creed, the Our Father, Hail Mary and Glory Be.

On this particular pilgrimage, there were more than four shrines that offered Plenary indulgences. The priest told us, we might want to use one Plenary Indulgence for ourselves; and the others could be offered for the Poor Souls in Purgatory, which would release Souls out of Purgatory into Heaven, immediately upon earning those indulgences. At other shrines there were indulgences available, only not Plenary; they were Partial. In those instances, we were advised to offer them *solely* for the dead. That also has tremendous merit. In addition to praying a Poor Soul out of Purgatory, we're building an army of supporters in Heaven. Once that soul enters into the Kingdom, he prays for those who helped him get out of Purgatory. We need all the help we can get, and we can get that help by sending souls in Purgatory to Heaven.

On this subject, the Catholic Catechism tells us:
  "In the communion of Saints,
  'a perennial link of charity exists between the faithful
  who have already reached their Heavenly home,
  those who are expiating their sins in Purgatory

and those who are still pilgrims on earth.
Between them there is, too,
an abundant exchange of all good things.'
In this wonderful exchange,
the holiness of one profits others,
well beyond the harm
that the sin of one could cause others.
Thus recourse to the Communion of Saints
lets the contrite sinner be
more promptly and efficaciously purified
of the punishments for sin."[12]

Purgatory and the Old Testament

Isaiah speaks of Purgatory when we read:
"The people that walked in darkness have seen a great light; to them that dwelt in the region of the shadow of death, light is risen."[13]

Isaiah speaks of Purgatory when he mentions *"the region of the shadow of death."* God created us to be in His Light, in His likeness, perfect and unblemished, for all time. Through disobedience and the sins of our first parents, Adam and Eve, we lost the gift that God had in store for us, that great and wonderful moment when He planned our existence.

When God created us in His likeness, He had in His Mind's Eye, creatures who resembled in every way all that is holy and immaculate, as He is Holy and Immaculate, not equal with Him, but like Him in His goodness. He created us to be without blemish, sinless. Our Lord's plan for us was to live *eternally*.

Because of the sin of Adam and Eve, death and *darkness* came into the world. But the Father so loved us, He sent His only begotten Son, the *Light* of the World to conquer darkness, and by His death on the Cross, conquer

---

[12]Catholic Catechism #1475 - Page 371
[13]Isaiah 9:2

death. When Jesus *rose* from the dead, new Hope rose with Him; but because of our sinfulness, we continue to sin and offend God. Does God give up on us? No, He created Purgatory so that we can still be with Him, someday.

Those outside our Church, who do not understand Purgatory, and God's Mercy in providing this gift to us, often argue there is no reference to Purgatory in the Bible. Listen to Machabees in the Old Testament! Hear what the Jews believed, and you will see that it was not only in *life after death*, but in the cleansing, necessary to free them of sin.

"On the following day,
since the task had now become urgent,
Judas and his men went to gather the bodies of the slain
and bury them with their kinsmen in their ancestral tombs.
But under the tunic of each of the dead
they found amulets sacred to the idols of Jamnia,
which the law forbids the Jews to wear,
so it was clear to all that this was why these men had been slain.
They all therefore praised the ways of the Lord,
the just Judge Who brings light to the things that are hidden.
Turning to supplication, they prayed
that the sinful deed might be fully blotted out.
The noble Judas warned the soldiers
to keep themselves free from sin,
for they had seen with their own eyes
what had happened because of the sin of those who had fallen.
He then took up a collection among all his soldiers,
amounting to two thousand silver drachmas,
which he sent to Jerusalem to provide for an expiatory sacrifice.
In doing this he acted in a very excellent and noble way,
inasmuch as he had the resurrection of the dead in view;
for if he were not expecting the fallen to rise again,
it would have been useless and foolish
to pray for them in death.
But if he did this with the view to the splendid reward

that awaits those who had gone to rest in godliness,
it was a holy and pious thought.
Thus he made atonement for the dead
that they might be freed from this sin."[14]

Judas, the Machabean, was not satisfied with just recognizing the fallen with a grand funeral. Seeing the sins that had been hidden, he commanded a collection be taken up among the remaining soldiers. This he sent to the Temple in Jerusalem as an offering, so that sacrifice would be offered to wipe out the sins and transgressions they had committed against the law of the Jews, that of worshiping false idols. Is this not what we do, when we have Masses said for the dead?

In Machabees, we read:

"It is a holy and wholesome thought to pray for the dead, that they may be freed from sins."[15]

If there is no Purgatory, and death is final, why pray for the dead to be *"freed from their sins"?* And if there is no *middle place* between Heaven and Hell, then from where could they be wiped clean of their sins? It's not Heaven, as those who are there are sinless, nor Hell where sins are final. It has to be that *middle place* we call Purgatory.

The Jews, who have faithfully followed the Old Testament for thousands of years, have always believed in purification in the next world. The tradition, that of praying for the dead, has been passed down from generation to generation. For example, a child is required to pray for his deceased parent, for one year, a prayer that is called *"Kadis."*[16] If there are no surviving children, a person is hired to pray for the deceased. This prayer is so holy, so special, that one is never to recite this prayer except for the purpose of praying for a dead parent. If there is no life after

---

[14]IIMach 12:39-46
[15]IIMach 12:46
[16]pronounced Kadesh

death, then *why pray*; it is all over; this world is all there is; their prayers are for no purpose. *Why pray?* If there is no remedy, no hope for the soul of the departed parent, or if there is no need for remedy, or if there is no place where the soul can be remedied, then *why pray?*

Another tradition is that of lighting candles for the dead, called "*Yortsite*" candles. Now, if you do not believe in life after death and the resurrection of the dead, why would you *light candles* for them? And if the Jews did not believe that there is a middle place between the earth and Heaven, that which we Catholics call Purgatory, then it would be foolishness to *light candles* for someone who is beyond help. When they *light candles* for the dead are they not, by the smoke of the candle, sending up a sweet sacrifice to the Lord, as their ancestors did before them.

"Before these stood seventy of the elders of the House of Israel ...each of them with his censor in his hand and the fragrance of the incense was rising upward."[17]

By these traditions: lighting a light and praying for the dead, the Jewish people[18] show that they believe:
(1) there is a *need* for purification, that their parents did not die and go straight to Heaven, and
(2) there is *hope* for sanctification, as they did not die and go to Hell, and
(3) there is a necessity for those who are left behind to pray for those who have departed.

We teach in the Catholic Church that one way to alleviate or lessen the sufferings of the Poor Souls in Purgatory is by the giving of alms. Another way that the Jewish people pray for purification of their departed loved ones is by alms giving; they are very philanthropic, giving all forms of charity in their dead parents' names. Why would

---

[17]Ezekiel 8:11

[18]In the time of Jesus, the Pharisees believed in the resurrection and the Sadducees did not. (Acts 23:6-10)

they do this, if they did not believe in life after death? It would be foolishness! After all, their parents cannot see or benefit from these generous acts, if there is no *purification* after death. What point is there to all this, if there is no *life after death*?

With so many of us, because our traditions and their true meanings are not passed down, we do things by rote, repeating what went on before us, simply because our parents did it, missing the deep meaning of the action in relationship to God and His Eternal Love for His children. Could this be another reason you are reading this book, to share this with our Jewish brothers and sisters, God's chosen people whom He has always loved so dearly?

When **Our Lord** walked the earth, He did not hesitate to correct abuses against His Father in Heaven. He knew that the Jews believed in praying for the dead. Why did He not correct this practice? He not only did not, he spoke plainly, when He spoke of the seriousness of blasphemy:

"And whosoever shall speak a word (blasphemes) against the Holy Spirit, it shall not be forgiven him neither in the this world, nor in the world to come."[19]

Then, if this practice was against the Commandments passed down by His Father to Moses, you can be sure Jesus would have spoken out, loud and clear.

St. Paul knew the Jewish Law. When he was converted by the Lord, he used this knowledge of the law, to try to bring his brothers and sisters of the Hebrew Faith to the Messiah they had been awaiting, Jesus the Christ. Paul built a bridge for his Jewish brethren to walk over, and that was the Old Law. He explained how the Lord Jesus had come and fulfilled all that had been prophesied centuries before. Once they crossed that bridge, he could then lead them to the Truth Who is Jesus Christ.

---

[19]Matt 12:32

Now, Paul had been a Pharisee. Like them, he believed in a middle state between Heaven and Hell.   At one point, to explain the teaching of the Resurrection, St. Paul referred to the Jewish custom of devoutly praying for the dead:

"If the dead are not raised, what about those who have themselves baptized on behalf of the dead? If the raising of the dead is not a reality, why be baptized on their behalf? And why are we continually putting ourselves in danger? I swear to you, brothers, by the very pride you take in me, which I cherish in Jesus Christ our Lord, that I face death every day. If I fought those beasts at Ephesus for purely human motives, what profit was there for me? If the dead are not raised, let us eat and drink, for tomorrow we die."[20]

What St. Paul was saying was: If there is no resurrection, then why pray for the dead, why go through all the pious rituals for the dead? Is he not also saying: If there is no place where the dead can be purified, why pray for the dead? For if they are in Heaven, there is no necessity as they are already sanctified; or if they are in Hell there is no hope of sanctification, as they are already damned. So, there has to be a place where the dead are forgiven; although he does not specifically use the word Purgatory, he is affirming a place of purification which we call Purgatory.

Purgatory and the New Testament

Jesus affirms Purgatory in Matthew's Gospel:[21]

"Whoever says anything against the Son of Man will be forgiven, but whoever says anything against the Holy Spirit will not be forgiven, either in this age or the one to come."

What is He saying here, you may ask, in reference to Purgatory? Jesus said that *"whoever blasphemes against the Holy Spirit will not be forgiven, either in this age or the world to*

---

[20]1Cor 15:29-33
[21]Matt 12:32

come." What did He mean by "*the one to come?*" He could not be referring to Heaven. Those who are already in Heaven have no need for forgiveness; their garments (souls) are spotless, made clean by the Blood of the Lamb. He cannot be speaking of Hell as that is irrevocable; the place from where no one returns. Those who are in Hell made the decision to sin against God and not seeking forgiveness, condemned themselves to this inferno of eternal damnation. Jesus must be referring to Purgatory.

Saints Augustine, Gregory the Great, and Bernard, to mention a few, teach that Jesus is plainly "*declaring that there is a place between Heaven and Hell where certain sins can be forgiven, in the world, beyond.*" - Purgatory.

"*Whether Jesus is referring to the obstinacy of the Jews or other unbelievers, in refusing to acknowledge the Truth, when He said: 'whosoever shall speak a word against the Holy Spirit,' one thing rings out clear and indisputable, Jesus is declaring that there is a place between Heaven and Hell where certain sins can be forgiven, in the world, beyond.*"

We hear Jesus speaking out about "*getting angry,*" that he who does so will be liable to judgment. He warns:

"*Lose no time; settle with your opponent while on your way to court with him. Otherwise your opponent may hand you over to the judge, who will hand you over to the guard, who will throw you into prison. I warn you, you will not be released until you have paid the last penny.*"[22]

Again, is He not referring here to Purgatory? Is Jesus not saying, make retribution here on earth rather than suffer the pains of Purgatory from which you will not be released until the debt is fully paid?

Early Church Fathers, such as Saint Ambrose, Saint Augustine, Saint Jerome and countless others have all *taught*

---

[22]Matt 5:25-26

that this passage from Holy Scripture refers to Purgatory, when Jesus speaks of the debt being *"fully paid."*

It is true that the pain suffered in Purgatory is like that of Hell, with one great exception; in Purgatory it is temporary. The Poor Souls suffer that crushing pain of separation from the Beatific Vision. But although they do not know how long it will be until they are in Heaven, they know that this is only for a time, and then they will be with the Lord and their loved ones for all eternity. Our hope and joy is that God will allow us to pay *"the last penny"* in Purgatory, or here on earth, or by loved ones who will pray and offer sacrifice for us.

The Sacraments and Purgatory - the Father's Gifts to us

Our hope for eternal life in Heaven lies in the great gifts that we were given - the Sacraments. The Lord, in His compassionate Love and most generous Heart, is constantly offering us through His Ambassadors-His holy Priests, the Sacraments to aid us on our journey.

Through **Baptism**, we were cleansed of Original Sin, the sin we inherited from our first parents, Adam and Eve. With the Sacrament of **Penance**, we are freed from the endless pain of Hell. When we receive the **Eucharist**, His Body, Blood, Soul and Divinity, we are strengthened for the journey to everlasting life with the Lord in Heaven. Through the Sacrament of **Holy Orders**, we are given the instruments, His Priests, by which we receive these life-saving Sacraments.

In the Garden of Gethsemane, as Our Lord was sweating Blood and Tears over our sins, His thoughts were of us, His Eyes on the Cross which would save us. As He carried the Cross, laden down by our sins, He walked, more dead than alive, falling and getting up three times, all out of love for us. His last words were to the Father to forgive us, *"they know not what they do."* How very much He loves us and how very much we have wounded Him, when we have put the world and its creatures before Him and His Love!

Our sins are forgiven through the **Sacrament of Penance**[23] and our confessor who is "*in persona Christi Capitas,*"[24] by virtue of the **Sacrament of Holy Orders** he received on the day of his ordination. These sins that are forgiven are called "*Actual Sins.*"[25] Even though we have been absolved, the stain of these sins has to be removed, either on earth or in Purgatory. When we confess to a crime in a civil matter, we have to make restitution. How much more so, in a matter more far-reaching, that of our immortal souls!

What does His Love deserve, that great and unsparing Love that God has for us? When we behold the Love that the Holy Trinity has for us, we will beg to go to Purgatory, to be cleansed of any blemishes and all impediments that would block us from being the spotless soul He created us to be.

Speaking of the Sacraments, we need to address the **Sacrament of Matrimony**. Jesus thought so highly of this union formed by God with the couple, uniting them not only with each other, but making them one with Him, He performed His first Miracle at the Wedding Feast in Cana.

---

[23]Jesus left this mission to His Apostles. "*Receive the Holy Spirit. For those whose sins you forgive, they are forgiven; for those whose sins you retain, they are retained.*" John 20:23

[24]in the personhood of Jesus Christ

[25]Actual Sin: A *personal act* that is morally bad, or the omission of some obliged good, or an act against right reason or the law of God is an Actual Sin. It is a *voluntary transgression* of a moral law or a law obliging the will, resulting in sins of either commission or omission. According to the manner of their commission such sins may be interior or exterior; committed against God, one's neighbor, or one's self according to their object; in gravity, either mortal or venial; from their cause, either committed in ignorance, weakness or malice; and capital or non-capital with regard to whether they do or do not give rise to other sins. (The Catholic Encyclopedia-Broderick)

My spouse and I believe[26] that we, and our Sacrament of Matrimony, were in God's Heart and Mind when He created the world. When we went on our first Marriage Encounter weekend,[27] the priest called us *to holiness*; he said we were to revere one another; he informed us that this is the only Sacrament that comes directly from God, and that the priest is there as a witness of God's people. We looked at each other differently from that moment to this day, over twenty years later. My spouse is precious; my spouse is holy; I am called to holiness. Now, most of us do not commit adultery; but do we commit it in our minds? Jesus tells us, sin begins in the mind. Do you remember what He said about sin?

"You have heard the commandment imposed on your forefathers, 'You shall not commit adultery.' What I say to you is: anyone who looks lustfully at a woman has already committed adultery with her in his thoughts. If your right eye is your trouble, gouge it out and throw it away! Better to lose part of your body than to have it all cast into Gehenna (Hell). Again, if your right hand is your trouble, cut it off and throw it away! Better to lose part of your body than to have it all cast into Gehenna."[28]

Therefore, although our sins are remitted through the Sacrament of Penance, the payment must be made, when through our own fault we were unfaithful to our spouse, whether in thought or action. This is why it is necessary we pray for our spouse, for all our loved ones, for our friends, for the Poor Souls who have no one to pray for them; pray that their suffering be shortened. As we do not know the hearts of our separated brothers and sisters in Christ and only God reads their hearts, we should offer prayers and sacrifice for their sanctification, begging God's Mercy. And

---

[26]not theological, but a personal feeling

[27]a weekend for good marriages that want to be great! You learn communication skills that will enrich your marriage.

[28]Matt 5:30

we will not go unrewarded, for although the Poor Souls cannot pray for themselves, they can pray for us.

The answer to the disciples' question to Jesus: *"Who then can be saved?"*[29] is to be found in the Treasury of our Faith. We have read how God planned for our salvation, how He sent His only Son to redeem our sins. Our God wants us to be with Him in Heaven! Do we not want to be eternally with our loved ones? Then imagine how much the Lord Who is the perfect Lover, the eternal loving Father, the most benevolent King of the Universe wants His children to be with Him in Paradise. We would move Heaven and earth for our children, and we are imperfect parents. How much will He do for us to be eternally with Him! It's up to us!

That's what Free Will is all about; God gave us Free Will to love Him. We can pay our debts on earth and be purified, or be purged of them in Purgatory. We can also try to live our lives pleasing to God, loving Him and our neighbor with all that is in us, in our imperfect state. I think that when we are standing before the Throne of God in Heaven and behold the love He has always had for us, we will, in true repentance for all the times we have failed to love Him as we should, flee to Purgatory. I think the greatest pain has to be that once having seen Jesus, our hearts long to be with Him, and we have to wait.

Addressing the last Sacrament that prayerfully we will all receive, that of the **Sacrament of the Blessing of the Sick,** our thoughts travel to those last few moments of our lives when our eyes are focused on the ceiling, that painful time when we know that we must leave all that we have known and loved on earth. Yet, I know that the anticipation of seeing Our Lord, at last, as He is in His Glory, will be our consolation, at this time of carrying the cross. *But will we know Him?* Will we be with Him in Paradise? Part of the

---

[29]Matt 19:25

joy that softens the pain of separation from our loved ones on earth, is the hope that we will be reunited with our loved ones in Paradise. *How will that be, if we do not pray for them?*

If you are reading this book, your heart is with the Lord and you do desire to be with Him; but remember that God's Mind is not ours; we must do *more* and must give *more* - toward the salvation of our immortal soul. For the body is dying; but the soul lives forever.

"Who then can be saved?" Our God loves us! He loves us so much, He opened His Arms on the Cross - for us! If He would suffer and die on the Cross out of love for us, He would not abandon us on earth to be lost to Him forever. God the Father planned our salvation, even as our first parents were sinning against Him. Even as we were betraying Him, He was working out the means to save us. Loving Father, knowing how difficult the path is that we must travel here on earth, He offers the Sacraments to us, to strengthen us in our walk. And that Last Supper, thinking only of us and not Himself and His Pain, He left us His Ambassadors, our Priests, the instruments by which He could be with us until the end of the world. Then, as one of His last acts of love, He left us the Church which flowed from His bleeding Heart, to direct our walk.

"Who then can be saved?" Hope did not die on the Cross. From the Holy Cave of Jesus' Heart, opened by the centurion's sword, Hope came to us, once again. Whereas in the Cave of Bethlehem, Hope was born into the world, on Calvary, from His Side *new Hope* came into the world, Mother Church. And that's how we will be saved, by this Hope!

Visions of St. Nicholas of Tolentino
Champion of the Souls in Purgatory

Nicholas was the pride of the Augustinian Community which flourished in the northeastern section of Italy known as the Marches. He was born in the year 1245, not too far from Tolentino where he spent most of his life as a religious. His elderly parents had not been able to bear a child. Late in life, they made a pilgrimage to Bari, petitioning Saint Nicholas of Bari to intercede with the Lord that they might bring a child into the world, never suspecting the impact that child would have on the history of the Church. St. Nicholas was born and his parents named him after Saint Nicholas of Bari in thanksgiving. He was the gift of their golden years. They offered him back to the Lord, as his mother committed him to God at his baptism. Parents, having a problem conceiving, often turn to St. Nicholas of Tolentino, Patron Saint of difficult births because of his miraculous birth.

From an early age, Nicholas longed for the religious life. The lives of the Saints, his mother had read to him filled him with the desire to be holy. The stories about Our Lord Jesus and Mother Mary brought him each day closer and closer to being her *son* and sharing in her *Son's* Way of the Cross.

There were those in the clergy who wanted to take him under their wing so that he could be a professional priest in the secular clergy, but that was not what Nicholas felt burning deep in his heart. Instead, he searched for wherever the *Lord* wanted him to serve. Not only had the life of Saint Augustine been one that his mother had read to him, but he was to hear about the Saint in school. When the Lord wants you to do something, He makes it perfectly clear. Just in case the young Nicholas had not understood the call to be an Augustinian, the Lord brought him to an *Augustinian* church, to hear an *Augustinian* preach; and in case he had not heard his commandment to follow Him in the religious life, what

Left:
St. Nicholas of Tolentino
Note the star on his chest. There is a tradition that, when meditating on where he should go, he saw an unusually bright star in the sky and followed the star to Tolentino.

Right:
The altar in the Shrine of St. Nicholas of Tolentino with a depiction of the Saint celebrating Mass for the Poor Souls in Purgatory revealing a Poor Soul coming out of Purgatory on its way to Heaven.

should the priest preach on in his homily but the following Gospel passage, *"Love not the world, nor the things that are in the world....the world is passing away."*[1] We never know when we are planting seeds, what will flower and bloom. Did he become an Augustinian because of his mother's instructions on her knee? I would say *"Yes!"* Did he become an Augustinian because of the lessons learned in school? Again we must say *"Yes!"* But it is believed that it was the preacher who filled Nicholas with the great desire which would catapult him into serving the Lord and only the Lord for the rest of his life.

He entered the Augustinian community while still a child, and before he was eighteen, he joined the community as a brother. His first task was as *doorkeeper* at the monastery. He loved this job. He was able to meet the poor, and instruct them gently in the ways of the Lord. He would also give them food, sometimes too much food for the liking of his superior, but that was who Nicholas was. He willingly gave up all that he had, but the problem was that he also gave up all the community had.

It was during this time, his early days in the Augustinian community, while being doorkeeper, that we hear of Nicholas' first miracle. A child came to the door with his parents. It was obvious he suffered a serious physical malady. Nicholas put his hand on the child's head and said, *"The good God will heal you."* The afflicted child was immediately healed.

He traveled up and down the provinces of Italy near to his home town. He spent time in Cingoli, where he was ordained a priest at age 25. He healed a blind woman in that village, and became well-loved by the people there. But he had to move on. The Lord had a plan for Nicholas, and that was to eventually bring his ministry to Tolentino. There, he

---

[1] 1 John 2:15

would spend the rest of his days, evangelizing to everyone and anyone he could.

On all the paintings and statues of St. Nicholas, you see a star on his chest. There is a tradition that when meditating on where he should go, he saw an unusually bright star in the sky and followed that star to Tolentino. This reminds us of the Magi who followed the star to Bethlehem that led them to the Baby Jesus, born to redeem the world. Why had the star led Nicholas to Tolentino? The situation was not good in Tolentino when he arrived. People were not attending Mass. The churches were empty. His superiors held the belief the only way was to go door-to-door evangelizing. If the people would not come to God, His disciples would go to them; and so they sent Brother Nicholas (among others) to the people. Now, he had not done this before, but he obeyed and set out among the villagers. What he found was that the faithful were actually *starving* for the Word of God; he was immediately accepted by the people. During his teachings on the Gospel, he simply glorified *God*. He could hear people crying as they listened to him. He spoke with, as St. Augustine taught, "*the heart and mind*" of the Church and conversions took place *en masse*. Even those who hated him, could not resist the love with which he preached; they too, soon came around.

There is an instance which is attributed to the Saint, where there was one angry man, a heretic, who not only did not believe, but became violent when Nicholas preached in the town squares. He did everything in his power to disrupt Nicholas, or distract the people so that they could not pay attention to Nicholas. But our little saint just kept plugging, exchanging anger and violence with love. This infuriated the man all the more.

One day, when Nicholas was preaching to the people, in the town square, sharing how much God loved them, the angry man decided to disrupt the proceedings by fencing with his friends. The sound of steel blades slicing against steel blades, the swords threatened to drown out Nicholas, but that didn't stop him. He kept sharing about the God Who unconditionally loves us, even as we are rejecting Him. The angry man, who could not help hearing everything Nicholas was saying, finally stopped fencing, leaned on his sword and listened to the rest of Nicholas' talk. Needless to say, he was converted and became one of Nicholas' greatest supporters.

St. Nicholas' devotion to the Poor Souls

There are many gifts for which St. Nicholas of Tolentino is best known. One is his great devotion to the Poor Souls in Purgatory. When his superiors encouraged him to enter the seminary in preparation for the priesthood, he hesitated. He wanted nothing to take away from his prayer time for the Poor Souls. It wasn't until he was convinced that the greatest prayer he could pray for those suffering in Purgatory was the *Sacrifice of the Mass*, and that he could do best as a priest of God, that he finally consented to enter the seminary. He was ordained a priest in the order of St. Augustine.

He remained a man of prayer, praying day and night for the Poor Souls in Purgatory, sometimes as much as six to eight hours a night. But his devotion to those in Purgatory had to take a back seat to his vow of obedience.

One evening, while he was in prayer, a friar who had recently passed away, Pellegrino of Osimo, appeared to Nicholas. It was all too obvious from the expression on his face that Pellegrino was in agony. He mournfully shared with Nicholas that he was in the pits of Purgatory, suffering the most excruciating pain. He knew of Nicholas' devotion to the Poor Souls in Purgatory, and so he pleaded with his old friend to offer Mass, not only for himself, but for the many other souls who had asked him to implore the aid of

Nicholas.   Nicholas   immediately   consented.   *Then* he
remembered   that   he   was   under   obedience   to   offer   the
conventual Mass of the Order for the next week.

Pellegrino brought Nicholas into the pits of Purgatory,
so that he could see first-hand, the suffering of all those who
had asked for his intercession.   Before him were a multitude
of souls of all ages and conditions, experiencing terrible
torment. Pellegrino turned to Nicholas and said,

*"Behold the state of those who sent me to you.   Since
you are agreeable in the sight of God, we have confidence
that He will refuse nothing to the oblation of the Sacrifice
offered by you,[2] and that His Divine Mercy will deliver us."*

Nicholas could not hold back the tears.   He went into
prayer, after which he went to his superior and asked
permission to pray *the Mass for the Dead*.   When he shared
his vision, and the agonizing condition of the souls who had
asked for his help, the superior, too, broke down into tears.
He gave Nicholas a special dispensation from praying the
conventual Mass for that next week, and granted him
permission to dedicate his Masses as well as all his prayers,
toward the deliverance of the Poor Souls from Purgatory.
Nicholas celebrated those Masses *passionately* as (and with)
the *Victim Priest*[3] before him, the One Who came that no one
would have to suffer the pains of eternal damnation.

At the end of a week, Pellegrino of Osimo appeared to
Nicholas again, only this time he was not in agonizing pain.
He had been released from Purgatory, and was on his way to
Heaven. The other souls were in the same way, clad in white
garments and enveloped with a bright, heavenly light. They
called him their liberator, and as they rose up to Heaven,
they chanted the prayer,

---

[2]when the priest consecrates the host during the Sacrifice of the
Mass

[3]Jesus Christ on the Cross offering Himself to the Father for the
Redemption of the world

"Thou has saved us from them that afflict us, and thou has put them to shame that hate us."[4]

There were many instances of Nicholas' intercession for the Poor Souls in Purgatory. It became one of the greatest goals of his vocation, to help as many souls be released from Purgatory as he possibly could. But there is another thing for which St. Nicholas of Tolentino is famous, and that is the bread of St. Nicholas.

The Miraculous bread of St. Nicholas of Tolentino

The tradition began when Nicholas was quite ill and beginning to show the ravages of old age; he was so sick and so debilitated, he was about to die. His superiors asked him to eat a little meat and some nourishing foods. After all, they pleaded, they needed him, they and the community *and his Souls in Purgatory*! He wanted to obey his superiors, but he also knew the power of fasting toward moving God's Heart. So he prayed to Our Lady. Now, we know how much she loves her priests, her favorite sons, especially ones like Nicholas of Tolentino. Mother Mary appeared with the Baby Jesus in her arms. She handed Nicholas a small bit of bread; the Infant Jesus was holding a chalice filled with water; Mother Mary enjoined Nicholas to dip the bread into the chalice and then to eat it. Upon obeying the Mother of God, *his* Mother, he immediately recovered from his illness, and had more strength than he had ever known before.

From that time on, St. Nicholas would bless little pieces of bread, which he would distribute among the people. Healings abounded. *Author's note: When we visited Tolentino for the first time in 1977, the nun at the Shrine gave us some "St. Nicholas' bread." There were approximately six little crackers[5] enclosed in cellophane packages. Just having returned*

---

[4]Psalm 43

[5]little round crackers which look like small oysterette crackers that are sometimes put into soup

*to the Church two years before, and not having had much real
education in the Faith at the time, Penny asked how much we
were to give someone who was suffering, to bring about a cure.
The nun made a very wise statement, a teaching which has
stayed with us these many years. She said:*

   "It takes a little bread and a lot of faith."

Eight days before his death, our Lady appeared to St.
Nicholas and prophesied that he would die on September
the 10th, the third day after the anniversary of Mary's birth.[6]
St. Nicholas was on his death bed and suffering. The *enemy*
was attacking him mercilessly, these his last days. His soul
was in anguish, as the enemy persisted, taunting him,
disrupting his praying to the point he could barely remember
the prayers. St. Nicholas turned to his Mother Mary and
pleaded with her, saying he had endured the torments of the
devil all his life; could he, his last hours on earth be
undisturbed so that he could prepare properly for his
entrance before the Lord. Our Lady left without giving him
an answer. St. Nicholas continued praying. An Angel
appeared to him, told him his prayers had been heard, and
he would have the peace he desired. St. Nicholas spent his
last days in peace, without any attacks from the devil. Not
only that but he spent his last days, as if he were already in
Paradise, his face illuminated.

As Mother Mary had predicted, St. Nicholas of
Tolentino died on September 10, 1305. At his death, his
tomb became immediately a shrine of veneration. Twenty
years after his death, Pope John XXII ordered the Process
for Beatification to be opened. But during the investigation,
the popes moved from Italy to Avignon, France, and the
process was held up until they came back to Rome.

Three hundred and seventy-three miracles were
attributed to his intercession. They were investigated, and

---

[6]September the 8th

Left:
The Shrine of St. Nicholas of Tolentino in Tolentino, Italy

Right:
Jesus comes down off the Cross to embrace St. Nicholas of Tolentino

Above: ***The Tomb of St. Nicholas of Tolentino***

over 300 miracles were accepted by Mother Church. Pope Eugene IV canonized St. Nicholas on the Feast of Pentecost, June 5, 1446. The Pope had a special devotion to St. Nicholas. He had prayed to him, for the success of the Council of Florence; it had been called to make smooth the path to unification of all Christians, the Greek church with the Latin. Because many of the Eastern churches returned to the Chair of Peter through that Council, Pope Eugene IV attributed it to the intercession of St. Nicholas.

Forty years after his death, a tomb was erected where the faithful could come to venerate the Saint. One day, a disturbed fanatic, desiring to have part of the Saint to bring back to his country,[7] decided to cut off his arms. When he performed this sacrilegious operation on the Saint's body, the Saint's arms began to bleed profusely, *forty years after his death*. The rest of the body has decomposed, but from that time on, the miraculous arms have been incorrupt and were venerated in their own special chapel. They are still solemnly processed on the Saint's Feast Day. In 1926, the body was investigated and the Church verified that it was the body of the Saint. At that time, the arms were reunited with the rest of the body, a silver mask was placed over the Saint's face and the remains of the Saint are exposed for veneration, at the base of the Altar of Sacrifice, fitting for a priest who had prayed for so many Souls as he celebrated Mass.

Because of the many Souls that were released from Purgatory through his prayers, and the Masses he celebrated for the Poor Souls, he became and is known as the *Saint of Purgatory*.

Great pilgrimages began immediately to Tolentino. St. Nicholas was declared *Patron Saint* of many large cities in the rest of Italy, due to the miraculous deliverance from plagues and pestilences, through the intercession of St.

---

[7] it is written that he was a foreigner

Nicholas. Devotion to him came about in all of Europe, and then in the whole world. In Mexico, there are over 30 villages named after St. Nicholas, as well as a village in the Canary Islands. He is also venerated in South America.

He has among those who have been devoted: many Popes, many Saints and Blesseds who spent much time in Tolentino, praying to our Saint.

Saint of the Suffering on Earth and in Purgatory

St. Nicholas was *Saint of the Suffering on earth*, feeding them with earthly food and *Heavenly* Food in the Eucharist. He is known as well as *Saint of the Suffering Poor Souls in Purgatory*, having prayed for them all his life as a religious, and celebrating Mass for them as a priest. Because of His devotion to the Poor Souls, *Pope Leo XIII* declared the Basilica of St. Nicholas - *Church of the Poor Souls in Purgatory*. Mass is celebrated, there, every afternoon, for the Poor Souls in Purgatory.

Miracles abound through the intercession of St. Nicholas

One miracle came about in a village in *Spain*. There was a deadly plague spreading throughout Europe and was now claiming many lives in Spain. In petition and supplication, the faithful were processing through the streets, carrying a Crucifix and a statue of St. Nicholas. They were praying, with faith, for the intercession of our Saint. The priests were following, distributing Holy Bread of St. Nicholas. The procession was passing before the hospital, which was filled with the dying, when at that moment, Christ bent down from the Cross and embraced the statue of St. Nicholas. [This is another indication of the great love and devotion that St. Nicholas had for our Lord Crucified and His Passion.] Miracles began immediately. The plague stopped. People were miraculously healed.

In *Genoa*, they revere St. Nicholas and pray to him, because he answered the prayers of the Genovese and put down the pestilence that was spreading through that port city.

Another miracle attributed to St. Nicholas took place in *Venice*. The ducal palace of the Doge was on fire and was burning down, when they saw a vision of St. Nicholas in the sky. He threw a piece of blessed bread into the flames and the fire was extinguished. A beautiful painting was made of this miracle by the Venetians and hangs in the Basilica of St. Nicholas, till today.

One of the miracles accepted for his canonization, was the bringing to life of a young woman who had died, through the intercession of St. Nicholas.

Many miracles happened and continue to happen. One person was cured of her blindness. People were saved from drowning through his intercession. A farmer prayed to St. Nicholas and was saved. He had been tied up by outlaws, who had come to steal his cattle and kill him, when he turned to our Saint. It is not said what happened; only that they fled and left him and the livestock untouched. Why? Why do you think? Anyhow, this was considered another of the many miracles through our Saint's intervention. Another miracle through the intercession of St. Nicholas was when a man was about to be hanged. He was miraculously proven innocent and was freed, at the last moment, through the intercession of St. Nicholas.

The world and the people of God have always been plagued by the *deceiver* and his band of *deceivers*. And although there have always been those who accommodate the devil by teaching there is no such spirit, we have always needed the exorcism of fallen angels. Through St. Nicholas' intercession, demons have been known to be exorcised.

†††

We met St. Nicholas of Tolentino, so to speak, through the other Augustinian saints with whom we have become very close. In the same region of Italy, you will find the shrines to St. Rita of Cascia, St. Clare of Montefalco, and St. Nicholas of Tolentino. While their lives are separate, they are distinctly interconnected with each other *spiritually*. The common denominator, of course, is their founder and father in Faith, St. Augustine, a powerful role model and intercessor.

We have found great warmth and consolation from these Augustinian Saints. We have felt a brotherhood also to the different communities we have met at their shrines. It's like being with family. Learn about these Saints. Meet the community of believers who continue to espouse their charism. You will be home; you will be with family.

And most of all, have Masses said for the Poor Souls in Purgatory. You will then have Great Friends in High Places when they are released and go to live with Jesus in Paradise.

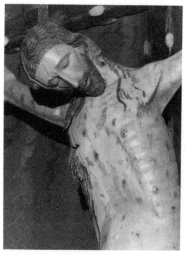

Above:
Jesus spoke to St. Margaret of Cortona from this Crucifix

Above:
St. Margaret of Cortona "Magdalen of the 13th Century"

Above:
The birth place of St. Margaret of Cortona

Saint Margaret of Cortona
Magdalen of the Thirteenth Century

As we begin our story of Saint Margaret, we need to add another name that has been used to paint a portrait of this gentle, yet powerful Saint: *"Magdalen of the Seraphic Order."* A book could be written around that one title. But then let Jesus speak to you, as He spoke to Margaret:

> *"Thou art the third light granted to the order of My beloved St. Francis. He was the first, among the Friars Minor; Clare was the second, among the nuns; thou shalt be the third, in the Order of Penance."*[1]

†

Magdalen of the Seraphic Order! When we begin to throw stones whether it be *literally*, as in Holy Scripture, or *figuratively* through rejection and condemnation, spreading scandal, slandering one's reputation, we must by God's Justice pause and reflect on the Mary Magdalen of Jesus' time and the special privilege God afforded her to allow her to be beside his Mother, prostrate at His Feet, as He gave His last ounce of Blood for the Redemption of the World. If you will also recall, it was to this repentant sinner that He first showed Himself after the Resurrection.

St. Therese of the Child Jesus once complained, misunderstanding Jesus' love for sinners, *"I do not want to be a sinner to have your Love."* To which, Jesus replied, *"With Mary Magdalen, I picked her up and brushed her off when she tripped on the stones and fell; with you, I went before you and took away the stones before you could fall."*[2] With some of us, the Lord is with us, calling us to be all that He planned we be at the moment of our conception, and although we fall, as in the case of Saint Margaret of Cortona, He is lovingly

---

[1]Under obedience to her confessor, Saint Margaret shared the conversation she had with the Lord where He said this to her.

[2]cf *"Autobiography of a Saint"* - St. Therese of Lisieux

standing by patiently wanting to forgive us and call us to holiness. We love The Little Flower and she touches many; but we also know that there are those who feel that God will never forgive them and they need a Saint like Margaret of Cortona. This life that we want to briefly share with you is one of a beloved repentant, another Magdalen whom Jesus loved.

Margaret of Cortona is one whom the Lord held in great favor, as He did David, another sinner who also repented and God chose to be an ancestor of Our Lord Himself. We would be remiss if we told you *only* of Saint Margaret of Cortona's love for the Poor Souls in Purgatory. There is so much more that we believe the Lord wants to teach you through this great Saint. In a time when people are committing murders and abusing God's children because of their claims of childhood abuse, we feel with all our hearts that God wants you to learn about a sinner who became a Saint; rejected by man she was specially chosen for His own by her Lord.

We have written about many Saints, and we love them all, but somehow we find our Margaret of Cortona to be a Saint of Reconciliation, a Saint of Hope in this world screaming for hope. If you learn nothing else from this Saint's story, it would have been worth writing if you walk away with God's message that *there is a God and He loves you, even when you are sinning.*

†

Our Saint began her life on earth in the Thirteenth Century. Let us go back to that time, to a little farmhouse in Laviano, in the province of Tuscany. There was a flurry in the quiet kitchen. Dusk had no sooner settled into night when dawn was desperately trying to break through. Water was boiling; the mid-wife was there to assist the bringing into the world of a new life. It was a girl! The pain of childbirth soon disappeared, as the mother held her new baby in her arms. We can just picture Baby Margaret's eyes opening to this new world outside of her mother's womb. Did you cry, Margaret? I wonder if babies cry upon leaving the security of their mother's womb because they have been whacked on the bottom, or are they whacked as a reminder of what life has in store for them?

I have always been affirmed by loved-ones, maybe that's why the vision of a Loving Father in Heaven is so easy for me to accept. I have always believed that God loved me. My parents showed their love in word and deed. They always made me feel special. My father said that I was the only one of his children that did not cause my mother pain when she gave birth. I do not know what that means, but maybe that's one of the reasons that I tried never to hurt my parents. Do we call our children by loving names, affirming complementing them, telling them how very beautiful they are? We cannot tell you how many wounded adults, children in grown-up bodies, are scarred because their parents did not affirm them.

Margaret was born in the region of Italy that has always been known as the *haughty* part of the boot. The citizens of Tuscany pride themselves as being descendants of the ancient Etruscan tribe, which is purported to having entered this region from the Far East over 5000 years ago. They have always been a proud people! This will be important to remember, as our story progresses.

Although life started simply enough for Margaret, her father putting bread on the table by farming, her mother showering little Margaret with love and attention, this was to come to a cruel end, when at age seven her mother died, suddenly. The woman who came to take her mother's place was as hard and stern, as her natural mother had been loving and compassionate, patient and understanding. Margaret was starved for love; her father, fearing angry reprisal from his new demanding wife, turned his back on Margaret, agreeing with her step-mother that she was worthless and would amount to no good.

Now, Margaret grew into a most beautiful young woman, full of life. But there was an emptiness. She hungered for love and acceptance; so just imagine when a handsome young lord spotted her and persistently courted her, flattering her, promising her marriage, how trusting she was, maybe too anxious to be number one in someone's life. Whatever the attraction or the reason, the young man swept her off her feet and carried her off to his castle. Marriage never came. She was faithful to him. He, on his part showed his love by showering her with everything but what she desired most - marriage. She rode through town on the finest horse, sporting superb finery. Now, this was just what the town gossips needed; here was an ideal opportunity to throw mud at her reputation. In their sickness of soul, did they think that perhaps by tearing her down they could gain some of the self worth they were possibly longing for?

Margaret never stopped pleading with her young lover to marry her. She gave the young lord a son. She never stopped loving him. Although he was faithful to her, looking at no one but her, he never would consent to marry her, even after their child was born. At heart, she was a good girl and her state of life pained her. She knew that this was displeasing to God and she loved Him even then, but her need of love on earth kept her from choosing God to the exclusion of all else. This was all to change.

One day, her young lord went off to inspect his estates; when night came and he had not returned, she became worried. The next day, she and her little boy waited anxiously, but there was no sign of him. When night came and he had still not returned, she became alarmed; this was not like him. Suddenly she saw something running through the woods toward the castle. It was the dog who had accompanied her lord. He scratched on the door; after she let him in, he began pulling at her dress, desperately trying to get her to follow him. When they reached a tree, the dog stopped and started to dig. Imagine her grief, when she saw the mangled body of her lover. He had been assassinated and buried under the tree, his murderers confident no one would find him.

Margaret took this as a sign the Lord was angry, and she was experiencing some of God's Justice. She gave everything the lord had given to her, to his family and to the poor, many of whom had scorned her. Taking nothing for herself and her son, they left Montepulciano[3] for her father's home. She entered the little town of her birth, not on a fine steed, adorned in the fine clothes and jewels of the past, but donned in the most humble clothes of a penitent.

Her father and stepmother, true to form, would have nothing to do with her or the little child. Penniless, with no where to turn, she left the town of her birth, desolate, despondent and all alone. Was it her Guardian Angel who reminded her of the Franciscans[4] in Cortona who were well known for their outreach and compassion toward penitents? When she arrived in Cortona, she was noticed by two sisters, who, seeing her alone with her little boy, befriended her and gave them a place in their home. They brought Margaret to the Franciscans and two of the Friars began to provide Margaret with Spiritual Direction.

Margaret asked permission to return to Montepulciano, to the villagers she judged she had scandalized by her former life. Her spiritual directors said Yes, and she set out. Arriving in town, dressed as a penitent, she processed through the streets, pleading for their forgiveness. That accomplished, she asked permission from the Friars to go to the town of her birth, and confess to all the villagers with

---

[3]where the lord had his castle
[4]They were known as the Grey Penitents

whom she had grown up. They said no, judging it would not be prudent at that time to do so.

Margaret begins to live, at last

Margaret prepared for three years, as a novice, and that glorious day arrived when she was admitted and vested in the Third Order of St. Francis. She sent her son to study in Arezzo (Italy) and he later became a Friar Minor. Her life became more and more a life dedicated to holiness. Her austere penances were sustained by the extremely strong will that brought her through all her years of suffering.

Never forgetting the hopelessness she and her son had felt when they had no place to go, she spent the rest of her life serving the poor and the sick. She founded a hospital, St. Mary of Mercy, which serves all who come to the door, till today, sending no one away who cannot pay. She selflessly gave of herself, at times to the point of exhaustion, but always entirely strengthened by the Divine Will of the Lord in Whom she trusted.

After sixteen years, her Savior gave her the mandate to retire to the abandoned Oratory of St. Basil. But her Lord never deserted her, if anything He was closer to her than ever, as she beheld His Precious Self and heard His Heart addressing her heart, as I'm sure He had the other Magdalen. But as the first Magdalen chose to walk the *Way of the Cross* with Jesus on the way to Calvary, so this, the *new Magdalen* spent the last nine years of her life, doing severe penance for her sins and the sins of the world (maybe also doing penance for those young girls who are trapped in unhealthy relationships, and do not have the strength to say "No!"). She continued having frequent ecstasies until the 22nd of February when she went Home to her Lord in Heaven.

The townspeople of Cortona immediately proclaimed her a Saint because of her generosity in serving them and the many miracles that had come to pass during her lifetime and were still occurring through her intercession even after death. Mother Church officially canonized her in 1728 and declared St. Margaret *Co-Patron of Cortona*.

Margaret and her special empathy for the Poor Souls

The Souls in Purgatory would appear to Margaret and beg her to offer all her suffering to diminish their pain and anguish. In particular, there were two merchants who had been slain on the road and died suddenly without having made restitution to those with whom they had dealt unfairly, cheating them while still alive. Death had come upon them so unexpectedly, they had not had time to go to a priest and confess their sins. They said that only by the Grace of God with His Most merciful Compassion, and with the intercession of His most precious Mother, were they able to make a last minute act of contrition, before taking their final breath and were spared from eternal damnation. They now pleaded with her to help them, as their suffering was excruciating, to pay for the wrongs they had committed against people who had trusted in them. They told Margaret they would have no relief until these debts were paid on earth. Would she go to their families and ask them to make amends to those whom they had cheated, giving them back all the money they had unjustly taken from them. Having imparted to our Saint where she could find them, the souls of the merchants disappeared. Margaret fulfilled their wishes and the souls never reappeared.

Margaret did not only show undying love and compassion for all the Poor Souls in Purgatory, but most passionately for her deceased mother and father, the father who had rejected her and her son, and her most unloving stepmother who had shown so little charity toward her. She never stopped offering up all her suffering for them; she sacrificed much needed sleep; she handed to the Lord her

Left:
Scene from the War Memorial Chapel in the Sanctuary of St. Margaret of Cortona. She is often shown with a dog near her. It was this dog that led her to her assassinated lover. After his death she gave all, that he had given her, to the poor and donned the humble clothes of a penitent.

Right:
St. Margaret of Cortona in glory going to Heaven.
She was very compassionate toward the Poor Souls in Purgatory, offering all her mortification and suffering, for their release.
When she was dying, she saw an Army of Souls that had been delivered from Purgatory forming an honor guard, a royal escort to Heaven.

dear and precious Holy Communions and all the Masses in which she had most reverently participated for their deliverance from Purgatory. The Lord heard His little bride; He appeared to her and declared, because of her supplications, not only had she lessened the immeasurable period of suffering, her parents would have had to endure, through her pleading they had been released from Purgatory and were in Paradise.

Was Margaret compassionate and caring for the Poor Souls in Purgatory, offering all her mortification and suffering for their release, because she felt herself such a great sinner? We do not know the innermost regions of her heart; we only know that when she was dying, she saw an Army of Souls that had been delivered from Purgatory forming an *honor guard*, a *royal escort to Heaven*. On her deathbed, she had become enraptured in ecstasy and when she came to briefly, she shared with those surrounding her bed, how the Lord had shown her a precious Army of Saints whom He said, through her prayers and mortification, were with Him and His Father in Paradise.

Left:
St. Gertrude the Great
No matter where she was, St. Gertrude's crucifix was nearby. One day, Gertrude held her crucifix up to her lips and kissed it. Her Lord appeared to her and said that every time someone kisses the crucifix or reverently adores the Christ represented on the crucifix, "God's Eyes of Mercy become a stamp on his soul."

Right:
One day St. Gertrude was praying for the Poor Souls, when Jesus admonished her for not praying with the confident assurance, the faith and realized hope that God hears and answers our prayers.

Visions of St. Gertrude the Great

When Our Lord wants a message to get out to His Church, he raises up a powerful Saint to do the task. Such a Saint was *Gertrude the Great*! She was the one to plant the seed which would bloom through the hands of another powerful Saint and visionary, St. Margaret Mary Alacoque, four centuries later, and subsequently through Blessed Sr. Faustina Kowalska in this century, through the Mission of Divine Mercy. Our Lord's mandate to St. Gertrude was to herald devotion to His Most Sacred Heart.

She came to us in the Thirteenth Century, a time of rampant heresy[1] and glorious victory. The Lord promised that His Church, although besieged by persecution, would triumph in the end; in the Thirteenth Century, with His Infinite Humility, He raised up great Saints to bring this about. St. Gertrude received the title "*the Great*" partially because of the extraordinary gifts she received from the Lord, but we believe more for her total dedication to her Spouse Jesus.

Why did the Lord want devotion to His Most Sacred Heart to begin at this time? We know that He brought about the Miracle of the Eucharist at Bolsena to dispel the heresy of *Berengarianism* in this century, but why did He give the message to St. Gertrude to bring about an awareness and love of His Most Sacred *Heart*, the Furnace of His Love?

Six centuries before, in around the year 720, His children were being led astray, innocent lambs being led to slaughter by some "*judas goats*," and so God in His *Mercy* gave His *little ones* a Miracle of the Eucharist in the Form of a *Human Heart*! Then six centuries later, He sends a Saint to herald devotion to His Most *Sacred Heart*, to let us know

---

[1]Albigensianism and Berengarianism - you can read more about these heresies, with the battles fought and won in Bob and Penny Lord's book: "*Scandal of the Cross and Its Triumph.*"

how much He loves us, how we can find refuge and strength in the *Mercy* of His Sacred Heart. Is this book not about His Mercy? God could not have shown more Mercy and Compassion than to give us an opportunity to be made ready for Him by gracing us with Purgatory.

He gave us Miracles of the Eucharist, whenever we were in danger of losing our faith. Why? Because He wanted us to know that He is with us, reachable and waiting for us, coming to dwell in us during the ongoing Sacrifice of the Cross, the Sacrifice of the Mass. He told St. Gertrude:

"You can find Me in no place where I delight more, or which is more suitable for Me, than in the Sacrament of the Altar."

This reaffirms a theme that runs through our books on *Visionaries, Mystics and Stigmatists, Saints, Angels, Mother Mary and Miracles of the Eucharist* that *no one, nothing* is more dear and precious to the Lord than us sharing in the Sacrifice of the Cross. You will read throughout this book how the most powerful arrow that can pierce the loving Heart of God the Father, moving Him to have mercy on us, is Our Lord's Passion, Death and Resurrection, that ongoing Sacrifice of the Cross - the Sacrifice of the Mass.

†

Our story begins in the village of Helfta, Germany. A little girl, barely five years old entered a Benedictine convent, a community filled with holy cloistered nuns whose whole life was the Lord. They knew and believed that the Lord was as truly present in the Blessed Sacrament as He was in Heaven and so they spent much of their lives on earth adoring Him.[2] From this fountain of faith flowed a desire to praise him morning, day and night, praying the Divine

---

[2]like Mother Angelica and her Poor Clare Nuns of Perpetual Eucharistic Adoration, whose Apostolate is Adoring the Lord in the Blessed Sacrament

Office. Gertrude grew in holiness and when she came of age, she became a Bride of Christ.

Gertrude receives her first vision

Her Bridegroom Jesus appeared to her when she was twenty-six years old. During Advent, she had been filled with a restlessness and longing to be closer to Jesus. The more she meditated, the more she began to have a disdain for the things of the world. One evening, she was about to retire, when Our Lord appeared to her as a very handsome young Man. He said: "*Thy salvation is at hand. Why are you so consumed by sorrow?*" She had received her first vision!

Now, she *knew* that she was in her dormitory, but it seemed as if she was being transported to the corner of the choir.[3] Jesus spoke to her:

"*I will save and deliver you. Fear not.*"

Our Lord opened His Arms wide to embrace her. She tried to approach Him, but a hedge, made thick with long menacing thorns barred the way, looming between them, separating her from Him. As she knew that the hedge and thorns were the times she had sinned and displeased the Lord, she began to weep. The Lord extended His Hand, and as if some unseen force had lifted her, she was beside Him. He invited her to rest her head on His Precious Chest. Her eyes went from His pierced Heart to His Hands and Feet; and there before her were His five Wounds, bleeding out of love for her and us "*the radiant jewels of His Sacred Wounds.*"[4]

St. Gertrude tells us that after this she was *converted*, not that she had been anything but virtuous. She had always been a good student, excelling in Latin, History and other worldly subjects. But after this, she had eyes only for the Word of God in Holy Scripture and the works of such Church Fathers as Saints Augustine, Gregory and Bernard.

---

[3]where the Nuns prayed the Divine Office
[4]St. Gertrude's words

St. Gertrude lived to love Jesus *alone*; pleasing Him was her sole objective in life. She sought and found Him everywhere, but most especially in the Eucharist. Jesus was consistently in her mind and on her heart; she took to heart His words, when Our Lord said:

"I delight so much in her, I have chosen to dwell in her. All that others see and love in her is My work; and whoever loves My work in her, loves Me. I have decreed that she stand alone, without friends or relatives, that none may love her from ties of relationship, but that I Myself may be the sole cause of her being loved and esteemed."

She had ultimate confidence in Jesus' Love and Mercy. He told her:

"It is impossible that anyone should not receive all that he has believed and hoped to obtain. It gives Me great pleasure when men hope great things from Me and I will always grant them more than they expect."

She turned to Jesus, as she would to an earthly father, with the complete trust of a child. No petition was too small or too great. On one occasion, when she had lost a needle in a pile of straw, she asked the Lord to find it for her:

"It would be in vain that I would search for this needle and so very much a waste of time. If You would be so kind, find it for me!"[5]

She turned her head, groped with one of her hands and immediately found the needle. Our Lord delighted in her simplicity and innocence, and always rewarded her faith in Him with gifts affirming that faith.

After that first vision, she continued to see Her Lord, only *"indistinctly"* as we say - with the eyes of the heart, when she would receive Holy Communion. This went on until the vigil of the Annunciation, when Our Lord visited her again and helped her to understand Him *more clearly*. From this

---

[5]cf "Saint Gertrude the Great, herald of Divine Love"-Tan Publishers

time on she would correct her faults out of love for the God of Mercy, not out of fear of the God of Justice!

She was so filled with God's Grace, she committed this prayer to memory, reciting it over and over again:

"O most merciful Lord, engrave Thy Wounds upon my heart with Thy most Precious Blood, that I may read in them both Thy grief and Thy Love; and that the memory of Thy Wounds may ever remain in my inmost heart, to excite my compassion for Thy sufferings and to increase in me Thy Love. Grant also that I may despise all creatures, and that my heart may delight in Thee alone. Amen."

Then, one day, she *knew* that the Lord had heard her prayer and, in response, had imprinted the Wounds that had pierced His most Sacred Body on the Cross, on her body. She had received the *stigmata* and would from that day on, experience the agony that her Lord had known.

Her heart is pierced by an arrow of Love

Seven years passed.   Gertrude did not believe it possible, she could receive any more Graces than she already had. Then during Advent, she had just received the Lord in Holy Communion when she saw a beam of light shoot forth from the Wound in Our Lord's Side on the Crucifix, and with the force of an arrow pierce her heart. With this stamp on *her* heart, the Lord expressed *His* Heart's desire :

"May all your love and compassion be centered on Me, so that all your delight, your hope, your joy, your grief, your fear and every feeling you have may be sustained by Me."[6]

Then, the last year of her life, Gertrude received the great grace to have Jesus exchange His Heart for her heart. She wrote that from that day on, she no longer lived but that she could truly feel Jesus living in her, loving through her.

---

[6]cf "Saint Gertrude the Great, herald of Divine Love"-Tan Publishers

Mary places the Infant Jesus into Gertrude's heart

She had been united with Jesus, the God-Man and now, it was time for the *Infant* King to touch her soul. Gertrude was meditating; it was Christmas Eve, and she was trying to place herself spiritually in the little barn in Bethlehem. She so wished she could have assisted Mother Mary bring the Baby Jesus into the world. As she was meditating, she felt the Blessed Mother place the Infant Jesus into her heart. She was being transfigured, the Lord her God becoming *all* in *all things*, to the exclusion of *all else*. Her soul was so filled with her Beloved Spouse's Presence, and she so delighted in this Spouse, alone, Who so strongly dwelled in her that she was blind to all the distractions around her.

Jesus places Gertrude's hand in His Open Wound

St. Gertrude had many visions. And they were all beautiful and special, but the one that touches my heart most is when Jesus appeared to Gertrude and asked for her hand. She stretched out her hand and he placed it in the open Wound in His Side. He promised to continue endowing her with His Graces, but should He subject her to the pain of being deprived of His Presence,[7] and she persevered, He would return and bless her a *hundredfold*. When Gertrude withdrew her hand, she saw three rings on her ring finger and one on each of the other four making seven (rings) in all. They were to represent, Our Lord said, the Graces that He had bestowed on the world through her.

When we read about Our Lord placing Gertrude's hand *in the open Wound in His Side, and read again his promise to her, and His assurance that should He deprive her of His Presence, and she persevered, He would return and bless her a hundredfold*, we could not help thinking of our beloved Church which flowed from the Wound in His Side, from His Most Sacred Heart, and it seemed the Lord was talking to

---

[7]Some of the Saints called this "The Dark Night of the Soul"

us, the Mystical Body of Christ. If we persevere and remain faithful to our Church, even should she appear near death, she will rise again more alive and glorious than ever.

The Sacred Heart and the Eucharist in the *Latter Days*

Jesus told Gertrude that His *Sacred Heart* is the Treasure He has reserved for the "*Latter Days*." A word that has been coming to us is that the Third Millennium will be *The Age of the Eucharist,* where everyone's eyes will be open and they will be able to see clearly Our Lord present in the Sacrament of the Eucharist. Statistics say that only 30% of Catholics believe that Jesus is truly Present in the Eucharist. Well, we are not into statistics but this we do know, that those who do believe, believe with their whole hearts; and some of them (believe), with an awareness of His Presence that the Saints like St. Gertrude had before them.

Many times, she was given the gift of having the veil lifted from her eyes; so that at those times, she could *see* the Divine Love and Mercy that Jesus in the Eucharist had for His children. He revealed how He longed to be united with them through this Sacrament. Jesus said that His Delight was to be with His children and that is why He left us Himself. He said that when He enters a soul in Holy Communion, He fills not only that soul with Graces but all the inhabitants of Heaven and earth benefit, as well as the *Poor Souls in Purgatory* who at the same time are experiencing some of the Lord's abounding Love and Mercy.

Jesus also told His little spouse that His Heart is the Altar upon which He, the Eternal High Priest, offers Himself to the Father during the ongoing Sacrifice of the Cross, the Sacrifice of the Mass, the Angels once again encircling Him as He goes through His Passion and Resurrection. Just thinking of the Altar in our churches as the Lord's Heart, how can we enter the church and not genuflect; or if our

Lord is not present (the tabernacle not being in the church) at least not bow? Do we know? Do we believe?

St. Gertrude has a vision of St. John the Beloved

She had a vision of St. John the Beloved and he invited her to rest her head on Jesus' Chest. She stood on one side and he on the other side of Jesus. Gertrude asked St. John if his heart beat excitedly when he rested on the Lord's Bosom during the Last Supper, and if he could not hear the blessed beating of her Lord's Most Sacred Heart at that time? St. John said that not only had he, but his *soul* could feel the sweet rhythm of the Lord's Heart beating down to its very core, leaving an indelible mark forever on his heart. Then, she asked why he had not written about the Lord's Sacred Heart. To which St. John replied, he was chosen to bring the *Eternal Word of God* to the faithful, but the message of the compassionate roaring flame of Our Lord's Sacred Heart has been reserved for the *Latter Days*.

When we think that what we hear, when we listen to *a human* heart beating, is a heart pumping *life* to the rest of the body, we understand some of the great Gift that God has reserved for us, to bring us through these rough days, these days that are so bewildering at times. He is filling us *with Life through the Eucharist, and hope through His Sacred Heart*.

Jesus tells us in Holy Scripture not to be afraid. Let us center our minds and hearts on this Lord of Mercy Who is sharing His Sacred Heart with us to strengthen us and to carry us through the Latter Days. Believe in Him, as Gertrude and all the Saints did; He will never betray you.

The Lord told St. Gertrude that every time, God the Father was sorely wounded by the sins of men, Jesus would show His Wounded Hands to His Father in atonement for their sins. So, he said, if only men will repent for their sins, they will obtain ready pardon from God the Father, His anger having been appeased because of His Son's Sacrifice.

Jesus speaks to St. Gertrude about the Crucifix

No matter where she was, St. Gertrude's crucifix was nearby. Even during the evening, in bed, she would reach out to touch her crucifix, holding her Lord on the cross close to her heart. One day, Gertrude held her crucifix up to her lips and kissed it. Her Lord appeared to her and said that every time someone kisses the crucifix or reverently adores the Christ represented on the crucifix, *"God's Eyes of Mercy become a stamp on his soul."* To us it also becomes a shield, a suit of armor upon our souls, protecting us from all harm.

St. Gertrude and the Blessed Mother

Gertrude had visions not only of Jesus but of Mother Mary and the Saints, who came and spoke to her. The Lord revealed the holy profits received by a soul who petitions Him through His Mother. He said that it was *He* Who chose to *only* bestow His Graces on God's children, through the hands and the Immaculate Heart of His Mother Mary. He told Gertrude that whenever she was afraid of weakening and succumbing to the snares of the devil, or felt incapable of doing His Will, to call on His Mother who would be her strength, her guide and her protectress.

On Mother Mary's birthday, September 8th, Gertrude had a vision of the Lord. She asked what rewards would be theirs who celebrated this Feast Day, with true devotion. He replied He would grant them a share in the *"special joys He possesses in Heaven, and in the virtues with which the most Glorious Blessed Trinity adorns Him."*

One time, when Gertrude asked Jesus what most pleased Him, He replied: *"Place yourself before My Mother, who reigns by My side, and endeavor to praise her."* St. Gertrude did so and *"our Lady adorned her with the rose of love, the lily of chastity and the violet of obedience."*[8]

---

[8]cf"Saint Gertrude the Great, herald of Divine Love" -Tan Publishers

Yet, we hear people foolishly questioning the love and devotion we have for our, and Jesus' Mother Mary. If for no other reason than, it so pleases Her Son, we should honor her. If for no other reason than, as one of His last acts of love on the Cross, Jesus gave Mary to us, as our Mother, we should love her.

"When Jesus saw His Mother and the Disciple there whom He loved, He said to His Mother, 'Woman, behold, your son.' Then He said to the Disciple, 'Behold, your mother.' And from that hour, the Disciple took her into his home."[9]

Once her Son had entrusted His bride to Our Lady, she never left Gertrude alone. She revealed to her, the place of the Holy Trinity in her life. Mother Mary appeared as a Lily with three petals, one upright and the other two gently draped downward, as if reaching out. [One of Our Lady's titles is *"Resplendent Lily of the Trinity,"* having been the only one, above all God's creatures, who most perfectly deserved and received the Graces of the *Three in One God*. She earned this honor, her perfect soul[10] never soiled with even the slightest stain of sin.] St. Gertrude understood that the upright petal represented the *"Omnipotence"* of God the Father, and the other two petals, the *"Wisdom"* of Jesus the Son and the *"Purity"* of the Holy Spirit.

Daughter of the Father, Mother of the Son, Spouse of the Holy Spirit, it was only fitting she be represented by this strong symbol of her relationship with the Triune God.

Gertrude was an instrument of healing

Even during her lifetime, people heard of Gertrude's holiness and asked her to intercede for them with Jesus. She

---

[9]John 19:26-27

[10]Mary was born without the stain of original sin; that was a gift from the Father; her gift to Him was she never stained her perfect soul with *actual sin*.

did, and many miraculous healings came about, physical and spiritual, equally.   If she could so powerfully move the Father's Heart for the living who were still sinning, how much more would the Lord listen to her prayers for those Souls who no longer sin, those suffering Souls in Purgatory, and answer them!

St. Gertrude's love and compassion for the Poor Souls

St. Gertrude felt great tenderness toward the Poor Souls in Purgatory. She constantly prayed for the Lord's Mercy on these Souls who were suffering, as they longed to enter Heaven. One day, before receiving Holy Communion, as she was praying for the Poor Souls, she seemed to descend with Jesus into the depths of Purgatory. She was devastated by what she saw. The Lord told her that He would allow her to bring forth from Purgatory all for whom she prayed.   After Communion, she saw more Souls ascending to Heaven than for whom she had dared to ask.

One day, Gertrude was praying for the Poor Souls, when Jesus admonished her for not praying with the confident assurance, the faith and realized hope that God hears and answers our prayers.[11] He assured her:

"It would not be past My Justice to release those Suffering Souls for whom you are praying, immediately, if you would pray with confidence for this petition."

St. Gertrude's greatest delight was in seeing a multitude of souls being released from Purgatory. But she received her greatest joy on the days she received Holy Communion, because on those days the numbers were infinitely greater. When she questioned the Lord, He replied,

---

[11]*"Faith is confident assurance concerning what we hope for and conviction about things we do not see."*(Hebrews 11:1)

"What makes you think I could refuse your prayers for the Poor Souls, especially on those days you are joined to Me in Holy Communion?"[12]

Our Lord, at another time, stressing how dear it was to Him to have Masses said, told St. Gertrude:

"At the hour of death, I will send to My children, as many saints to console and assist them, as Holy Masses they have reverently attended during their lifetime."[13]

One day, when she was praying for the Poor Souls, she asked Jesus how many Souls His Mercy would release from Purgatory. He replied that His Love desires to release *all* Souls from Purgatory. He used the following parable.

When a compassionate king has to imprison a friend, guilty of a crime, for the sake of equal justice for all his people, he longs for someone to plead for his friend and offer some sort of ransom for his release. You can imagine the joy, the king has when he is able to free his friend, and how kindly he feels toward those who arranged for his friend's freedom, those who paid off his debt.

If a king who is an imperfect ruler feels so for a friend, how much more so, Our Lord Who died for the Poor Souls in Purgatory! Jesus told St. Gertrude that every time someone prays for a Poor Soul, His Heart eagerly reaches out to send this loved one to join Him in Heaven.

It is not God's Will or design that we be separated from Him. We are part of the Creator, and He longs to be reunited with that part of Himself that He has created, that is so precious to Him. It is we who condemn ourselves to Hell or, who out of love for the Father, send ourselves to Purgatory to be made more presentable to Him. When God fashioned us, He created us in His Image with Free Will to know Him, to love Him and to serve Him. When we stand

---

[12]cf In author's language

[13]cf"Saint Gertrude the Great, herald of Divine Love"-Tan Publishers

before Him, we see how many times we have failed to love Him as we should, how many times we have put matters of the world before serving Him, how we have *reluctantly* spent time getting to know Him better by spending time, quiet quality time during the Sacrifice of the Mass or adoring Him in the Blessed Sacrament. At that time, He will look into our eyes and His Eyes of Perfect Love will meet ours and we will condemn ourselves, and we will willingly fly to Purgatory.

Who is My brother and My sister?

Our Lord instructed St. Gertrude *whom* to pray for in Purgatory. On All Souls Day, as her community was praying for the deceased parents of the sisters, St. Gertrude could see many rejoicing souls ascending up to Heaven, cutting through the darkness, lighting the sky with their brilliance. She asked the Lord if these were all their relatives and Our Precious Lord replied:

"I am your nearest Relative, your Father and your Mother. Therefore My nearest friends are your nearest relatives, and these are among those whom I have freed."[14]

When she wrote for her sisters' education, her writings reflected her attitude towards *death*:

"I wish with my whole heart to be strengthened by those health-giving last Sacraments; nevertheless the Will and appointment of God seem to be the best and surest preparation. I am certain that, whatever the manner of my death, sudden or foreseen, I shall never lack His Mercy, without which I cannot possibly be saved in either case."

Jesus told St. Gertrude that He had revealed His Heart to her, that she might pass His messages of love down to His children. And when St. Gertrude was reluctant to reveal her revelations, the Lord told her emphatically that she would

---

[14]cf"Saint Gertrude the Great, herald of Divine Love"-Tan Publishers

not be released from the *"prison of her flesh"* until she had obeyed Him in this matter. And so, she did.

It is time for St. Gertrude to go Home, at last

Although her life had been one of *almost daily* visions of Jesus, with an intimacy and communication rarely known on earth, her heart was restless until it rested in Him, in the Kingdom, for all eternity. She was on fire! Her whole being yearned for her God. Instead of these heavenly privileges making her resolute with this time on earth, the splendor and the intense joy of seeing Him, hearing Him, being in Our Lord's Presence gave her a greater desire each day, and a growing holy impatience to be with Him in *Heaven*.

One time, she cried out: *"When are You going to release me from the prison of this body and permit me to enter the gates of Heaven to begin our life eternal together?*[15]

Now, St. Gertrude and Jesus had a wonderful relationship. As she was complaining to her beloved Spouse about Him not granting her request, He revealed how she was to die. She went into deep ecstasy and saw a Heavenly Army of Angels and Saints, coming to escort her Home, followed by the Patriarchs, the Prophets, the Apostles, the Martyrs, the Virgins, and the Holy Innocents. The fallen angels were afraid to venture near this Heavenly court.

St. Gertrude became very ill. She spoke to Jesus and said that although she longed to be with Him, if He willed she remain on earth, she willingly obeyed Him, although her heart was with Him. It seemed that was what Jesus was waiting to hear. He told her, she had fulfilled His Will for her on earth and He was ready to escort her to His Father. Her last months on earth were filled with excruciating pain, but although she had to be carried to Mass, she would not

---

[15]cf"Saint Gertrude the Great, herald of Divine Love"-Tan Publishers

miss a day being near her Spouse in the Word and in the Eucharist.

All the sisters surrounded her bed, their sorrow inconsolable. It was painfully obvious she was leaving them. Jesus appeared to His bride, His Face radiant. His Mother was on His right, and as at the foot of the Cross, St. John was on His left. As He had told her, there were the *Heavenly host of Angels, the Saints, the Martyrs, the Innocents, the Virgins;* it seemed all Heaven had turned out for her welcome into Heaven.

The sisters were reading the Passion when they pronounced the words: "*And bowing His Head, He gave up His Spirit,*" Jesus opened His Heart welcoming her within. The Angels began singing Alleluia, and the next thing you know, one of the sisters heard the Lord say:

"Behold you are united to Me and to become My own forever....I will present you to My Father by the close embrace of My Heart."

You can be sure that there was a Heavenly Court made up of all the Souls who had been released from Purgatory through her intercession, also awaiting her in Heaven with big signs welcoming her Home!

Left:
St. Clare of Montefalco
Jesus thrust His Cross into her heart and said, *"How long I have waited for someone I could trust with My Cross."*

Right:
Just before St. Clare of Montefalco died, she sat up in bed and appeared completely recovered. She remained seated upright in the bed, her eyes turned toward heaven, not moving, without even the smallest quiver. She said, "Now I have nothing more to say to you. You are with God because I am going to Him." Then she died.

Above: ***The Incorrupt body of St. Clare of Montefalco***

Saint Clare of Montefalco

*"If you seek the Cross of Christ, take my heart;
there you will find the Suffering Lord."*

The above statement was made by St. Clare of Montefalco, an Augustinian Nun, *and Mother* to her Community of Nuns. These were words, to them and us, to *hope in,* and *to have an understanding of* the crosses we are called to carry in our own lives. Jesus could bear the Cross, because He knew and believed in the Love of the Father and His Promise of the Resurrection. Clare adored and carried the Cross of Jesus, confident that she could trust in Him and His Promise to her.

†

"Clare was born in 1268. Her eldest sister Giovanna established a hermitage in the year 1271. The first candidate was her sister Clare, all of six years old.

"Even without a Religious Rule, Clare faithfully practiced *strict* obedience to her sister Giovanna, the leader of the group. Once when she broke the rule of silence prescribed by Giovanna, Clare imposed on herself a penance of standing in a bucket of ice cold water with her arms outstretched high above her head, praying the Lord's Prayer one hundred times.

"According to one of the rulings instituted by the Council of Lyons (1274) and subsequently decreed by a Papal Bull, the little band of hermits of *Santa Croce*, or Holy Cross, was required to adopt one of the established Rules of the Church. Their choice was the Rule of St. Augustine, that is to live a shared life, like that of the first Christian Community, with one mind, one spirit, one heart centered in God; in short, *to be what we are all called to be, One, Holy, Catholic and Apostolic.* The Rule was granted to them by the Bishop of Spoleto on June 10, 1290.

"They had started with a Community of two, Giovanna and Andreola. Clare joined and they became three. She was followed by Marina, and they became four. One by one, young women came and stayed. What began as a small raggedy remnant of hermits became a *Community* of Nuns. Their hermitage which had started very humbly, grew very slowly and painfully into what is today a Monastery. The life begun by those first Nuns of the Holy Cross, a life in common structured after that of the Rule of St. Augustine, has been faithfully followed for close to 730 years."[1]

Sister Giovanna goes Home

"On November 22, 1291, Clare's sister Giovanna went to dwell with her Lord and Master, Jesus. People, soon after her death, began calling her *Blessed.*

"For Clare, the loss of her sister was to cause her pain unlike anything she had ever experienced before. Not even at the death of her father, had Clare cried. Not even when her mother died in Clare's Monastery, did Clare cry. She loved her mother and father very much, but she *had not* cried. Now she cried for three days and nights. Inconsolable, allowing no one inside her, she grieved alone, privately. The Nuns were puzzled to see her cry at the death of her sister, as she had not cried for her parents. Concerned and troubled, they approached her asking her the reason for her tears.

"She replied, *'How is it you do not understand? I weep neither for her (Giovanna) soul or her body, but only for myself. Isn't that who we cry for? Giovanna was to me an example and a mirror of life; everyday she spoke to me of God and of always new and profound and spiritual matters. For this I weep, for nothing else.'*"[2]

---

[1]excerpts from chapter, Saint Clare of Montefalco in Bob and Penny's book: "*Saints and other Powerful Women in the Church*"

[2]excerpts from "*Saints and other Powerful Women in the Church*"

Giovanna passed on. Clare's grief was inconsolable, but she put her pain aside, and reflected more on the state of her sister's soul. Although she was fully aware of her sister's holiness, she did not take for granted, she would be in Heaven. Three days after Giovanna's death, during her morning prayers, she had a vision. Before her was a large torch, something resembling a beam; it shot across the room toward her and rested above her head. It was brilliant, the flame lighting the room, filling her with an unexplainable joy. As she had been imploring the Lord to reveal her sister's fate, the vision made Clare understand that her sister was with Him in the Kingdom. Trusting in the Lord and His faithfulness, Clare was suddenly filled with such peace, that if she had the gift of having her sister remain on earth, it could not have surpassed this assurance she had of her sister's salvation. In the same vision, she saw persons, who were godly and those who were evil, and the extent of their holiness and sinfulness. At the end of the vision, her sister Giovanna appeared to her. Clare asked her, "*Giovanna, are you not dead?*" To which her sister replied, "*My death was not death but a passage to life.*" And my brothers and sisters *this* is what we are all preparing for, that "*passage to life.*"

Clare has a vision of a Poor Soul in Purgatory

When we researched Saint Clare and became a part of this Community, we discovered that she had the faithful from all walks of life coming to her for spiritual direction. Now, as the Community of nuns were cloistered,[3] Giovanna and Clare counselled all who came seeking spiritual help, anonymously, from behind a dark screen, their faces further covered by a black veil.

One day, a grieving widower, a simple farmer, came and appealed to Giovanna to pray to the Lord and ask Him

---

[3]They are still cloistered, living faithfully the almost 730 year Rule of their foundress Giovanna.

where his recently deceased wife was. Clare overheard the man's petition, and out of compassion, returned to her cell and began to pray. She had a Divine vision, where she was advised, the woman was suffering excruciating pain in Purgatory. She asked the Lord for permission to partake in this Poor Soul's agony, and He said Yes! Clare shared the stripes meant for the woman, paying in part for the sins of the Poor Soul, as her Savior, before her, had accepted the flagellation due us for our sins. After enduring unfathomable suffering, it was revealed that the Soul could be helped by her husband giving alms to those whom she had named. The man was still crying to Giovanna, when Clare called her aside, and spoke to her, *quietly*, so the man would not know that she had had a vision. Giovanna shared his wife's message and the man went away sad, but filled with hope, knowing he could do something to relieve his wife's pain and possibly shorten her time in Purgatory.

Clare would be called to intercede many times for the Suffering Souls in Purgatory. But there was a price to be paid, an ongoing war between God and the enemy of God raging inside her, making all her intense suffering as nothing, compared with this battle for her soul. If the enemy could win her, what good he could block, and what evil he could bring about. But the Shepherd of Souls never leaves us, and so, He was always there protecting His precious Bride, never allowing her to bear more than she could bear.

Clare Soars to Heaven at the Nativity

One year, during Advent, Clare felt herself continually being drawn up in rapture. She was in the presence of our Lord Jesus; she could actually see Him all the time. This began three weeks before the Birth of Our dear Lord Jesus, and continued on until Christmas Eve. At that time, she could feel herself being brought to an open field. She was holding the newborn Baby Jesus in her arms. She walked along the road until she arrived at a large house. A brilliant light emanated from the house. She was in the brilliance of the presence of God Himself. The light went from the Lord to her, enveloping her and the Baby Jesus completely. She was swallowed up in it.

She felt surrounded by the Holy Spirit. She was given a spiritual anointing. Clare could feel herself in the company of the Angels and Saints. She was caught up in the light that was descending from the Father. The Angels and Saints were all around her, embracing her, singing praises to God and the newborn Baby Jesus. She began to sing with them; the voice was not even hers. It was coming from the Holy Spirit. Although she was singing very softly, she knew from the responses of the Angels and Saints that her voice was ringing out all over the world.

Nuns in the monastery heard Clare singing, but her words were unintelligible. She was singing in tongues, a gift given to her on that night by the Holy Spirit. She knew she was taking part in the celestial celebration of the birth of the Savior. It was such an exciting time. She cradled the Christ Child in her arms. She was in a complete state of ecstasy as the Angels and Saints sang softly, putting her into the sleep of the joyful. She had never felt closer to Heaven than on that blessed evening.

Clare sees the Judgment of the Souls

Clare was given gifts of Heavenly Visions often during the time of Christmas. On another occasion, on the Feast of the Epiphany, she felt herself being drawn up again into the Celestial surroundings. She went into such a rapture, she was lost to the entire world for thirty days. During this time, she witnessed God's Judgment of the Souls. But it was like nothing she had ever heard or seen. There was no anger, no guilt, no trial. Actually, God did not judge anyone; they judged themselves. She could see them convicting themselves of all they had done in their lives, and condemning themselves because of their sins, and exacting for themselves their own punishment, their own condemnation.

It was a time where all that was hidden in the darkness was seen in the light. She could see her own sins; defects which she never would have considered wrong before, all of a sudden took on a grave significance, calling for severe consequences. She saw thousands and thousands of demons in front of her. They shrieked at her: *"You must come down here! We're waiting for you!"* A condemned soul rushed past her, being pulled by demons with rakes and hooks; they were hurled into the darkness, right in the line of a huge demon who smashed the soul with a huge iron.

The fury of the shrieking and the pitch of the outcries were impossible to describe, they were so horrible. The frightening thing for Clare was, she was not sure if these souls were going down into Hell or Purgatory.

But during this time of ecstasy, she also saw a beautiful round mountain, marvelous and beautiful to behold. Bows in the sky shone all around; some were like rays of the sunlight; others were colored like rainbows. They inspired her; they filled her with such joy. She could not help but want to do good; she wanted to glorify God in everything she did. She could see, on the center of the mountain, God, the source of the light, surrounded by the Angels. The Saints sang out to her, *"Come! Come!"* Another voice, (she didn't say if this was God) spoke softly: *"She will certainly come, but not now."*

Clare has a vision of the Blessed Trinity

After having these painful visions, God graced her with one of the Divine, *The Blessed Trinity*. She beheld her Triune God in Three distinct Persons, yet in One substance, Equal. Clare wrote that, even should God come to her and

ask what gift, He could give her, there would be nothing sh..
could desire that would equal this vision of Her Lord, in His
Glorious Trinity. When she died, they found inside her
incorrupt body, three kidney stones, weighing equally: three
weighing as much as one, two as three and etc., a gift from
the Lord, representing the Trinity, left as a sign of the special
relationship she had with the Holy Trinity.

Clare prepares to go the her Lord

During one of her ecstasies, she saw the Heavenly court
of Saints inviting her into Heaven. The sisters heard her say,
"*Tell Mother Mary to welcome my soul.*" Then, she turned to
the grieving nuns and said, "*Let us all rejoice in the Lord and
sing 'Te Deum, Laudamus,' because my Lord desires to take
me with Him to His Father's House.*" She shared that, her
bridal party, the Saints and Angels were awaiting her, her
Bridegroom was standing at the High Altar and God the
Father was presiding. She exclaimed that she wished she
could invite the whole world to be present at what has been
prepared for her.

"On the evening of August the 15th, she called the Nuns
together and left them her spiritual last will and testament, '*I
offer my soul and all of you, the death of Lord Jesus Christ. Be
blessed by God and by me. And I pray, my daughters, that you
behave well and that all the work God has had me do for you
be blessed. Be humble, obedient; be such women that God
may always be praised through you.*'

"After speaking to all of the weeping Nuns, trying to
leave them consoled and strengthened, she asked for the
Sacrament of *Extreme Unction*.

"When a Nun is dying, each of the Sisters make a sign of
the Cross on her. As they attempted to do so to Clare, she
gently but firmly protested over and over again, '*Why do you
sign me, Sisters? I have the crucified Jesus in my heart.*'

"Friday, late in the afternoon, she called for her brother Francesco, who was guardian of a Convent in Spoleto. That night, when he arrived, he found his sister very tired. But the following morning a very happy Dr. Simone greeted him with the good news that Clare had slept well and was resting comfortably. Francesco started to leave when he was called back by two of the Nuns. He followed them into the Chapel of the Holy Cross, her bedroom. She appeared completely recovered, was sitting up, the color back in her face, smiling, looking so well he suggested they give her something to eat. She gave her brother Spiritual Direction, as she was his Spiritual Director and teacher, talking at great length with him. As much joy and a mood of anticipated celebration began to spread among the Nuns and Francesco, Clare turned to Fra Tommaso, the Chaplain of the Monastery, *'I confess to God and to you my faults, all my offenses.'* And a little later, turning to her Nuns, *'Now I have nothing more to say to you. You are with God because I am going to Him.'*

"She remained like that, seated upright in her bed, her eyes turned toward Heaven, not moving, without even the smallest quiver. Several minutes passed. Clare was no longer speaking. Francesco took his sister's pulse; He turned to the Nuns circled about the bed and announced, tears running down his face, *'She is dead.'* The doctor teased Francesco and the Nuns, believing Clare had gone into ecstasy. Nothing Francesco could say would satisfy him until he reluctantly took her pulse himself. Having done so, he agreed that she was gone, and he too, broke into tears. A friend was dead. The world would never be the same. It was 9 a.m. on a *Saturday* morning, the 17th of August. We're sure that Mary, the Mother of God, was there waiting to bring this faithful daughter to her Spouse, her Bridegroom Who had a place ready for her in His Father's Mansion."[4]

---

[4]excerpts from "*Saints and other Powerful Women in the Church*"

Her body kept exuding a heavenly fragrance. They couldn't put their beloved Mother in the grave. There was an investigation of the body; scientists as well as the local Bishop and other Church dignitaries were there. During that investigation, they opened her heart, because of her words, "*Look to my heart; there you will find the Crucified Lord.*" This is what they found:

When you visit the church, where the incorrupt body of Saint Clare is visible for veneration, you will see on the right side of the altar, Saint Clare's *heart*, and on the left side, a Cross. In the center of the Cross is the shape of our *Crucified Lord*, formed out of muscle, found on the inside of the heart of the Saint. Nerve endings form *a Crown of Thorns* on His Head. Underneath the shape is a tendon, which looks like the *whip of flagellation*. On the three corners of the Cross are the kidney stones we spoke of, above.

There is so much more, we could tell you in this chapter, but sadly, not enough space. But please read more about this very timely Saint, for this time and all time.

✝

We want to express our heartfelt thanks to Mother Paola of the Sisters of the Holy Cross of Saint Clare of Montefalco for the research done for this chapter, digging into all the material on our great Augustinian Saint.

We want to also give our deepest thanks to Father John Rotelle, O.S.A, for taking time out of his very busy schedule to undertake the great but arduous task of translating the text from Italian into English.

We thank God for the opportunity to, once again, write about our Patron Saint, *St. Clare of Montefalco*. We can never thank her enough for the blessings, received from her intercession and all the life-giving support and direction we have received from her Community of Nuns, for the almost twenty years, we have been going to her Shrine.

Left:
St. Catherine of Siena in ecstasy
"I have seen the hidden things of
God and now I am thrust back into
the prison of the body."

Below:
St. Catherine of Siena being
Mystically Married to Jesus

Below:
St. Catherine's father,
remembering the time that he had
seen a dove hovering over her
head, ordered the family not to
interfere with her vow to the Lord.
When Catherine knelt beside her
father's deathbed, she asked to
suffer in his place.

St. Catherine of Siena
Glimpses Heaven

In each century, when the Church has been in need, the Lord has raised up powerful men and women to save her. Catherine was one of those powerful women, a light in the darkness of the Fourteenth Century. She had been chosen by her Lord and Savior to be His bride. And then, when He believed she was ready, He commissioned her to save His Church. She had lived for the Church and she died for the Church, one of those *"Dry Martyrs"*[1] we so often speak of in our books.

There is so much we could write about Saint Catherine in this chapter. But we have written about her in three of our books[2] and here we would like to focus our attention on her visions of Heaven and her experiences with souls from Purgatory.

Catherine and Heaven

This one August morning in 1370,[3] Saint Catherine was not seated with her fellow *Mantellate*[4] at the back of the Church of Saint Dominic, as she usually was.[5] This one Sunday, the priest was preaching, when suddenly there was a commotion in the church. Her Mantellate companions were

---

[1] Archbishop Fulton J. Sheen used this expression to describe those who do not shed their blood for Mother Church, but *"who suffer over a period of years pain that far exceeds that of the Wet Martyrs."*

[2] *"Saints and other Powerful Women in the Church"*
"Scandal of the Cross and Its Triumph"
"This is My Body This is My Blood, Miracles of the Eucharist, Book I"

[3] 10 years before her death

[4] a form of Tertiaries

[5] We visited this church many times and stood where this great Mystic went into ecstasy. She would, upon reception of Holy Communion, go into ecstasy and remain so for hours, most times levitating in mid-air. At times, she had to be carried out of the church because the sacristan had to close it for the night.

all whispering nervously. Father Bartolomeo realized no one
was listening to him.   It seemed, he overheard *"Catherine
Benincasa[6] is dead!"* He quickly finished his homily and after
Mass was over, hurried into the sacristy to find a lay brother
wringing his hands over the devastating news that Catherine
was dead!

The priest rushed over to Catherine's house.   The
streets were lined with mourners. He plowed through the
many people who jammed the staircase up to her home. The
priest and lay brother forced their way into her room. What
they saw brought tears to their eyes; it was Saint Catherine
lying *motionless* in a coffin.   Father Bartolomeo had seen
Catherine many times in a trance where she appeared dead,
but somehow this was not the same. He groaned, his voice
shaking, barely able to pronounce the words: "When did she
die?" Lapa, one of her close companions, said that she had
found her like this when she went to awaken her at six in the
morning.

The brother with Father Bartolomeo began to sob
uncontrollably, so much so, a blood vessel broke in his chest
and he began to hemorrhage profusely, blood gushing forth
from his mouth. Everyone was alarmed, as it was apparent
the brother was in grave danger. There was no way to stop
the bleeding. Father Della Fonte, a priest who had been
summoned, raised the brother's limp body up to the edge of
the coffin. He took Catherine's still, lifeless hand and placed
it on the brother's breast.   The bleeding stopped,
immediately. Color slowly returned to Catherine's pale face,
which by this time had taken on the appearance of marble.
Everyone excitedly came close to the coffin. Their joy and
eagerness, in anticipation of once again seeing their
Catherine's radiant eyes looking back at them, turned to
utter dismay.   She looked back at them, completely

---

[6]Saint Catherine's full name

devastated, and then turned toward the wall, sobbing uncontrollably.

Her companions all filed out, to spread the good news that Catherine was alive! But their *good* news was her *bad* news. Her trance had lasted over four *hours*, but her grief at having returned to life lasted two *days*. When she did speak, all she could say was:

"I have seen the hidden things of God and now I am thrust back into the prison of the body."[7]

The mystical *death* she experienced was different from the other ecstasies she'd had. For the next (and last) ten years of her life, she could not speak of what she had seen and felt, without bursting into tears. She would look away, her eyes far off, remembering. It was as if she were communicating with her Spouse: *How long, how long before I go to You, my Lord?* What glorious light had she witnessed that made her life on earth appear so dark and lonely? Not to over simplify, but to try to equate the darkness on earth for Catherine with something we possibly can understand, would be for me, like being in a room filled with people, yet feeling all alone because my spouse was not there. Although it would be a joyful party for everyone, for me it would be empty and lonely, and I would not be able to stand it till I was reunited with my love. Catherine and Jesus were mystically married. She had been instructed by Jesus on earth; she had seen Him in her room at home, when she went into ecstasy in St. Dominic's Church. How was this so different, so earth-shattering, that life on earth became such a burden? How much we have to look forward to!

Although her grief was inconsolable at times, she never was a burden to anyone. She never shirked from the task the Lord had assigned her. It was during this sorrowful period in her life that she brought Pope Gregory XI back

---

[7]St. Catherine intimates that she has had visions of Heaven

from Avignon to Rome, and upon his death, supported his successor. When a new Pope, Pope Urban VI was elected, she was horrified that anyone would turn against him. She loved her Pope and had a few words for those who might think themselves autonomous of the Pope and criticize him:

"Even if he were the devil incarnate, we should not raise our heads against him because he is sweet Christ on earth."

Although she had seen the Lord in Heaven and had received countless gifts, she did not put herself above the Church and its traditions. She was a formidable fighter who would wage battle with the devil himself to save Mother Church.

Catherine chooses Purgatory on earth

Catherine loved her father Giacomo very much. When life with the family became very difficult, (not being able to accept her way of life), he believed in her, remembering the time he had seen a dove hovering over Catherine's head. It was her father Giacomo who ordered his family not to interfere with Catherine's vow to the Lord.

The time came when Giacomo became so ill, the end was near. Catherine, as was her custom, began to pray to her Spouse to cure her father, if it be His Will. The Lord responded that it would not be for Giacomo's best interest for him to remain on earth, any longer. When Catherine knelt beside her father's bedside, she saw how ready he was to leave this world, and she knew peace. But that did not stop her from praying for her Spouse's Mercy. She asked the Lord, not only to pardon her father's sins, but at the moment of death to grant that he enter Heaven, without going through the purifying fires of Purgatory. Jesus could do nothing but deny her petition, explaining that God's Justice had to be satisfied; the soul of her father had to be pure, without blemish, to enter Paradise. He said that although he had led an exemplary life as a husband and father (the Lord particularly pleased with his treatment of Catherine), he had stains on his soul that had to be removed by the purifying flames of Purgatory.

Then Catherine pleaded with the Lord: *"Please Lord, do not allow my father to die before his soul has been purified on earth, so that he might not suffer torment passing through the raging flames of Purgatory."*[8] Giacomo lingered, his strength ebbing away, unable to die because of the battle between the Lord's demand for Justice and Catherine's plea for mercy. Realizing the Lord would not grant her father that special Grace without exacting full payment, Catherine countered with: *"If my father cannot go directly to Heaven without satisfying God's Justice, then please allow me to bear my father's pain in his stead."*[9] Jesus accepted her selfless act of love toward her father, because of her faithful love for Him and assured her she would suffer as long as she lived, the pain destined for him. Catherine cried out joyfully: *"Thank You, Lord for Your Compassion on my father; Thy Will be done."*[10] As Giacomo's soul was leaving his body, Catherine's body was being filled with the most excruciating pain, which lasted the rest of her life.

While everyone was grieving, Catherine was glowing, offering consolation to her mother and all the members of her family; for you see, she had seen her father's beloved soul leave his body and soar like a beautiful bird to eternal happiness in Heaven. The Lord, prior to her father's death and ascent to Heaven, had mercifully given Catherine a glimpse of Paradise.[11] As He had done with Peter, James and John when He brought them onto Mount Tabor, and showed them His transfigured Self, prior to His Crucifixion, so now Jesus brought His bride to Heaven that she might

---

[8]Cf.Blessed Raymond of Capua
[9]Cf.Blessed Raymond of Capua
[10]Cf.Blessed Raymond of Capua
[11]Cf.Blessed Raymond of Capua

keep this Image in her mind and heart through her days of suffering.

Blessed Raymond further writes that Catherine shared that her father visited her many times and thanked her for the happiness she had purchased for him, with her suffering. He revealed many hidden things and warned her of the traps the devil sets for those who relax their guard.

Catherine and a Poor Soul doomed to Purgatory

Catherine spent much of her time, when she was not dictating the Lord's messages to her many secretaries, ministering to the sick[12] and the needy. There was a woman named Palmerina to whom she had shown great charity. But as can happen, the recipient of love will often bite the hand of the giver. The woman spread all kinds of false gossip about Catherine. And the more that Catherine responded to her abuse with love, the more the hate grew in the heart of Palmerina. Seeing her helplessness in aiding this poor victim of her own hate, Catherine turned to prayer. Knowing that this hate which had spread like a cancer, blocking out all reason, would finally consume Palmerina so completely that she would be lost forever, Catherine implored God to soften the woman's heart and consequently save her soul.

The Lord answered her prayer; the woman fell seriously ill. You would think that would do it; but instead she grew more angry and bitter. Catherine, caring selflessly for her and her wounds, only made Palmerina's fury grow. When her insults failed to drive Catherine away, Palmerina ordered her out of her room at the hospital.

---

[12]We visited the hospital where she served so selflessly and the little cave *"Santa Caterina della Notte"* (which is now a shrine to the Saint across from the Cathedral in Siena), where she would spend the night when she had finished working too late to return home.

A short time later, Catherine received word that Palmerina was dying. A priest was called, but he could not administer Last Rites, her heart was so full of vindictiveness and malice. Her unrepentant anger and hatred was blocking her from God's Mercy. Knowing that, without receiving the Last Sacraments, the woman was flirting with Hell, Catherine cried inconsolably, imploring God's Mercy. This went on for three days and three nights, Catherine adding fasting to her prayers. She pleaded:

"Lord will You allow this soul to be lost because of me? I entreat you to grant me, at any price, her conversion and salvation. Punish me instead of her, as I am the reason for the state of her soul. Do not chastise her, but strike me. I beg You, most merciful Savior to not allow my sister's soul to leave her body until it has been restored to Your Grace."[13]

Catherine's prayers powerfully reached her Spouse and the woman did not die immediately, to the amazement of her nurses and doctors. She suffered agony for three days and three nights. Catherine continued to pray! God could no longer resist His little spouse. A heavenly ray penetrated the dying woman's heart and her faults were exposed. Upon seeing them, she repented. God revealed this to Catherine and she hurried to her bedside. As soon as the woman spotted Catherine, she confessed, accusing herself of spreading false rumors and slander against Catherine whose only sin was being kind and loving to her. She piously received the Last Sacraments and died in the state of Grace.

Although Palmerina had been truly sorry for her sins, Catherine knew this did not wipe away the debt owed, for all the harm she had done. She was concerned that a sinner who had so narrowly escaped Hell would most certainly suffer severely in Purgatory. Catherine continued to pray

---

[13]Cf.Blessed Raymond of Capua

and fast for the speedy release of Palmerina from Purgatory to Heaven. The Lord rewarded Catherine by showing her the soul saved by her prayers. Blessed Raymond said that Catherine told him, it was so brilliant, she could not find the words to describe its beauty. Although it had not, as yet been granted the gift of beholding the Beatific Vision, it shone with the brightness which the grace of Baptism confers upon us. Catherine shared that Our Lord said to her:

"Behold, my daughter the lost soul which you found. Does she appear to you most beautiful and precious? Who would not endure all kinds of suffering to save a creature so perfect and introduce it into eternal life? If I Who am the Supreme Beauty, from Whom all beauty emanates, have been so captivated by the beauty of souls to descend upon earth and shed My Blood to redeem them; how much greater reason should you have to labor one for another, that such admirable creatures not be lost. If I showed you this soul, it was that you should be all the more zealous in all that concerns the salvation of souls."[14]

Catherine gave her last ounce of blood for her Church. Near the end of her painful journey on earth, her friends heard her say,

"O eternal God, accept the sacrifice of my life for the mystical body of Thy Holy Church. I have nothing to give save that which Thou hast given to me. Take my heart then and press it over the face of Thy Spouse!

"She saw God take her heart from her body and squeeze it over the Church. As long as Catherine had a breath of life in her to give, she prayed and sacrificed for her love on earth, Mother Church. She instructed her companions she would continue to fight for her Church even after death."[15]

---

[14]Cf.Blessed Raymond of Capua
[15]Excerpt from Bob and Penny Lord's *"Saints and other Powerful Women in the Church"*

"*She had had a Vision in the early part of 1380, in which the ship of the Church crushed her to earth. At that moment, she offered herself as a willing sacrifice. She was to be ill from that time until April 21 of that year, when she suffered a paralytic stroke from the waist down. Catherine, with her last faint breath of life, continued to gaze at her Spouse on the Cross, whispering over and over again, 'Blood, blood, blood.' She was joining Christ on the Cross, for the last time on earth; His last Great Act of Love becoming her last great act. On April 29, she went to her reward.*"[16]

Catherine, please pray for our Church and our Pope.

---

[16]excerpts from Bob and Penny Lord's "*This is My Body, This is My Blood, Miracles of the Eucharist*" and "*Saints and other Powerful Women in the Church*"

Above:
After the death of son Evangelista,
Jesus gave St. Frances of Rome
an Archangel to be her companion
and guide for the next 23 years.
Above left:
St. Frances of Rome and her family shared
all the provisions they had in their palace
until there were none left.
Left:
St. Frances fed the poor of Rome. Crops
affected, work was curtailed; starvation
became a natural progression for the
already fractured Rome.

Saint Frances of Rome
Wife, Mother, Visionary

We have been asked to write on Lay people who became Saints. As we researched our last book, *Visionaries, Mystics and Stigmatists*, we found ourselves writing on many Saints and Blesseds, brothers and sisters who came from a life very much like our own; they never entered the Religious life, but instead served the Lord right where He had planted them, within their families.

St. Frances of Rome is one such Saint and Visionary. True Saints are remembered long past their life here on earth; they are an everlasting remembrance of how very much God loves us and when we accept that love, how very much He can change our lives. Till today, if you visit Rome, you can pray before her tomb, seeking her intercession - powerful in life and powerful in death. If you were to visit the Church on her Feast Day, you would be among the countless faithful who still pray *hopefully*, petitioning her to intervene for them with the Lord, their families having passed down the Good News of miracles through her intercession. St. Frances of Rome's story is one of joy and sorrow, of faith and of hope at a dire time in the world and in the Church.

I do not know about you, but I am tired of reading over and over again how, throughout the last twenty centuries, the world has influenced the Church, instead of the Church influencing the world. It's time for a change, I say! The more we read about these great Saints who have brought us messages from our Celestial Family of what joy is awaiting us in Heaven, and from the Church Suffering what agony our brothers and sisters are enduring in Purgatory, it gives us reason to pause in our busy, worldly-filled days and meditate on what is really important. Will we pay for every soul who does not choose everlasting life with Jesus in Paradise and instead chooses the temporary rewards of life on earth, because we did not tell him about the *Treasures* of our most precious Roman Catholic Church? Will we share in the punishment of those who have sinned grievously against the Lord because we said and did nothing?

†

Our story begins in the Fourteenth Century, and the birth of *The Great Western Schism* which would have devastating consequences on the Church and on St. Frances' family.

"Towards the end of the Thirteenth Century, many factions within Italy were trying to take over Rome, and the Papal States. One family in particular, the Colonna family, was attacking the Popes. In 1304, Pope Benedict XI fled Rome to Perugia, near Assisi, where he died the same year.

"Pope Clement V, the first Pope of Avignon, was elected in Perugia on June 5, 1305. He was a Frenchman, who accepted the offer of the King of France to rule the Church from France. He had ulterior motives. While it was true that Italy was a battleground and the Pope one of the main targets, he also wanted to reconcile France and England in order to get them to help him launch a new crusade in the Holy Land. It was not until March of 1309 that he actually took up residence in Avignon.

"The first two popes who had residency in Avignon, Clement V, and John XXII considered Avignon as temporary living quarters, and the last two, Urban V, and Gregory XI, wanted to return to Rome. Urban V did go back to Rome in 1367, but returned to Avignon in 1370.

"Gregory XI had made a secret promise to the Lord before he became Pope, to bring the Papacy back to Rome. Only he and Jesus were aware of this promise. So, when Catherine of Siena reminded him of the promise he had made, Pope Gregory XI knew it was the Lord who

*was speaking to him. He returned to Rome in 1376. This caused what has been termed **The Great Western Schism**, in which there was a Pope of Avignon who was recognized only by France, Spain, and the Kingdom of Sicily, and another Pope, the Roman Pope, successor of St. Peter. This sorrowful situation lasted until 1409.*[1]

Although the Schism ended in 1409, Frances never saw peace and harmony return to Rome and the Church.

†

Frances was born in the year 1384, into nobility and great wealth. The luxurious life they led in their palace,[2] did not affect the spirituality of the family. As they were deeply devout, it should have come as no surprise that Frances, at the age of only eleven years, would ask to be allowed to enter a convent. They refused, emphatically! Although her parents were holy and pious people, they would not acquiesce. They had very different plans for this beautiful and talented daughter, their budding rose! For a year her tearful requests and persistent pleading to become a nun, fell on deaf ears. At the end of that time, the family introduced her to the man who was to be her spouse. He was young and wealthy, came from a fine family, equal in stature and position with that of her family. All in all, *Lorenzo Ponziano*, her future husband was a perfect match for the fair Frances. Seeing his kindness and gentleness, Frances finally gave in and at thirteen years old, she was betrothed to Lorenzo and settled in the Ponziano Palace.

Their apartment in the palace was elegant. But although she tried to please both her young husband and his family, she became more and more despondent. There was something missing in her life, or was it Someone? One day,

---

[1]Excerpt from Bob and Penny Lord's book: "*This is My Body, This is My Blood, Miracles of the Eucharist*"
[2]Palazzo Ponziano

her brother-in-law Paluzzo's wife, Vannozza, came upon her crying. When she discovered why little Frances was so heartbroken, she revealed that she too, had always desired a life of prayer and quiet. A close friendship began and lasted to the end of their lives. The two young ladies of the nobility put aside all their finery and jewels and exchanged them for very simple, unadorned dresses of coarse fabric. Adopting the clothes of the peasantry, they ventured into the most rundown sections of Rome to serve the poor and destitute, each day. Although this was not *their husbands'* walk, they did not object to this new austere lifestyle their wives had adopted and did not place any obstacles in their way.

At one point, all charitable activities had to be curtailed as Frances had become seriously ill with a disease that had all the doctors in Rome stumped. Did Frances' family lose faith in the One True God and return to the false gods of paganism? They called in witches and resorted to the use of *magic* to attempt to cure their loved one. Can you just picture God, shaking His Head sadly, as He looks down upon His creation once again giving into the enemy who led Adam and Eve astray? It makes us wonder if He is not thinking, *"How many times do I have to suffer and die for them to understand that there is only One God and no other; wasn't once enough?"*

After a year of this foolishness, the Lord had had enough. He sent Saint Alex to Frances. In a vision, he asked her if she was prepared to die or did she wish to remain here on earth. Frances responded, as the Saints before and after her, *"It is not my will I want, but the Will of my Father."* *"Then,"* Saint Alex responded, *"it is the Will of God that you recover and that you work for His glory!"* With that, the Saint placed his cloak over her and she was cured!

If the family had thought their former lifestyle was austere, it was a party compared to the life the two daughters-in-law now adopted. They left their lovely palace early each day for the *Ospedale Santo Spirito*[3] to serve not only the poorest and sickest, but those suffering from the most highly contagious and repugnant diseases. Their mother-in-law was upset because she was worried they would catch one of the diseases and/or transmit it to the rest of the family. She also complained to her sons that it was not fitting for ladies of their station to be seen doing such menial work and that she felt they were causing scandal by ignoring the duties connected with the nobility - such as entertaining at dinner parties and attending formal banquets. Thank God, her sons felt differently and told their mother they would not interfere with their wives' acts of charity.

In the year 1400, a baby was born to Frances. They named him *Battista* after St. John the Baptist. This new life now dominated most her waking hours, but she still found time to serve, although not as much as before the baby was born. When the baby was almost one year old, her mother-in-law died and her father-in-law asked Frances to take her place as hostess and head of the household. Although she protested that Vannozza, as wife of the eldest son was the natural one to succeed the mother-in-law, they all (including Vannozza) insisted she would best serve. Their faith in her was well-founded; she discharged her responsibilities joyfully and faithfully, treating the servants as family rather than as serfs beneath her. She never stopped serving God. In her position as head-mistress, she was in a position to share her Faith with her servants, and because of the love she showed them, she was responsible for many of them returning to Church and receiving the Sacraments.

Her husband and family came first; serving God was also serving her family. Whenever her husband and children called her, she stopped praying and tended to them, making her action her prayer at that time. We call that serving the

---

[3]Hospital of the Holy Spirit

small church. She loved God with all her heart and might; but that did not take away from the love she bore her husband and children; it only enhanced it. Lorenzo and Frances were the happiest couple; never a harsh word was heard between them, the forty years they were married. There were three children in all, and she personally reared all of them. She said of her commitment:

"It is commendable in a married woman to be devout, but she must never forget that she is first and foremost a housewife."

God rewards those who are obedient to their immediate superior, whether a religious obeying his or her superior, or a wife obeying her husband, or a child obeying a parent; this is a way on earth we can obey God. This one day, one of the servants interrupted Frances, saying her Office, *five* times with, "Madonna, my master begs you to come to him." Each time, she closed her Office and went peacefully to her spouse. When she returned to her Office the fifth time, she found the words imprinted in *Gold*!

As with the other Saints, Frances was attacked her entire life by all sorts of temptations, sometimes savage and ferocious, other times lewd and repulsive, the devil never sleeping, never missing a moment or occasion to try to drain her of all her energy or detract her from doing God's Will. But she fought! And won, battle by battle! When he saw that all his antics did not get the desired effect, he proceeded to inflict the most brutal physical attacks.

But one area where she and her family were not affected was *financially*; that is not until unrest and wars between the provinces broke out, eating away at the flesh of the little boot[4] like a giant spreading cancer. Plagues accompanied the pestilence of violence that bred more violence. People were dying in the streets, with barely

---

[4]Italy has the shape of a boot

enough help at times to take the bodies away; consequently, the spread of highly infectious disease. The stench of death choked the hope out of the people. Crops were affected; work was curtailed; starvation became a natural progression for an already fractured Rome. It seemed as if the sun would never shine over Rome again. The once proud *Romano* no longer strutted in the streets of his fair Rome, but instead searched the garbage for what he could find. Chaos and confusion accompanied desperation and despair.

Frances and her family shared all the provisions they had in the palace until there were none left. Then, Frances asked her father-in-law's permission to sell her jewels to feed the poor, and he gave his consent. From that time on, Frances wore the plainest peasant clothing.

Rome was taken over by an ally of the anti-pope. He appointed one of his henchmen as governor. As the Ponziano family always defended the Apostolic succession of the legitimate Pope, the family was attacked and Lorenzo was wounded. They carried him home, near dead, to the palace. But as his wife had selflessly tended others and been an instrument of healing for them, the Lord healed and completely restored her beloved spouse to his former self. The governor, believing he had completely destroyed the morale of the people, decided to take all leadership from them, so that they would have no one to lead them to recovery. [All the monsters of the world have always killed the leaders and the *intelligentsia* of a nation, beginning with the members of the hierarchy of the Roman Catholic Church, so that the lambs are left without shepherds and die.]

Her brother-in-law, Vannozza's husband Paluzzo, was taken prisoner and then they came for little *Battista*. Frances turned to her Lord and Savior; while she was praying in church, word came that the governor, without any *earthly* reason, released the little hostage Battista. A sigh of relief filled the palace. But, it was short-lived for Rome was again taken over by the followers of the anti-pope. Lorenzo, who was head of the party supporting the Pope, had to flee! He escaped but his family was not able to, and had to remain behind. Little Battista was once again taken hostage, but got away and joined his father. The palace was looted; the family's possessions were seized and that which the thugs of that day could not carry, they destroyed. They killed all the livestock, burned the farm to the ground and murdered the peasants. Frances retired to a small corner of her ruined home with her remaining children, Evangelist and Agnes, and her sister-in-law Vannozza. They took care not only of *their* families but, as much as they could, the poorer families around them, sharing what little they had.

Three years later, a plague attacked Rome and Frances' son Evangelist died. Frances mourned the dead by caring for the living; she turned part of her home into a hospital, open to all who came. God always rewards sacrifice. He also gives us all we need, to do His Will. He gave Frances the *Gift of Healing*. One year after his death, Evangelist appeared to his mother. As she was praying, a bright light filled the room, and before her stood her beautiful son accompanied by an Archangel. He told his mother how wonderful it was in Heaven and how very happy he was there. She was overjoyed. How she had longed to see him, once more. But her joy turned to sorrow, as he said he had another reason for coming, to warn her that Agnes, her daughter was going to die. But Our Lord did not leave her bereft of companionship and love; He left her the Archangel, who had accompanied her son, to be her companion and guide for the next twenty-three years, to be then replaced by another Archangel who would remain with her the rest of her life.

Just as her son had forewarned, Agnes soon became ill and after a year's illness, she died at sixteen years old. From the moment her beloved daughter departed this world, Frances could see the Archangel. He took on the appearance of a beautiful eight year old boy. But this gift was only for her. No one else could see the Angel and when she committed a serious fault, she was denied the presence of the Angel. He faded away, leaving her all alone. As soon as she was heartily sorry, confessed her sins, and was absolved, he returned.

As with many of the Saints, she was completely poured out. The tragedy in her life had drained her of all her strength; she became a victim of the plague and was dying. But, God not finished with her yet, she recovered!

Purgatory, *a Stopover of Hope*

It was at this time Frances saw a vision of Hell.[5] It was so horrendous, she could not speak of it without sobbing uncontrollably. The vision of Hell and its horror, the excruciating agony of its tenants, tormented her more than any suffering she had endured on earth.

Frances wrote that having passed through this unbearable inferno, she was carried into Purgatory by her Heavenly Angel. There, she saw neither the utter hopelessness nor the endless pitch-black gloom she had seen in Hell. Instead, it seemed as if they were in a fog where the *bright* hope of *life eternal* with Jesus was trying to cut through. It must be like when you awaken to the dawn. It is still dark from the cover of night, but the promise of a new day begins, as you see a glimmer of the sun trying to filter through. Here, in this level of Purgatory, the pain of the Poor Souls was seeing that glimmer of *Divine Hope* and yet not being able to see God in His Beatific Vision. Although these souls suffered intensely, their pain was lessened by the

---

[5]Saint Frances reluctantly later wrote of this horrible experience as well as that of Purgatory at the insistence of her superiors.

presence of the Angels who came to visit and help them in their suffering. *Oh, how good and merciful is our God.*

She said that Purgatory is composed of three *distinctly different* levels, as diverse as being in three different countries of one continent. One level is located beneath another, the souls consigned to a level based on the seriousness of the offense and the debt owed. The deeper they are interred, the longer the time before their delivery.

St. Frances is led to the deepest Dungeon of Purgatory

The Angel brought Frances to the lowest level of Purgatory, to a a cavern filled with a roaring fire, its red-hot flames cutting through the black smoke that darkened the cave. But as horrible as it was, Frances said it was not as hot as in Hell. As her eyes adjusted to the darkness, she could see bodies being plunged into what appeared to be a cauldron of raging fire, its flames enveloping them, pulling them down. She was told that these were souls who had been guilty of committing serious sins, had confessed and were absolved of their sins by a priest, but had not satisfied the wrong done by their act against God.[6]

In this vision, she was told that for each mortal sin committed and forgiven, a payment of seven years of reparation[7] in Purgatory was necessary to erase it from the soul. Since the damage done by each mortal sin affects the world differently, some more deadly and lasting, the length of time and punishment differs. The type of pain and suffering measured out to each of these souls, was in proportion to the *type* of sin, the *damage* done by the sins, and the *number* of wounds inflicted on our Lord's Sacred Heart by these sins.

In this level, she found the Poor Souls of the Laity and Religious, alike. Those of the *Laity* were souls who had led a

---

[6]Every mortal sin is a sin against God.
[7]make amends, restitution

life of sin, and converted toward the end of their lives.
Conversion to the Lord and His Church is God's gift to us,
as only the Holy Spirit can convert men's hearts. As they
had not paid their debt on earth, they had to clear the
invoice due the Lord here in Purgatory.

The Souls of the *Religious* were those who had not kept
the vows they had professed. No sooner had this been
explained to her than St. Frances saw the soul of a priest
who was very well known. He had a covering on his face, to
try to hide the ugly blemish that had remained. Now, this
priest had led a truly priestly life, faithfully administering the
Sacraments and pastoring his flock. His only sin had been an
intemperate need to gouge himself at mealtime, seeking his
reward from God's creation rather than God alone.

The Angel then led Frances to the Intermediate Dungeon

This region was reserved for those souls who had not
sinned as seriously as those of the lowest dungeon, nor
caused irreparable damage by their transgressions. As their
souls were not free from the ugly blemishes that are a result
of sin, they were required to spend time in Purgatory; but
because of God's Justice they did not need to spend time
suffering the intense punishment of souls in the dungeons
below. This dungeon had three compartments:
(1) The first was a cavern of ice, sharp icicles threatening the
souls below. It was incredibly cold in here. She could see
the poor souls trying to warm themselves to no avail, as ice
seemed to be hemming them in, closing in on them,
surrounding them; the walls, the floor, the ceiling, nowhere
to get away from the endless freezing cold!
(2) Next, there was an underground prison of boiling oil and
pitch.[8] The sickening odor of burning flesh filled the area.
She could see the Poor Souls, covered with black pitch,

---

[8]a substance emanating from tar - used for waterproofing and
covering roofs

writhing in pain. No matter what they did, they could not escape the boiling petroleum nor the sticky hot, black mess which clung to them.

(3) In the third and last level she saw Souls struggling not to drown in what appeared to be a pool filled with liquefied ore, resembling melted gold and silver. Had these Souls attached too much importance to the rewards of the world, counting the Graces from the Lord as nothing in comparison?

The Saint visits the Upper Dungeon

Our Saint does not go into detail on this level of atonement, only that this is the place where the Poor Souls condemned themselves, upon seeing that *one time*[9] before the Lord, how they had transgressed against Him. The more we study about Purgatory, the more I find myself asking the question, *"Am I offending You, my Lord?"* This is not so much from the viewpoint of suffering in Purgatory (my foremost desire being Heaven), but the thought of Jesus and how He will look, as my unrequited sins pass before me, the many times I failed to put Him first, the missed opportunities to love Him by loving my brothers and sisters. Oh my Lord, how my heart breaks thinking I may have offended you!

The Souls in this dungeon have the anguish which the Poor Souls in Purgatory say is the most painful, the absence of the Beatific Vision. Can you imagine knowing that your loved one is somewhere but you cannot see him or her? Multiply that by a million-fold and you get a small idea of how it must be for those who, having seen Jesus that one time, can no longer see Him. Oh, Lord, how we long to see Your Face! The consolation of being in this place is that this is the last place before being united with Jesus, Mary and the whole Celestial Family; they know they are on their way.

---

[9]refer to chapter on St. Catherine of Genoa

†

It is the year 1414, and we find Pope John XXIII[10]
convening the Council of Constance[11] which was called to
end the Schism in the Western Church. After 45 sessions
Gregory XII, the *Roman* Pope agreed to step down and the
Council fathers deposed John XXIII, the Pope residing in
Avignon. Then the Council elected Pope Martin V.

Lorenzo and Battista returned to Rome and they along
with the rest of the family, were allowed to occupy their
palace once more. But Lorenzo was no longer a zealot on
fire; he was tired and broken. Tragedy had taken a toll on
him. Frances tenderly cared for her spouse. The miracles
connected with Frances began to spread throughout the
seven hills of Rome. People asked her to pray for them, and
they were healed. Others asked her to settle disputes
between families and even on civil matters. God was using
her. Lorenzo loved her more and more each day, but he
could see that she was to go another step in her walk with
Jesus; he released her from occupying his bed and living a
fully sacramental life as his wife. He just asked that she
remain under his roof, living as brother and sister.

Frances could see that this was the Lord's way to tell
her this was His Will and His timetable, and so she founded
a community of women. This dream had been growing in
her mind and heart and now, it was to become a reality: a
community of women living in the world, bound by no vows,
who would devote themselves to a life consecrated to doing
God's Will through serving the poor and helpless. She
received the full approval of her confessor and the first
community was called the *Oblates of Mary*, later to be known
as the *Oblates of Tor de' Specchi*.

---

[10]This was the anti-pope. This does not refer to Pope John XXIII of
Vatican Council II.

[11]called the 16th Ecumenical Council in the West.

The community of women continued to live at home and serve the poor for seven years when they were called to open a house for the women to meet and pray together. It was an old building, but they loved it and named it: *Tor de' Specchi*. Whenever she could get some free time from caring for her family (never neglecting them for one moment), she would go to the house and share the work and prayer life of the community of women she had founded. Three years passed when the Lord called Lorenzo *Home*. A grieving widow laid her dear spouse to rest beside his children Evangelist and Agnes. Her family no longer needing her (Battista was married), Frances told them she was thinking of entering her community.

On the Feast of St. Benedict, Frances requested she be allowed to enter as just another member of the community. The one whom she had chosen as Superior when the house had first opened, Agnes de Lellis, immediately insisted on stepping down and the community of women greeted their foundress as their Superior, all her objections failing to accomplish her desired effect. She continued living a life of extreme austerity and maintained all the forms of mortification and discipline she had practiced all her life.

Frances grew more and more in the Celestial world, than in the world around her, visions of her Lord and His Mother becoming more and more frequent. When the other sisters would look into her room to check up on her during the night, they said that many times they would see her deep in prayer; only to discover the following morning, her bed untouched, she had remained awake the entire evening.

Spring had come to the year 1440. Although only 56 years old, the wounds of the passing years were taking their toll. One evening, as she was returning from visiting her son Battista and his family, she was finding it difficult to walk. She had wanted to return home before her family could see how seriously ill she was. By the providence of God, who should come upon his charge at the point of death, but her spiritual director. He carried her to her son's home. The family thought she would pass on that evening, but she lasted seven days. I wonder, was she giving her precious son time to accept his mother going to join the rest of her family? March 9th, her family around her, Frances' face was suddenly illuminated with a light, unlike any they had ever seen. She looked beyond them and said: *"The Angel has finished his task; he is beckoning me to follow him."* And she was gone; now she would do her good from Heaven.

As soon as word got out that their Saint was dead the mourners filed into the Palace to see their beloved patron one more time, and to be healed through her intercession; knowing, as only the pure heart can, death would not rob them of this powerful instrument of healing. And they were right! They had to bring her body to the church of Santa Maria Nuova because of the multitude of believers who continued to come and pray for her intercession. Miracles upon miracles spread past the Italian borders, and the faithful from all parts of Europe still visit and pray before the tomb of Frances of Rome.

In 1608, what the faithful had believed for over 200 years, the Church made official, and Frances of Rome was canonized *Saint Frances of Rome*. Santa Maria Nuova was renamed Santa Francesca Romana after the Saint. Do you have a petition? Pray to a woman who led a faithful life, always, to husband, children, family, friends, the poor and the needy, to her community, but most of all to her Lord. She will speak to your heart. *Listen*!

Above:
St. Catherine of Genoa

Above:
*St. Catherine of Genoa
had many visions of Purgatory*

Above: *St. Catherine of Genoa in Glory*

St. Catherine of Genoa
Lay woman, Mystic and friend of the Souls in Purgatory

Catherine of Genoa was born into one of the most powerful and influential families of Genoa, Italy. Although Catherine desired to be a nun, her family arranged a marriage for her with the son of another well-known family. The union proved disastrous and soon Catherine was trying to lead her husband's wild life in an attempt to save her marriage. But the Lord stepped in; Catherine was converted; her husband lost everything and soon joined his wife in her acts of charity among the sick and the needy. He became a Franciscan tertiary and died in the state of Grace.

In addition to the great and philanthropic life she led, Catherine was gifted with Visions of *Heaven, Hell and Purgatory* by the Lord. Her writings on these areas are some of the best known accounts of what life is like after death. We have written about her life in our other book: *"Visionaries, Mystics and Stigmatists."*

Saint Catherine wrote extensively about the danger of self-love. She wrote: The *spirit* entrenched in self-love has, first and foremost, little or no concern whether it attacks its own body and soul or that of its neighbor. The soul, so absorbed with self-love, will go to any lengths to accomplish its end. When it has set its sites on a certain diabolical course, neither promises nor threats can dissuade it from wielding its lethal blows; causing enslavement and impoverishment, death of reputation through scandal. It cares not if the results are damaging to itself or others. Then finally, when there is not a glimpse of the goodness of the precious soul that God created, it cares not the cost and sounds the death knell, but not for its adversary but for itself, condemning itself to *Purgatory or even Hell.*[1]

---

[1] Cf. Saint Catherine of Genoa

She further said that once a soul has allowed self-love to take over, not even the promises of wealth, position, and fulfillment of every earthly desire, can persuade it to turn around, not even the knowledge, it will lose eternal happiness and peace in *Heaven*. And so, deafened and blinded to the Truth, the soul condemns itself willingly and openly to *Purgatory* or the never-ending agony of *Hell*.

A priest once said that if someone were to open the gates of Hell, no one would leave. How devastating! It causes our heart to break, when we think that possibly someone we love has taken that road. But the Lord is not finished with any of our souls and He will reach out, through our prayers and sacrifice to bring those we love home to Him, before it's too late; because He never stops loving!

She further shared that *self-love* is a subtle thief who steals even from God Himself; claiming souls as his own, he uses God's gifts against God and His loved ones. The evil of self-will is insidiously deluding the soul that is so inundated by its lies that it really believes *the end justifies the means*. It thinks nothing of robbing from others, in the name of doing good. The soul which is permeated with *self-love* is often difficult, and may appear impossible to detect.

Saint Catherine warned that *spiritual* self-love is far more deadly than bodily love, in that it is often disguised as sanctity and cannot be easily detected; it can appear as charity; it can arouse our pity, calling us to defend it against those who try to expose it. It uses so many deceitful masks, it makes one shudder, fearing for the innocent lambs of the world. But, we have seen it come to pass; the Lord in His Light, in His Love, will not allow His loved ones to be deceived, for long. God, in His Truth, will set us free!

Jesus reveals Purgatory and Hell to Catherine

Through the Divine fire Which burned inside Catherine, while she was still on earth, she was able to understand the state of souls in *Purgatory*. The Lord had purified her soul in the furnace of His Love, as gold is refined of all its impurities, by *fire!* Cleansing her of every stain of sin, while she was still in the flesh, He was perfecting her on earth, so that when she passed to the next world, she would be ready to appear before Him. God told her that the soul is like gold; once all the impurities are burned away, no matter how great the fire is, it can do no harm to the soul; He keeps the soul in the flames of His Divine Love until every stain of sin is burned away and the soul reaches the highest perfection it is capable of (each according to its own vocation and capacity), and once this is accomplished, the soul rests completely in Him.

In Catherine's Treatise on Purgatory, she writes:
"Either in this life or in the life to come, the soul that seeks union with God must be purged by 'The Fiery Love of God.' The holy souls are purged of all the rust and stains of sin which they have not rid themselves in this life. The fire of Purgatory is first of all The Fiery Love of God."

Reading that *"The fire of Purgatory is first of all The Fiery Love of God"*, is so consoling. We can handle almost anything, as long as we know that it is through the Loving God Who never stops loving us. We know that whatever God has for us, His Divine Justice will be mingled with His Divine Love. The Lord through the Mystics tells us that it is better to suffer a *thousand days on earth* (in reparation of our sins) than an *hour in Purgatory*.

St. Catherine said that he who purifies himself from his faults in the present life satisfies with a penny a debt of a thousand ducats[2] (what today would be more than a thousand dollars), and he who waits until the other life to

---

[2]coin bearing an image of a duke; gold or silver coins used in some European countries - Webster's Dictionary

pay off his debts, consents to pay a thousand dollars for that which he might before have paid with a penny.

None of us want to suffer Purgatory of any kind, on earth or in Purgatory, so we try to lead the kind of life that will present us pleasing to God, that moment we appear before Him. But more importantly, we try to avoid sin because we love Him and we do not want to hurt Him. Consequently, when we sin, are we not putting other gods before Him? Including ourselves? We, in this life either decide for God or against Him, with each step we take. Then when we die, and we face our Lord, we remember the many times we put the world and its attractions before Him.

Our souls are meant to be like a room flooded with sunlight, only the Light is the Light of the Son, not the sun; the Creator not the creation. The Lord told St. Catherine that the sun cannot penetrate a covered surface (like a dark shade, which will not allow light to flow into a room), not through any defect in the sun but simply from the blockage of the covering; so it is with the rust of sin which darkens the soul; it blocks the *Son's* Love from coming through.

Today, little is taught about sin; it is almost treated like a word from the past, irrelevant, and yet never has the world *been more inundated with sin than in this Twentieth Century.* The vision of Purgatory that the Lord revealed to Saint Catherine so impressed her, she could not wipe it from her mind and heart. She writes:

"The source of all suffering is either original or actual sin. God created the soul pure, simple, free from every stain, and with a certain beatific instinct toward Himself. It is drawn away from Him by Original Sin,[3] and when Actual Sin[4] is added afterwards, this draws the soul still

---

[3]Original Sin - Sin inherited from Adam and Eve - Removed by the Sacrament of Baptism

[4]Actual Sin - A personal act that is morally bad, committed with full knowledge and full acceptance

farther away from God; and as the soul removes itself more and more from Him, its sinfulness increases and its communing (or communication) with God decreases, till there is less and less of Him and more and more of the dark shade of sin blocking the soul from Him."[5]

Have you ever noticed, when people are living in sin, the first thing they do is stop going to Mass? Rather than going to confession, unburdening themselves of all that has separated them from God and living a new life in Him, they remain in the Hell that they have created on earth for themselves, walking farther and farther from God. Catherine further shares,

"The souls in Purgatory do not think about themselves. They do not even say: 'I deserve to be here because of such and such sin.' So happy are they to be within God's ordinance, and that He should do all which pleases Him, as it pleases Him that in their greatest pain they cannot think of themselves.

"Only once, as they pass from this life, do they see the cause of the Purgatory they endure; never again do they see it.

"The Poor Souls in Purgatory are in a state of the greatest joy. In fact no happiness can be found worthy to be compared with that of a soul in Purgatory except that of the Saints in Paradise; and day by day this happiness grows as God flows into these souls, more and more as the hindrance to His entrance is consumed. Sin's rust is the hindrance, and the fire burns the rust away so that more and more the soul opens itself to the Divine inflowing. At the same time, the souls endure a pain so extreme that no tongue can be found to tell it, nor could the mind understand its least pang (smallest pain) if God by special

---

[5]We have paraphrased Catherine's words, to a degree, to make them more understandable to today's reader.

Grace did not show (reveal) so much. All guilt has been removed from their souls. Only the rust remains."[6]

St. Catherine wrote on **Hell and the Soul**:

"As the purified spirit finds no repose but in God for Whom it was created, so the soul in sin can rest nowhere but in Hell, which by reason of its sin has become its end."

On Purgatory: *"The same thing is true of Purgatory: the soul leaving the body, and not finding in herself that purity in which it is created, and seeing also the hindrances which prevent her union with God, conscious also that only Purgatory can remove them, casts herself quickly and willingly therein. And if she did not find the means ordained for her purification, she would instantly create for herself a Hell worse than Purgatory, seeing that by reason of this impediment she is hindered from approaching her end, which is God; and this is so great an ill that in comparison with it the soul esteems Purgatory as nothing. True it is like Hell; and yet in comparison with the loss of God it is as nothing.*

"I will say furthermore: I see that as far as God is concerned, Paradise has no gates, but he who will may enter. For God is all Mercy, and His open Arms are ever extended to receive us into His glory. But I see that the Divine Essence is so pure - purer than the imagination can conceive - that the soul, finding in itself the slightest imperfection, would rather cast itself into a thousand hells than appear, so stained, in the presence of the Divine Majesty. Knowing, then, that Purgatory was intended for her cleansing, she throws herself therein, and finds there that great mercy, the removal of her stains.

"The great importance of Purgatory, neither mind can conceive nor tongue describe. I see only that its pains are as great as those of Hell; and yet I see that a soul, stained

---

[6]Cf. Saint Catherine of Genoa

with the slightest fault, receiving this Mercy, counts its pain as naught (nothing) in comparison with this hindrance to her love. And I know that the greatest misery of the souls in Purgatory is to behold in themselves anything that displeases God, and to discover that, in spite of His goodness, they had consented to it."

What St. Catherine is saying is that in Purgatory, the Lord is in charge; we are once again children. Remember how you felt when you were a child. You never worried where you were going to live or where your next meal was coming from. That was your parent's job. And you trusted that they would do what was best for you. When you misbehaved, you didn't want to be punished, but you felt safe that they were the ones doing it, knowing that they would do nothing to hurt you. The Poor Souls in Purgatory are suffering because of having sinned. Like our parents, our Lord forgives us when we admit our sins and say that we are truly sorry.[7] But, the punishment was there for us as children and is for us when we die. Purgatory is also like, when as children, we played in the mud and came in all soiled. We had to shower before going to Grandma and Grandpa's house. When we die, we need to be cleansed of the mud of ugly sin that has covered our souls, before dwelling with God in His House, Heaven. The great thing about being in Purgatory is that you are assured, you will be in Heaven with Jesus and your loved ones, some day. There is also that joy knowing that you are doing all you can to make God happy.

†

Catherine was a lay woman and a wife. After the Lord brought her back to that which He had planned for her in the first place, her life did a complete turnaround. She lived her life with her eyes and heart on Jesus. And He, in turn, shared with her that which would lead us to *Heaven, Hell or*

---

[7] go to Confession and have true contrition for our sins

Purgatory. These revelations were given to a woman at a time when women were not well educated. Again the Lord, as He did with Gideon,[8] is showing that it was *He*, and not Catherine, Who is bringing these messages to His children. As we read about the visions, these great saints have had of *Heaven, Hell and Purgatory*, you can better understand the lives these Saints led. So many times, those of us who do not know the full stories of these holy people, judge their acts of mortification as extreme, but as you read on and on about the price we have to pay for the smallest transgression not atoned for in this world, you look upon them and their lives with a different perspective.

We thank You Lord, for the gift of St. Catherine, and the teachings You have given us through her Visions on *Heaven, Hell and Purgatory*. We pray Lord, that we will accept the lessons from her teachings.

---

[8]The Lord asked Gideon to send away all his troops except the few men that He would choose, so that all would know that it was He, the Lord Who was defeating the enemy of His people Israel. When Gideon and *300* men blew their horns, the army of Midians that far outnumbered them by 125,000, fled. There could be no question that it was to the Lord that all glory be given; it was He Who was the victor, not Gideon and his few men.

St. Teresa of Avila's Visions

When we wrote on the life of St. Teresa in our book *"Saints and other Powerful Women in the Church,"* little did we think that we would some day, be using her visions of *Heaven, Hell and Purgatory* to affirm these important truths of our Catholic Faith. As we have said so many times, the lives of the Saints are not about old bones, long gone and forgotten, but *alive* in the lives they led, in their living examples of holiness and virtue for us to follow, in the path they have paved by the teachings they have left behind, as alive in a smaller degree as the Word of God found in Holy Scripture. As we delved into the many books on *Heaven, Hell and Purgatory* and combed Holy Scripture trying to discern what the Lord wanted in this book, we felt a haunting urgency to forge on despite many obstacles placed in our way, the kind of attacks mentioned by St. Teresa in her book, *"Vida,"*[1] often good things or good people with good intentions. But as we discover, day after day in our walk with the Lord and His Mother, when the Lord wants something done, He will do anything and everything to have it come to pass, not excluding using our Guardian Angels to persistently plant His Thoughts and Will in our minds. And so here we are, and we are once again writing about one of our most loved and precious Saints and Doctors of the Church,[2] Saint Teresa of Avila.

As you will discover in the lives of these Mystics who have experienced *Heaven, Hell and Purgatory* or had visions of those who were now subject to one or the other of these forms of life after death, there are many ways we can make

---

[1]life

[2]At the writing of this book, there are only 2 women Doctors of the Church - St. Teresa of Avila and St. Catherine of Siena (both of whom Bob and Penny have written about in their book: *"Saints and other Powerful Women in the Church"*).

retribution for debts owed to our Lord whether by us or by loved ones or friends.

Teresa experiences Purgatory on earth

At age fifteen, Teresa was sent away to a Convent of Augustinian Nuns in Avila where she would be educated with young women of her class. Although she got off to a bad start, Teresa began to enjoy the Convent, finding herself attracted to the Nuns and their way of life. But after a year and a half, Teresa became seriously ill and had to be taken home by her father. Teresa began to consider *seriously* a life as a Religious. But she had a huge battle going on, as if two suitors were after her. Part of her was drawn to the life of a Nun and part of her was repulsed by the thought of it.

When she presented her desire to become a Nun to her father, he replied, *"No, definitely no! Should you so desire after I am dead, so be it."* Against her father's wishes, afraid she might weaken in her resolve, she quickly ran away to the Convent of the Incarnation of the Carmelite Nuns outside of Avila. She recalls,

> *"while leaving my father's house, I knew I would not, even at the very moment and agony of my death, feel the anguish of separation more painfully than at that point in time."* She went on to say, *"not even the love of God I had inside me could make up for the love I felt for my father and friends."*

Her father did not contest her action, as she was twenty years old by this time. The following year she was professed, only to be removed from the Convent because of an illness that had begun before her profession and had progressively worsened. The countless doctors, failing to find a cure, diagnosed her illness as *hopeless*. Her father, refusing to give up hope, brought her to a place renowned for its cures. Instead of relief, her suffering grew worse. She had an interminable struggle with excruciating pain and inner

Above left:
Statue of St. Teresa of Avila in house where she was born.

Above right:
St. Teresa of Avila had many Visions of Heaven, Hell and Purgatory and went into ecstasy many times during her life in Spain.

Left:
St. Teresa of Avila in Glory, surrounded by the Heavenly hosts, receiving her Glorious mantle from the hands of St. Joseph and our Blessed Mother

turmoil, for almost a year. But it had given her time to reflect on her vocation. She came to the conclusion that the Purgatory she would suffer on earth as a Nun, was nothing compared to the eternal Hell she might know, otherwise. Her goal was to go straight to Heaven and she knew, for her, it was only through the *Religious Life*.

Teresa's condition deteriorated. She lay in bed, her tortured body finding no relief. She asked her father to call a Priest to hear her confession. She wished to prepare herself for the Feast of the Assumption. But her father refused, fearing if he granted her wish, she would take this as a sign she *was* dying and she would stop fighting to live. Teresa lost consciousness that evening. All attempts to revive her were in vain. Having proven to their satisfaction she was truly dead, the doctors left; the priest anointed her with holy oils; people recited prayers for the dead; and her poor father was beside himself. *Why hadn't he listened to her plea for a priest?*

A grave was prepared; the Nuns were waiting to escort the body to the Convent. There was only one stumbling block, *Teresa's father*. He insisted he could feel a *pulse!* No one believed him, pitying what they thought was a half-crazed old man. This battle raged on for four days. On the fourth night, Teresa's body was almost consumed by fire; a lit candle having fallen, igniting her bed clothes. Thank God, her brother, who had been keeping watch over the body, awoke just in time to put out the flames. During all the commotion, Teresa did not awaken.

Teresa has a vision of Heaven

Then, as her father and brothers were crying by her bedside, she suddenly sat up and complained, *"Why did you call me back?"* While all had been judging Teresa dead, she was having a Vision, seeing her family and communities of Nuns in Heaven through the intercession of her prayers and suffering. Attempting to describe her *Vision of Heaven*, like St. Paul, she found its splendor too *magnificent* for words.

Teresa recovered, if you can call being paralyzed, weak and disoriented, vomiting every morning, *recovery*. She felt as if her heart was being strangled by the pressure it had to endure. Her body was a pain-wracked network of crucified nerve-endings. She returned to the Incarnation Convent, her paralysis remaining with her for an *additional* three years. She turned to St. Joseph, trusting in his never-failing intercession with his Son Jesus; Teresa was completely cured of her paralysis at the end of the third year.

For twenty years, from age twenty four to forty four, Teresa was to know *Purgatory on Earth*. Her physical pains were to be joined by spiritual and mental ones, in the *metanoia*[3] from sinner (as she often called herself) into Saint.

Teresa has a vision of Purgatory

Four months before completing the Monastery of Malagón, Don Bernardino de Mendoza, a man well known in the area, approached Teresa and offered her a house, if she would start a Foundation in *Valladolid*. Tired, she reluctantly said "*Yes*." Two months later, the young man having suddenly contracted an illness which deprived him of all speech, was not able to make his confession, but did make signs pleading for God's forgiveness. Shortly after, he died.

The Lord came to Teresa and said that He had mercy on him because of the house he had given to Teresa which would do honor to *His Mother* through the Carmelite Order. But the Lord said the young man would not leave Purgatory until the first *Mass* was celebrated in that house. Teresa was so conscious of the terrible sufferings of that soul, she forestalled the opening of the Monastery in Toledo and plunged into the founding of this one in Valladolid.

---

[3]conversion

She left Malagón on the 19th of May, 1568, for Valladolid. She was delayed along the way. The Lord came to Teresa in a dream, "*While I was praying one day, He told me to hurry: that the soul (of Don Bernardino) was suffering a lot.*"[4] Needless to say, she went in much haste.

The house, Don Bernardino left them in Valladolid, was a disaster! Teresa hurriedly went about preparing the house to move in. God was in a hurry, so who do you think *just happened* to visit them, but the Vicar General of the City. Either he was terribly impressed or was it *a miracle*, but he issued the order for them to celebrate Mass immediately. Teresa had no idea the Lord's promise was being realized at this moment. Had she, in the rush of *doing good things*, of founding the house of Valladolid, forgotten the *reason* behind it in the first place? As Father Julian approached Teresa with Communion, she had a Vision of a young man standing beside the Priest. It was Don Bernardino; his face was *illuminated*, radiating joy. He thanked her for *her yes* that the Lord used to free him from Purgatory and welcome him into Heaven.

I think the greatest pain in Purgatory has to be, to *know* Jesus is just beyond and you cannot be with Him. It has to be like when a beloved has been left by the other spouse. You know he or she is alive, but not with you to love and to be loved by. The only relief is, we are promised that in the case of Purgatory, through the prayers of those on earth, there will someday be that union with Jesus that we long for as He welcomes us Home.

St. Teresa has visions of Hell

After much struggle and pain, St. Teresa's visions were tested and approved as genuine. She had every reason to believe that she was safe. Now she was prepared for anything God would have for her to do. Her answer came

---

[4]Foundations 10:3

with a vision of *Hell*! St. Teresa described it vividly in her *Autobiography*.

The Lord had given her many gifts. It was as if she was on a honeymoon. Imagine her shock when, while praying one day, she found herself in what appeared to be the middle of Hell. She was made to understand that the Lord wished her to see the place that the demons had prepared for her which, she writes, she *"merited by her sins."* She wrote that it lasted a very short time, but that if she lived many years she would never be able to forget it. The entrance resembled a very long straight alley, like a very low oven, dark and narrow. The ground was covered with what looked like very filthy, muddy water. A nauseatingly foul stench attacked her senses from the water that was stirred up by the many vile reptiles slithering through it. As her eyes adjusted to the darkness, she spotted on one side of the ominous pathway, a cavity pigeonholed in the wall. It could have been a cupboard, except for what she saw locked up tightly, within. The horrible, frightening sight before her, was as nothing compared to what she felt there.

She writes that she felt a fire in her soul. No stranger to suffering, she said that the most unbearable bodily pains she had ever known, including the excruciating spasms resulting from the shrinking of her limbs, the physical and spiritual torment caused by the devil, could not compare with the agony she experienced in her soul, *"a sense of being constrained, a stifling, an anguish so keen, a sorrow so abandoned and afflicted,"*[5] she could not describe it adequately. She said that it seemed as if *"her soul was cutting itself to pieces."* She felt herself crumbling into pieces, being in a place so evil and she so helpless to escape, with no hope or any consolation, no place to sit or to lie down, no room at all. The walls, where they had placed her, tightened around

---

[5]from the Autobiography of St. Teresa

her, closing in on her, suffocating her. Although she was enveloped in utter darkness, she could see everything that was horrible to behold in this deep black hole.

It was no less agonizing, knowing that the Lord was doing this to show her what His Mercy had saved her from suffering. All the horrible accounts of Hell she had read or heard about, were as nothing compared to what she was experiencing. It made such an impression on her, that six years later, when writing of this in her Autobiography, she could still feel the blood drain from her, all warmth leaving her body replaced by an icy chill. Whenever she suffered pain of any magnitude, whether physical or spiritual, she deemed it as nothing in comparison. She said that the Lord had truly done her a favor; because of this vision, she lost all fear of trials and tribulations on earth; it gave her the strength not only to endure them, but to praise the Lord in thanksgiving for all He had given her, in saving her from the pits of Hell.

As Teresa meditated more and more on what she had seen and experienced, her mind and heart became more and more filled with those wretched souls who were languishing in Hell and those who would end up there. She had an ongoing burning desire to save those poor wretches from the fate from which the Lord had saved her. Her greatest sorrow was for those who condemned themselves to Hell. She said she would gladly have died many deaths if she could save even one of them. As someone who had looked on Hell, she had no anger toward those who had unwittingly been led away from the true Church, who in their mis-placed zeal were burning down churches, killing priests and desecrating the Body of Christ, the Blessed Sacrament. Instead, she prayed for them and for God's mercy on them, especially those like Luther who were responsible for so many souls who, without full knowledge, had lost the precious Sacraments of the Church.

St. Teresa wrote:

"the human soul is like a beautiful castle, containing many mansions, in the center of which the Divine Majesty is enthroned. Souls in mortal sin cannot enter the palace, but remain outside among the foul, crawling things - servants of the devil, blackened in their living death, incapable of producing any good. It was once revealed to her in a vision that anyone who realized the effects of mortal sin would endure all conceivable torments rather than commit one."[6]

And so, Teresa, like her Savior before her, spent her days loving those who had sinned, praying for their immortal souls, not hating and condemning them as so many of her time did.

Not all of our Saint's visions were heavenly, as we have seen. There were those that wrenched at her soul as she literally *saw* the hideousness of sin in action, and the pitiable consequences of man giving into the father of sin and his demonic cohorts. When we think of one in particular, we know that the Lord shared these horrible moments with her that she might be used to warn not only those of the Fifteenth Century in which she lived,

but as an *"sos"*[7] to the faithful of the Church for centuries to come. What better way to weaken the Church than to attack our *"Ambassadors of Christ,"* our priests. In one of her more heart-rending visions, she saw a priest with two devils on top of his shoulders, wrapping themselves around his neck, as he was celebrating Holy Mass in a state of mortal sin.

How often are we too busy to go to confession; we say, we'll go next week; and then one week goes into one month

---

[6]*"Saint Teresa of Avila"* by William Thomas Walsh, Tan Publications

[7]When this signal goes out on the sea to other ships, it is from another ship in distress. The literal meaning is *"Save our ship!"* How apropos! When we sin, we weaken the Ship of the Church, which consists of the Mystical Body of Christ.

into one year and on and on until that day when the Angel of Death surprises us and we have died in a state of mortal sin. One of Saint Teresa's visions saw demons frolicking and reveling around the coffin of a poor soul who had died without having gone to confession. Like so many, this man had thought: *Let me have a good time, and then I'll go to confession; God will forgive me and I will not suffer the eternal pains of Hell.* For this man who had lived a sinful life, preferring the gifts of the devil to relationship with God, the giver of worldly temptations and lies[8] sent his enforcers to collect his soul. Not content to make sport with the lifeless body, mocking the prayers of the faithful who could not help him now, Saint Teresa saw them dragging his dead body about the coffin with meat hooks. She said: *"Would to God all in mortal sin might see what I saw!"*

If people in mortal sin could only *see* the ravages and utter destruction of mortal sin, would that stop them from giving into that first moment of temptation? What was it that Jesus said when speaking of Lazarus:

"There was a rich man who used to dress in purple and fine linen and feast magnificently every day. And at his gate there lay a poor man called Lazarus, covered with sores, who longed to fill himself with the scraps that fell from the rich man's table. Dogs came and even licked his sores. Now the poor man died and was carried away by the angels to the bosom of Abraham. The rich man also died and was buried.

"In his moment in Hades he looked up and saw Abraham a long way off with Lazarus in his bosom. So he cried out 'Father Abraham, pity me and send Lazarus to dip the tip of his finger in water and cool my tongue, for I am in agony in these flames.' 'My son,' Abraham replied, 'remember that during your life good things came

---

[8] the devil

your way, just as bad things came the way of Lazarus. Now he is being comforted here while you are in agony. But that is not all: between us and you a great gulf has been fixed, to stop anyone, if he wanted to, crossing from our side to yours, and to stop any crossing from your side to ours.'

"The rich man replied, 'Father, I beg you then to send Lazarus to my father's house, since I have five brothers, to give them warning so that they do not come to this place of torment too.' 'They have Moses and the prophets,' said Abraham, 'let them listen to them.' 'Ah no, father Abraham,' said the rich man, 'but if someone comes to them from the dead, they will repent.' Then Abraham said to him, 'If they will not listen either to Moses and the prophets, they will not be convinced if someone should rise from the dead.'"[9]

We are reading in this book the recounting over and over again of visions of *Heaven, Hell and Purgatory*. When we were children, we often resisted learning from our parents' experiences and wisdom. Mother Church has raised over the centuries Popes, Prophets, Saints, Visionaries, Mystics, and Stigmatists to warn us of the dangers and unimaginable misery we face in Hell eternal, to share the plight of those in Purgatory so that we pray for them, and to prophetically reveal the joys we will delight in as we rest in the arms of our Mother Mary, at the feet of Jesus in Heaven. Oh, the thought of being touched by Jesus and Mary, to see Their Eyes, to bask in the warmth and light of Their Love, at times makes us want to cry out with the Saints before us:

"I hear my Beloved.
See how He comes
leaping on the mountains,
bounding over the hills.

---

[9]Luke 16:19-31

My Beloved is like a gazelle,
Like a young stag.

"See where He stands
behind our wall.
He looks in at the window,
He peers through the lattice.

"My Beloved lifts up His Voice,
He says to me,
'Come then, My love,
My lovely one, come.
For see, the winter is past,
the rains are over and gone.
The flowers appear on the earth.

"The season of glad songs has come,
the cooing of the turtledove is heard
in our land.
The fig tree is forming its first figs
and the blossoming vines give out their fragrance.
Come then, My love,
My lovely one, come."[10]

Teresa's Visions of Heaven

There was a priest in Saint Teresa's life who had been of great spiritual help to her in her time of need.[11] As is God's way, her turn would come to return the favor. He came to see her one day; she was alarmed to see how his general health had deteriorated. She sensed there was something wrong other than physical; there appeared to be an emptiness in the priest. Now, it was not that he was not

---

[10]Song of Songs 2:8-13

[11]There are biographers who say St. Teresa is referring to a Dominican priest who had given the Last Rites to her father.

faithful to his priesthood or that he was not fulfilling all his obligations to his vocation. But because in his zeal to help others, he had neglected to care for the most important thing in his life, *his* immortal soul; he was just going through the motions, each day.

His eyes were not on Christ on the Cross, but below; and so like Peter before him, he was drowning. Was Jesus once more beckoning one of His chosen ones to come to Him? Knowing how powerfully he had been called to serve Christ and His Church, and knowing that *"he could not give what he did not have,"* [12] what did she do? She prayed, and she prayed, and she prayed! She pleaded with the Lord, reminding Him that His priest had been called to holiness, to sainthood. It seemed as if the Lord was not answering her; she prayed unceasingly. And when that did not get the desired result, she wept. [When we pray, do we pray passionately?] Her cry went up to the Lord and He appeared to her. He dictated a message she was to give to the priest. She did so, and although the miracle did not come as instantaneously as she would have hoped, change did come about, *a true metanoia*, the kind of conversion that can only come from above, and will last.

Then, what Teresa saw in her priest, the world must see in us, a radical change, a peace Jesus spoke of when He said: *"Peace I leave with you; My peace I give unto you; not as the world giveth, do I give unto you."* [13] He was giving back to the Lord that which was His, by allowing the Lord to fill Him. His prayer life became a strong part of his priesthood.

---

[12]Father Jim Plavcan OMF Conv, (now deceased) wrote to Bob and Penny before he died in an accident on the way to a Conference to further the Cause for Canonization of Blessed Kateri Tekakwitha *"Please keep up your prayer life. Without it you will not have the spirit or desire to continue in such marvelous efforts on His behalf. How does it go: 'You cannot give what you do not have!'"*
[13]Jn 14: 27

Because our prayers go up to the Lord as a sweet heavenly incense, they please the Lord, and He in turn transforms us into His creation, the creation He had in mind when He formed us.

Later, in one of her visions, Our Lord showed Saint Teresa the immense good this priest would do in his Order. Then another time, during an ecstasy, she saw him being transported upward by a *"Heavenly Army of Angels,"*[14] a sign from the Lord of the progress he was making in his ascent toward sanctity. His physical health improved to such a degree, he was able to resume the penances he had avoided out of fear he would jeopardize his health and consequently his apostolate. She saw the priest being handed a giant cross to carry: When someone he helped, attacked him, slandered him, spoke falsely about him, accused him unjustly, instead of defending himself, he was to humbly meet ingratitude with charity and patience. And so, he lived his life in this manner, from that moment on. Had he seen a tiny glimpse of Heaven? Had the Lord showed him how it would be with Him in the Kingdom?

In one vision of Heaven, Saint Teresa saw a Religious surrounded by Angels, standing very close to God. At that time, she was told of the great good that an Order would do in the last days, and the strength with which its members would defend and uphold the Faith. She did not mention the Order. We ask you, now, members of different Orders of the Church, is this God's Plan for you? Will you say *Yes?*

On many occasions, in her visions, she saw all the Jesuits, Franciscans, Carmelites, Dominicans and Augustinians *"together in Heaven, with white banners in their hands."* Saint Teresa goes on: *"and I have seen other wonderful things of them, and hold these Orders in great*

---

[14]Read more about the Angels in Bob and Penny's book: *"Heavenly Army of Angels."*

veneration, for I have dealt with them, and I see their lives conforming to what the Lord has given me to understand concerning them." Sons of Saint Ignatius, "*Army of the Pope,*" Sons and Daughters of Saint Francis, "*the Poor One,*" Sons and Daughters of Saint Dominic "*watch dogs of God,*" Sons and Daughters of Saint Augustine, "*one mind, one heart, one Spirit,*" and other members of Orders called to be faithful to Mother Church, this is what Our Lord disclosed to Saint Teresa about you! What an awesome heritage and what a formidable responsibility. Do you say Yes! like Jesus and Mary before you or do you say like Lucifer in the Garden, I will not serve?

Saint Teresa said that once, praying before the Blessed Sacrament, a Saint appeared to her whose Order had "*somewhat fallen.*"[15] He held a great book in his hands and read from it: "*In times to come this Order will flourish; it will have many martyrs.*"[16] Teresa did not say, this was the founder of the Jesuits, but we have gone to the places in Canada and upstate New York and have written about the Jesuit Martyrs who gave their lives that we in the North American Continent might have the gift of the Roman Catholic Faith, and we say, Why not! But then, it could have been Saint Francis referring to the many friars who were martyred in the Holy Land, alone, as they faithfully went about in their mission to evangelize and glorify the Lord's Name throughout the earth. We could go on and on, recalling the Maryknollers who were martyred and so many other brothers and sisters who gave their lives for the Faith. Was Saint Teresa speaking of any of you, or all of us? What do you think? If you for one moment believe this could be so, you must stand up and possibly suffer the greatest martyrdom of our Church's 2000 year history.

---

[15]"*Saint Teresa of Avila*" by William Thomas Walsh, Tan Publications
[16]from the Autobiography of St. Teresa

We know that it is difficult to remember that to die a martyr's death is to go straight up to Heaven, no stops on the way when you are burning at the stake. But nevertheless, that is the promise. And only God knows the value of dying a *Wet Martyr's* death versus dying a *Dry Martyr's* death. With the one, we die at once and it's over; with the other we die, little by little, day after day, by the sword that pierces our hearts as we hear those within the Church speak against her, her Pope and Bishops. If the rejection by those within and without the Church does not mortally wound you, then those who ridicule you because you hold fast to the teachings of the Church will try to finish you off. And it is that day in and day out faithfulness to Mother Church and her Magisterium, that *Dry Martyrdom* that will earn you your place in the Kingdom. And what can compare with that!

The closest we come to experiencing Heaven is at the Sacrifice of the Mass when Jesus is with us, Body, Blood, Soul and Divinity. We are seeing a preview of the Beatific Vision we will see when we are face to Face with Jesus in Heaven. As Saint Teresa said: *"The Mass and Holy Communion are the literal repetition of the Passion, Death, and Resurrection of the God-Man Jesus."* And this was from a woman who had seen and experienced *Heaven, Hell and Purgatory.*

Visions of St. Philip Neri
Apostle of Rome

In St. Philip's time, the Church was at a low point. Renaissance had taken its toll on the spirituality of most religious in Rome. The Medicis controlled the College of Cardinals. Choice candidates became princes of the land, rather than of the Church. The writings had become extremely secular and pagan. Morals and morale were at an all-time low. Severe abuses were occurring, as a result of giving into the worldliness of Renaissance, and all it stood for. *Everybody knew all about these abuses, but nobody did anything about them.* [Is this not happening today?]

†

To this mixed-up world, a Saint was born! St. Philip was born to a well-to-do family in Florence. From the time he was an infant, he demonstrated a gentleness and lovability that earned him the nickname *"Pippo buono",* or *"good little Phil."* He came from a *good* family, but not a particularly *spiritual* family. His father was a successful businessman; life was very normal and very happy. Then his mother died. He was very young; the little guy was lost; the Lord sent a caring step-mother to fill the void left by his most precious mother. His new mother loved him and his sisters dearly, and tended to them as if she had borne them. The attitudes and lifestyle of young Philip's family was typical of that time - *Do not harm your neighbor; support the Church financially; go to Mass* (all in that order), *and you will have nothing to worry about.* In contrast, Philip showed signs of holiness at an early age. But when he reached eighteen, it was time to prepare for the world and its demands.

Now the Neri family had a rich relative in Monte Cassino, who had succeeded handsomely in business. He asked Philip's parents to send their son to him. He not only wanted to train Philip in the affairs of the business world, but his intentions were to leave his entire operation to him, someday. Now, Philip was loved and trusted by everyone he met. His father believed, by sending him to his uncle he would receive the invaluable training which, with his outgoing disposition, would do him well in the world. This was his father's plan for sending him, his *earthly* father; but not his *Heavenly* Father!

He was obedient, and so, Philip, now 18 years old, was on his way to the grown up world of business, or so everyone thought. Although he was not particularly happy, he went to Monte Cassino and his uncle. Not many days passed, when he knew this life was not for him. The hounds of Heaven were gnawing at the eighteen year old's heart. He had always been spiritual. But now, in this new place, it was not as easy to pray, as it had been at home. Every chance he had, he'd finish his work quickly, run off and pray!

Now, as providence would have it, there was a place near Monte Cassino, called *Split Mountain*. When Our Lord gave up His Spirit to God the Father and died on the Cross, the curtain of the Temple ripped down the middle. We believe that the cry of the Angels was so anguished, at seeing their Lord and God die so horribly, the curtain could not withstand the furor and it tore in half. The tradition on Monte Cassino has always been that at the very same moment that the curtain split in Jerusalem, the mountain (Split Mountain) split in two, as well.

A Shrine was built; and a huge crucifix was placed there, which commemorates the death of Jesus Christ and our redemption. On this holy mountain, at this Shrine, St. Francis, in the Thirteenth Century, came and prayed; and then in the Sixteenth Century, Philip came and prayed in front of the same crucifix, on the same mountain.

When Philip first set out to pray at the Shrine, nestled in the crevice of the *Split Mountain*, his original focus was to pray and through prayer get closer to God. He would go to

Mass there and pray for God's Will in his life. Little did he know that God would talk to him on this remote mountain and change his life.

Now, it just happened, there is also a Shrine dedicated to the Blessed Trinity on this mountain. One day, while praying, he had a vision and was told to start a Confraternity of the Blessed Trinity. It was then and there that he received the inspiration to go to Rome! He made his decision based on this mystical experience, which he said brought about his "*conversion*". His life took a 180 degree turn. He converted from a *good* young man headed toward the world and all it had to offer, to a deeply *spiritual* young man willing to throw caution to the wind and go without hesitation, wherever the Lord sent him. Nothing of the world had any value to young Philip.

Philip goes to Rome

He set out for Rome with no possessions. When he arrived there, an Archduke who also came from Florence, provided him with shelter. His once-a-day ration was barely enough to eat - some bread, water and a few olives or other vegetables, his room - an unfinished attic with bare floors, a bed, a chair and a line upon which to hang his clothes. But for him, it was God's Will and he was quite content. Philip was hired to tutor the Archduke's young sons in exchange for his room and board. The boys' mother testified that the two, who had been unruly, became "*little saints*" under his direction. What developed was that soon they, too, wanted to devote their lives to God; and so, the three - Neri and the two young boys would go to the Basilicas and down to the Catacombs (specially St. Sebastian) to pray.

Outside of tutoring and praying with his two young friends and students, Philip spent the first two years in Rome, as a virtual *recluse*, his spare hours in solitary prayer. Then, he went from his little self-styled hermitage to studying

Left:
*St. Philip Neri
was known as
the "Apostle of
Rome."
He founded a
Confraternity of laity
who were formed
primarily to pray and
tend to the needs of the
pilgrims who were
coming to Rome for
the Holy Year.*

*St. Philip Neri saw a huge globe of fire come closer and closer to him.
He felt it go through his mouth and rest in his heart.*

at the Sapienza and the Sant'Agostino, two well-regarded schools, under the Augustinians. He became a brilliant student in philosophy and theology. Philip kept persevering, *full steam ahead*, in this direction for three years, and then, as urgently as he had begun, he just *stopped!*

For the last three years, whenever he had a chance, between his studies and classes, Philip would go off to pray. He would look upon Christ bleeding on the Crucifix. Then, he would go into ecstasy and enter so deeply into the Passion of Our Lord, it was as if he were there with the Lord on the Cross, suffering and dying. Was this what had precipitated his sudden change of heart?

Possibly the reason behind his *metanoia*,[1] his sudden change in direction, was due to the sad condition of the Church and her needs. In 1526, Rome had been sacked and she was slowly recovering from the rape and pillaging. The Church had been affected; priests rarely celebrated Mass; scandals spread about the clergy; no one went to church anymore in Rome.

We have to believe that Philip Neri had a very special relationship with Our Lord Jesus, because he made radical about-face modifications in his life at a minute's notice. Jesus knew that Philip was not someone content with just going through the motions, and He could and *would* work with that. If he had ever been made a cardinal, Philip would not have been a landowner, but a prince of the *Church*.

All we know is that he sold all his books. He felt the call to do something extreme. So, he went out and stood on the street corners of Rome and talked to whoever would listen. In short, he was answering the call to evangelize Rome. Through this, he earned the title: "*Apostle of Rome.*"

He had an overpowering urgency to create change. Something very interesting happened. Young people from

---

[1] conversion

the surrounding offices, banks, and shops, gathered around him and *listened!* The qualities that his father had seen in him, God would use to bring these young fertile minds and souls to do His Will. When he spoke, they gravitated toward this *troubadour* of the young; they joined in with his great sense of humor, laughed at his jokes, and cried when he spoke of that God Who had lived and died for them.

You would have thought that this being the early stages of Renaissance, everybody would be looking for things *not spiritual, not church*, more of the world - secular, artistic and fun. But that was not the case. Not everyone was caught up in the paganism that had become so fashionable. Actually, the rank and file, the little people in the Church like you and me, were looking for Jesus. But they didn't know where to go, or whom to ask, or what to do. They didn't want to join in the permissiveness that was rampant. But they needed someone to say it was all right not to want those things, but to want something of a higher level. *That someone was Philip.* He gave them that. He satisfied their hunger for more. First, he won them with his beautiful personality, and great sense of humor. Then, it didn't take long before he had them really *hearing* him with their minds and hearts.

When he greeted the young people he would ask: "*Well, brothers, when shall we begin to do good?*" And they responded, following him, joining him in corporal works of mercy, visiting hospitals, prisons, the elderly and the sick. They realized more gratification and self-worth from this, than from all the Renaissance perversion which was being thrown at them. They started to gather with Philip Neri in his small room, the laity, priests, nobility and commoners, all would come and pray; and through this, he formed what is now known as the *Oratory of the Laity.* Vatican Council II affirmed his Apostolate.

He founded a Confraternity of Laity who were formed primarily to pray and tend to the needs of the pilgrims who were coming to Rome for the Holy Year. The pilgrims of that day traveled with much love and devotion for Mother Church, but little more. They were hungry, needed shelter and often medical care, but mostly they came thirsting for the Word of God. As most pilgrims were extremely poor, the members of the Confraternity took full charge of them. They tended the sick *personally* and brought them to the Hospital of the Holy Spirit when they were in need of professional care. They provided food and lodging to those without a place to stay, which was most of the pilgrims.

Rome was not built up the way it is today; there were no hotels. Taking over homes, the members of the Confraternity made the first *pilgrimage* houses, one for men and one for women. If you came from a long distance, they gave you five days lodging, from near, three days lodging. When the Holy Year was over, some of the pilgrims were too sick to return home. The Confraternity stayed on and cared for them.

St. Philip is pierced with the Flame of Love

St. Philip Neri had a mystical experience, similar to those *of Padre Pio, St. Teresa of Avila* and *St. John of the Cross*. Theirs were called *Transverberation of the Heart*. They actually saw an Angel pierce their hearts. For the rest of their lives, they literally burned with love of Jesus. They all felt a swelling, an enlargement of the heart.

During the day, Philip Neri spent his every waking hour serving God's children, but at night he would retire to the catacombs and pray. He had been praying in St. Sebastian's Catacomb, when he saw a huge globe of fire soar toward him. He felt it go into his mouth, down his throat, through his entire body, and finally rest in his heart. The heat burned like an inner flame. He began to convulse with emotion. He was so full of love, he thought he would explode. Every part of his body tingled. He experienced so great an ecstasy, he cried out: *"Stop Lord! I cannot take anymore. Anymore and I will die."* This remained with him the rest of his life. His heart became so enlarged, when he died two prominent scientists from the Vatican examined him and discovered that two of his ribs had broken to accommodate the tremendously distended heart.

Saint of the Earthquake

He was known as *Saint of the Earthquake*, because when his heart beat, it made such a loud noise, it shook the room; it felt like an earthquake was rocking the house. They said, it could be felt all the way to St. Peter's Basilica.

From that day on, he never knew when he would be overcome with this fierce tremor, his heart beating with such intensity his whole body shook. Although this outward manifestation troubled him, the Lord so filled Him with His Love, he radiated! All this took place before he was ordained a priest.

He had been of the *Laity*; he had formed a Confraternity of *Laity* whose charism was to serve other *Laity*. He never felt called to be a priest. He never felt *worthy* to be a priest. No amount of persuasion would convince him to become a priest. It was only when his confessor *ordered* him that he was finally convinced, and Philip was ordained at age thirty-four. He continued his apostolate of speaking to people, and in that way bringing them back to the Church. However, now the main vehicle he used was the Confessional. He spent hours and hours each day counselling penitents.

He began a practice of having dialogues with the large group of penitents who spent hours, on long lines at the church, waiting to go to confession. A big room was set up above the church. Followers of the community of Philip Neri would flock there in great numbers to hear his lectures.

Now keep in mind, this was during the Renaissance, when there were so many distractions of every kind available down the block, or around the corner. Yet these people would rather be in church, listening to Philip Neri talk about Jesus.

The decadence and paganism of the past was hard to do away with in one day. At the time of carnivals, revelers lined the streets, engaging in all kinds of debauchery. Philip Neri gathered up young people who, rather than participate in this pagan behavior, instead processed through Rome from one church to another, to seven *churches*: St. Peter's, St. John Lateran, St. Mary Major, St. Paul, St. Sebastian, St. Lawrence, and The Church of the Holy Cross of Jerusalem.

When the procession was over, they all gathered together and broke bread. Now, when you want something done, enflame the hearts and minds of the Laity.[2] A group of people formed, quite a few of them from the aristocracy, and they became part of Philip Neri's Confraternity. They had started first by listening, and then making the lessons their own doing. They organized what we might call today, *outdoor picnics*; they hired the finest musicians to play, prepared small meals, and served all who had been in the procession, rich and poor alike. After the picnic was over, the nobility gathered all the dishes, cleaned the area, and tended the needs of all, while Philip Neri taught the Faith. *Conversions came about!*

The Oratory grew even more than before, after Philip Neri was ordained a priest, adding to its numbers those to whom he had ministered. When the Congregation was called to prayer in the Oratory, a bell was rung to get their attention. Thus began the tradition of the Oratorians, which ultimately became a Community. Fr. Philip Neri was its founder. Some years later, when Philip drew up a modest

---

[2]Read how the Laity built the first Oratory of St. Joseph in Montreal, Canada, in *"Visionaries, Mystics and Stigmatists"* by Bob and Penny Lord,

Above: ***The Poor Souls that St. Philip Neri had been praying for came to him upon his death and ushered him into the Kingdom of Heaven.***

St. Philip Neri in radiant glory

Rule for a small number of devotees who had become priests, they were called the Oratorians.

His Confraternity blossomed; more and more disciples joined. The Pope gave them a run-down church; they tore it down, and rebuilt on its foundation, a new church, designed to glorify the Lord. However, when it was ready, everybody moved into it except Philip Neri, the superior. He wanted to stay in his secluded living quarters, where he had spent so much of his life, where the Lord had worked so powerfully. *But obedience is the keyword.* It didn't make much sense for his whole community to headquarter out of this beautiful edifice, and for him not to be with them. So, out of obedience to the Pope and his Community, he joined them.

For the last twenty years of his life, he ministered to many people from his *room* at the church of *Santa Maria in Vallicella*. A veritable *Who's who* of the Church, and the world, passed through those doors, asking for guidance. It was in this way that he was most successful, and felt most comfortable. It was the same as he had done from the beginning, speaking in the streets, and then in the confessional. He was able to fight the evils of the Renaissance most powerfully from this intimate vantage point. The royalty of the world and of the Church came to him for advice, as well as those in his community.

On May 25, 1595, forty four years and two days after he was ordained, at age eighty, Philip Neri gave his body and soul over to his Lord. He joined the Communion of Saints in Heaven. But here on earth, his work continued vigorously. His followers begat more followers who begat more followers.

The Poor Souls in Purgatory

St. Philip had always had a great devotion to the Souls in Purgatory. He taught his Oratorians to pray for the Poor Souls, to do redemptive suffering for them, to offer up good works and especially have Masses said for them, as there is nothing that moves the Father's Heart like the Sacrifice of the Mass. Those who had been part of his Community, or under his spiritual direction, held a special place in his heart. Many times, he was visited by those of his Community, who had passed on, asking for prayers. Very often they returned to thank him for what he had done for them, how through his prayers, most powerfully during the Mass, he had kept them out of the pits of Hell, and instead brought them to Purgatory, where they had confident assurance that they would one day share in the *Beatific Vision*.

After our Saint's death, a holy priest was praying before his tomb when St. Philip Neri appeared to him in radiant glory. The priest recognized him - It was the glorified St. Philip, surrounded by blessed spirits! The priest asked him the meaning of these spirits. He replied that these were the souls who had been under his spiritual direction during life, and for whose release from Purgatory, he had prayed. Having attained entry into Heaven through him, they had come to meet him upon his death, and usher him into the Kingdom. They were so grateful to St. Philip for praying for them and offering Masses for their release from Purgatory, they had prayed for him till the day he died.

We're told that the Souls in Purgatory cannot do anything to help themselves. They can pray to our Guardian Angels to remind us to pray for them. The Poor Souls can pray for us, but they can't pray for each other or for themselves. We, on the other hand, can pray and have Masses offered for them, with full knowledge that we have Souls in Purgatory and Heaven who are praying for us and our salvation. We're told that upon entry into Heaven, these souls immediately intercede for those who have prayed for their release. Remember, *now* they are Saints in Heaven.

Then, when we breath our last, as with Philip Neri, maybe the Souls we prayed for, will escort us to Heaven.

Visions of St. Catherine de' Ricci

Suffered for the Souls in Purgatory

God is so good. He gives us so many gifts. He has given us the gift of researching these specially chosen Saints so that we can bring them to you. He gives *you* the gift of reading about them, so that you can share them with other brothers and sisters in Christ. We had a focus. We always have a focus and an agenda, and then God changes everything around to conform to *His* agenda and *His* focus. This book is about *Visions of Heaven, Hell and Purgatory.* We thought it important, however, to give you a thumbnail sketch of the lives of the Saints and Blesseds who have been granted the unique Grace to peer behind the curtain which separates Earth from *Heaven, Hell and Purgatory.*

But there is so much more. It is not difficult to understand that the Lord would grant extraordinary abilities to those who are completely committed to Him and His Kingdom. To those whom He gives one talent, He showers upon them many talents. St. Paul's words to the Romans ring out loud and clear, *"For those He foreknew, He also predestined ...And those He predestined, He also called, and those He called, He also justified; and those He justified, He also glorified."*[1] We sometimes wonder if the Lord doesn't put special people in our paths, not so much for the reason we think, but to glorify His Name! Such a person was St. Catherine de' Ricci.

A Saint extraordinare, she received the Stigmata, was mystically married to Jesus, *literally* shared in His Passion, and experienced many visions during her ecstasies, among which were *Heaven, Hell and Purgatory.* While our focus, in sharing with you the life of St. Catherine, has to do with *Visions of Heaven, Hell and Purgatory*, we would be remiss if

---

[1]Romans 8:28-30

we did not tell you something about this marvelous person, the Lord has put in our paths - Saint Catherine de' Ricci.

†

April 23, 1522, a baby's cry cut through the quiet of the palace and onto the streets of Florence,Italy and Alexandrina, who would someday be known as Saint Catherine de' Ricci, was born. She came from a prominent family of the nobility. Although they were not particularly known for their holiness, her piety and spirituality was evident from an early age. Therefore, it was no surprise to her family and friends when, at age thirteen, she entered the convent of *San Vicenzo* in Prato, a small town outside of Florence.

She immediately embraced her Dominican Community. She took the name Catherine as her religious name, in honor of her mentor, St. Catherine of Siena, a powerful Dominican Saint of the Fourteenth Century. As with her predecessor and namesake, she suffered greatly all her life. Saint Catherine de' Ricci was a virtuous young girl, never complaining or trying to bring attention to herself through an illness which would be with her the rest of her life. Like the Saint she was to become, she turned her afflictions into redemptive suffering, and used these sufferings to develop even stronger virtues. She exercised patience beyond the limits of human frailty, especially considering the severity of her physical afflictions. She was able to overcome the debilitating *consequences* of her illnesses by uniting her suffering with Her Lord's Passion, her eyes and heart constantly contemplating her Spouse Jesus as He agonized on the Cross.

We have to take a moment here and look at how the Lord chooses vessels who will stand out as contradictions in the world. Many of the people we write about in our books are from the Renaissance Era, and in particular from Florence where the Renaissance began. St. Catherine de'

Ricci was from nobility in Florence; St. Philip Neri came from wealth, also in Florence; St. Catherine of Siena was from a wealthy family from Siena; St. Bernardine of Siena was born of a noble family from a suburb of Siena. Siena and Florence are both in the Tuscany Province with only fifty miles distance between them.

The *Tuscani*[2] of Florence and Siena have always been extremely worldly. A proud people, they have given the world some of the greatest *maestri*[3] in music, art and literature. This province has been the home of some of the most profound and influential thinkers, down through the ages. Many times, being quite cultured and wise in the ways of the world, we lose touch with the One Who gave us these gifts in the first place, and we become proud! When the Renaissance hit, Florence and Siena were the *first areas* to embrace it. The Medicis, who ruled the Papacy during part of this time, were from Florence, as were the Pitti family, and the Sforzas. The Lord chose some of His greatest Defenders of the Faith, and powerful warriors of Jesus and Mary's army, from among the people of this region. And if that was not enough, many of them were either from royalty or nobility. *God always balances the scales.*

†

This chapter is about a holy contradiction. Let us travel back in time to the Sixteenth Century. Summer has arrived and Alexandrina's (Catherine) family has left Florence to go on pilgrimage to Prato, as they have done every year. There is a convent in Prato with a miraculous statue of Mother Mary to whom her family and many of the inhabitants of Tuscany have always had a great devotion. Years before, Spain had invaded Italy, her forces barreling through Florence and on to Prato, killing and destroying homes and

---

[2]Citizens of the Tuscany Province in Italy
[3]masters

everything in their path. They came upon the Dominican
Convent of *San Vicenzo*.[4] They entered the first level of the
convent, planning to invade the cloister and harm the nuns
within. As they were about to attack the nuns, the statue of
our Most Blessed Mother Mary came to life, and said: *"Do
not touch my sisters and I will promise you Paradise."* The
soldiers went down on their knees, and although 5000 lives
had already been taken, not one nun was touched.[5]

Nuns from the convent would come begging for olives,
oil, and wheat to make bread. Alexandrina's family was
always generous to the nuns, little knowing the gift they
would exact from them. Now, Alexandrina could not help
but be attracted to the simple piety and humility of these
Brides of Christ. She grew to love them. At eleven years old,
she decided she would become one of them. Her family said
absolutely not and quickly returned with her to Florence.
She had lost her mother when she was four years old and
had no one to turn to when, at thirteen years old, a marriage
was arranged. But her *Mother Mary* was watching over her.
Alexandrina became seriously ill! Her family allowed her to
enter the convent. The illness left her.

Right from the beginning of her religious life, she had
problems. The other sisters wanted to send her away. They
did not understand her; she was an outsider; she was of the
nobility; they did not trust her; they wanted her out, and they
systematically went about executing their campaign. That is,
until one day when, upon returning from Communion, they
saw the Lord bend down from the Cross and embrace her.

Five years later, on Easter Sunday, she prayed to the
Lord to give her a new heart, because she said *"With this*

---

[4]St. Vincent Ferrer

[5]This happened the 29th of August and the faithful of Prato
celebrate this miracle each year at this time. The statue is processed
through the streets, the Mother of God protecting this village and the
monastery through many wars including the 1st and 2nd world wars.

Left:
On Easter Sunday, St. Catherine de' Ricci prayed, *"With this weak heart of mine, I cannot love you properly."* Then on the Feast of Corpus Christi, she went into ecstasy, and Our Lord appeared to her and gave her a new heart. She said that her heart felt as if it was on fire.

Right:
St. Catherine de' Ricci had mystical conversations with St. Philip Neri of Rome. She bi-located to Rome. They corresponded about matters of Faith, but they had never actually met.

Below:
The incorrupt body of St. Catherine de' Ricci in Prato, Italy

weak heart of mine, I cannot love you properly." Then, on the Feast of Corpus Christi, she went into ecstasy, and Our Lord appeared to Catherine and gave her a new heart, made of flesh. She said that her heart felt as if it was on fire. She had asked to love Him with a heart that could love Him as He deserved. Whose heart could better love Him than that of Mother Mary! Who knew *how* to truly love her Son, if not His Mother? Our Lord, when she asked for a new heart that could properly love Him, gave her the heart of His Mother Mary. From that time on, she said her heart was no longer hers, but that of Jesus, Mother.

The following year, the 15th of April, 1542,[6] *she was mystically married to Jesus.* [Now, many Saints we have written about have been given that special blessing by the Lord: St. Catherine of Siena, St. Gemma Galgani, St. Veronica Giuliani to mention just a few. But the outward sign of St. Catherine de' Ricci's marriage was the most unusual we have ever heard.] Our Lord appeared to the young girl in a brilliance, reminiscent of the Transfiguration. He took her hand in His and kissed it; then He took a gleaming ring off His own finger and placed it on the ring finger on her left hand, saying,

"My daughter, receive this ring as pledge and proof that thou dost now, and ever shalt, belong to Me."

Now, this has happened before to many Saints. The difference with this Mystical Marriage was that there were *witnesses* to this miracle! The ring actually manifested itself in a *physical* ring of gold and diamonds. That's how St. Catherine saw it all her life. It was seen and testified to by three of the nuns in the community, all of whom were mature nuns. Only they saw something different from Catherine. They saw a red mark around the finger, as if the

---

[6]Many of the great gifts Catherine received came to her in 1542, when she was just twenty years old.

ring had made a mark on her finger. There was a larger red mark, in the form of a stone, but not a stone, appearing where a stone would be on an actual ring.

One description given was that it looked like a ring had been buried under the skin. This miraculous manifestation was seen by all on Ascension Thursday and the Feast of Corpus Christi, lasting for the entire day, each time.

The only exception to this was when the governor of Prato asked to see it. On the Feast of Corpus Christi, Catherine was brought into the church so that he would be able to view the ring. As soon as she approached him, the ring disappeared, and did not reappear until he left.

The ring became an important area of contention not only in her lifetime, but later, in the process of her Beatification and Canonization. [However, the Lord triumphed; her sincerity and spirituality were authenticated and she was *officially* added to the Communion of Saints.] Catherine's superior tried to find a way to remove the cause of the problem, the red mark on her finger. Catherine was open to any methods the superior chose to remove the mark. But all the time, Catherine insisted, she couldn't see any mark on her finger; what she could see was a magnificent ring of gold adorned with brilliant diamonds that Our Lord Jesus had given her.

When she had been mystically married to Jesus, there was a truly celestial celebration, as is proper for such a monumental event. But she was to learn that, as she was married to *Jesus Resurrected*, she was also married to *Christ Crucified*. A year after the mystical marriage, she went into a long ecstasy which lasted *twenty-eight hours*! She saw a beautiful Angel approach her with the arrows of the Passion, and felt the pains shoot into her hands, feet and side. She collapsed in complete ecstasy mingled with agony; now, she was truly the Bride of Christ.

Left:
St. Catherine de' Ricci was Mystically Married to our Lord Jesus. Jesus took a gleaming ring off His finger, and placed it on her ring finger, saying *"My daughter, receive this ring as pledge and proof that thou dost now, and ever shalt, belong to Me."*

Right:
Jesus on the Cross speaks to St. Catherine de' Ricci. These visions began when she was in her early twenties and continued until her mid-thirties. They took place every week. She actually went through Christ's agony, as if she were doing it in place of Jesus, or as if He was suffering in her body.

Her Stigmata[7] was somewhat different from any we have ever researched, in that it was manifested in different ways to different people. Some saw what is considered the *traditional* Stigmata, that is the hands, feet and side pierced and bleeding. Others saw a brilliant light coming from the wounds, so dazzling they had to look away. Then there were those who saw healed wounds, with just the red puffiness and swelling of wounds that had healed, black spots appearing in the center (of the wounds). In these instances, the blood under the skin appeared to be flowing in a circular movement around the black center. Catherine actually experienced, in a mystical sense, the agonies suffered by Our Lord Jesus Christ during His Passion and His Crucifixion.

The following Monday, she saw a beautiful lady dressed in red, coming out of one of the cells in the convent. She walked down the corridor of the dormitory toward Catherine. *It was Saint Mary Magdalen![8]* She beckoned Catherine to follow her. Now, Catherine was bleeding and weak from the agony she had endured during the twenty-eight hours of the Passion. At first, she tried to beg off, but in the end she obeyed. She walked, her back bent, her shoulder aching and bruised from carrying the cross. But this all passed, for before her stood her Risen Lord, bathed in a shower of light and He was splendid to behold. She fell to her knees in adoration. All her aches and pains turned into joy!

These visions began when she was in her early twenties, and continued until her mid-thirties. They took place every week. She actually went through Christ's agony, as if she were doing it in place of Jesus, or as if He was suffering in

---

[7]The stigmata refers to the wounds, scars, or skin abrasions that appear on the flesh of individuals. They correspond to the wounds suffered by Christ in the Crucifixion. (Catholic Encyclopedia - Broderick)

[8]the Mary Magdalen of Jesus' time

her body. This would begin Thursday evening, in memory of Holy Thursday and the Agony in the Garden, through to Friday in communion with Our Lord's Crucifixion on Good Friday, ending on Saturday. She was lost in deep meditation, the entire time. The only time she came out of it, for a short period, was when she received the Eucharist each morning. She would regain consciousness, receive her Lord, and sink right back into the sorrowful mystery of the Passion.

This went on continuously for twelve years. Looking at it in the light of the tempest it caused when word got out, it became a real cross for the rest of the sisters in the convent. Prayers and penance were offered by all, *including Catherine*, for it to end. Finally, in 1554, as an answer to prayer, it stopped. A gentle sigh of relief was breathed by all concerned. However, this did not mean, by any stretch of the imagination, that her ecstasies ended.

Catherine was to be given an additional gift; she received the Crown of Thorns. One day, our Blessed Mother appeared to Catherine. She was holding crowns and offered them to Catherine: one of thorns and one of silver. She already had the Stigmata and was experiencing great pain; weak, she asked for the crown of silver. Our Lady said: "*Catherine which crown did your spouse wear?*" Catherine replied: "*Then Mother Mary, place on my head the one my Lord wore.*" When we were interviewing the Mother Superior and one of her nuns, they shared: *Catherine was very human!* She did not desire *pain*; she desired to share in *Jesus' pain*, out of love for Him.

This period was difficult for the community, because they were not getting the full attention of this most special sister of theirs. *But with all of this, they elected her prioress!*

Her reputation for holiness spread far and wide. She became the counselor and advisor to priests, bishops and three cardinals who later became Popes. Kings and Queens came to her! Imagine hierarchy in the Church and powerful figures in the world, asking for the direction of a young girl, not yet thirty years old.

St. Catherine bi-locates and meets with St. Philip Neri

St. Catherine de' Ricci had mystical conversations with *St. Philip Neri*,[9] a most holy man, who confirmed this. When shown a painting of Catherine, he replied, she was far more beautiful. They had corresponded about matters of the Faith, but had never actually met. It would have been difficult, because Catherine was cloistered in Prato, and Philip's workplace was Rome. Nevertheless, she appeared to him in Rome and they had long conversations. Not only did St. Philip verify this, but also witnesses who actually saw the two saints conversing. St. Catherine and St. Philip were bonded together by the Lord, through Catherine's bi-locations bridging a distance of almost one hundred ninety seven miles.

Catherine and her devotion for the Poor Souls in Purgatory.

She constantly prayed for the release of the Suffering Souls in Purgatory. She performed acts of charity; she offered up her Masses and Communions on their behalf. She was even willing to suffer in their place, and there are many accounts where the Lord allowed her to do so. The Poor Souls were allowed to enter the Kingdom before they had suffered for the period assigned them, as Catherine suffered unbelievable pain on their behalf.

One incident of her involvement with the Poor Souls in Purgatory, well known in the life of St. Catherine, concerned the Granduke Francesco de' Medici. As we mentioned before, Catherine was advisor and friend of the Medicis and other nobility; one could almost call her *Saint of the Nobility*. Francesco's wife, the Granduchess (also Princess of Austria) was the spiritual daughter of Catherine. She was holy and

---

[9]Read about St. Philip Neri in the chapter on him in this book

virtuous, whereas her husband was cruel and totally insensitive to his wife's suffering. He even had a mistress living in the same house with him and his wife! This hurt the Granduchess, terribly. His whole court knew! He didn't care. But although he wounded her deeply, the Granduchess never stopped praying for his soul. She asked Catherine to pray for his conversion, that he might not be condemned to Hell. She also asked her to plead with God that when her husband died, he not suffer horribly in Purgatory. The Granduchess died before her husband, and he married the mistress. Although Catherine did not approve of her behavior, she nevertheless paid the new Granduchess the respect due her new station in life.

Now as far as the Granduke was concerned, the Church, the Lord, his immortal soul were all things which were way back in the recesses of his heart and mind. Catherine prayed for his conversion for *twenty years*. She pleaded with him to convert. He paid no attention to her. The Granduke died. Because of all her prayers, on his death bed, he asked for a priest, confessed his sins and received absolution before he died. He was spared the fires and everlasting pains of Hell; but was sent to the pits of Purgatory to suffer the temporal punishment due him for his sins. There, he would undergo the cleansing of his soul to such a state, he would be acceptable to enter into the presence of God.

St. Catherine kept her promise to the Granduchess and *pleaded* with the Lord, to allow her to take over the temporal punishment, due the Granduke. The Lord accepted, and the Granduke was led through the gates of Heaven.

We have to believe that Catherine had a great love for the poor suffering souls in Purgatory, to be willing to take on the type of horrendous reparation due for their acts on earth. She was given to understand that she would have to bear forty days of unbearable, excruciating, virtually impossible to describe - pain. In exchange, the Granduke would enter Heaven without suffering the agony that had been prepared for him. She said *Yes!*

The following account comes from eyewitnesses who stayed with St. Catherine during those nightmarish forty days of anguish and torment. Her body was covered with blisters, on top of her skin. The heat which emanated from the fire inside her, made her so warm that her room was described as being *hot as an oven.* Those who tried to help her, who wanted to pray with her in her room, could only stay for short intervals, as the heat was so intense they could not breathe. There were times when the blistering stopped. Then, her skin took on the appearance of being roasted. When the fire inside her started to rage again, the blisters began to discharge such unbearable heat, her followers were forced to leave the room.

It was obvious to all in her cell that Catherine was really in the depths of Purgatory, where the heat gets as intense as if she were in the pits of Hell. The only difference in Purgatory over Hell is *hope* and that promise that Jesus made to those souls in Purgatory that they would one day be released, and experience the Beatific Vision.

During this time, the suffering became so fierce that she lost her speech for as much as twelve minutes at a time. She suffered patiently and quietly until someone told her she was carrying this thing a little too far. One of her sisters reprimanded her for allowing herself to be tortured this way. St. Catherine reared herself up and addressed the comment:

"Pardon me, my dear sisters, if I answer you. Jesus has so much love for souls, that all we do for their salvation is infinitely agreeable to Him; that is why I gladly endure any pain, whatsoever it may be, as well for the conversion of sinners as for the deliverance of the souls detained in Purgatory. It is His Will they be with Him in Heaven; I am only His vessel."

The forty days ended; St. Catherine returned to her normal self again. The relatives of the Granduke, knowing that St. Catherine had been praying for him, inquired about the state of his soul. Catherine smiled and told them not to worry; he had been led out of the darkness, into the *Sonlight* of the Beatific Vision. Although she would never take credit, his family knew it was because of her suffering and prayers that this had come about. He had been forgiven his sins; his debt had been paid to the last penny, and he would enjoy life eternal in the Kingdom of God.

There's nothing mentioned as to whether the Granduke came back to earth in an apparition to St. Catherine to thank her for the suffering she had endured on his account. But it's really not important. As a matter of fact, it would probably be more desirable that neither he nor anyone else showed appreciation, so that when the Lord accompanied St. Catherine into Heaven, amidst much fanfare from the Heavenly Army of Angels and the Royal Court of Saints, the reward would come from Him.

All Catherine wanted to do was to serve her Lord. Redemptive suffering is a tool which the Lord gave her, and gives us, to help our brothers and sisters during their struggle to complete their journey to the Kingdom. It is also a way for us to give a little back to Jesus for all that He does for us. Thank You, Jesus, for allowing us to share in Your Love for the Poor Souls in Purgatory.

†

One of Catherine's brothers, Andrew led a wild life. At the end of his life, as he was dying in France, he refused the Sacraments. When Catherine heard he had died, she immediately began to plead his case with the Lord, invoking Him to have mercy on her brother, out of His love for her. This is one of the rare times that the Lord refused her, saying most decidedly that since her brother had refused the merciful Sacraments of the Church, he *wanted* to go to Hell;

and because He loved him so, the Lord was allowing him to go to Hell. God had given him the free will to love Him and he had chosen to use that gift to condemn himself to eternal damnation without Him.

These are just some of the incidents in the life of St. Catherine de' Ricci, her devotion and intercession for the Poor Souls in Purgatory. She suffered, and then watched many souls enter into the Kingdom because of her suffering. In addition, she lived the life of a model prioress of her community, as well as a mother and sister to the wards[10] the Lord had given her to protect and lead into the Kingdom.

St. Catherine died when she was sixty-eight years old, on February 2, 1590, after much suffering. She was a very holy lady. The ring she received when she was mystically married to Jesus, the stigmata, and her ecstasies, were all gifts from Jesus; her virtuous life was her gift to Him. When her cause for Beatification was opened in 1614, most of the sisters who had been eyewitnesses were dead. The Devil's Advocate was a very renowned priest, who went on to become Pope Benedict XIV. He was disturbed about what appeared to be confusion and unrest over the mystical ring. However, the Lord worked through this diversion, and Catherine became a member of the Communion of Saints. She was canonized in 1747. Her body has never decomposed. While it is hard and leathery, there is a peace and serenity which reflects who she was in her life. She lies in state in a glass coffin for the Faithful to venerate. She has been named the Co-Patroness of the city of Prato.

She suffered greatly all her life, but she accepted her role as a redemptive sufferer with celestial joy, and this was seen by everyone with whom she came in contact. She reacted to the great gifts the Lord gave her with humility, love and thanksgiving.

---

[10]the nuns in her charge

The day she died, all eternity waited for that beautiful moment when Catherine would be reunited with her Heavenly Spouse and her Mother Mary. We can just picture Our Lord Jesus and Our Lady, with Their Heavenly Army of Angels forming an honor guard, waiting to usher Catherine into the Kingdom. We can see that long army of Souls whom she had been instrumental in releasing from Purgatory, processing alongside their benefactress as her royal escorts. Great doings and rejoicing must have gone on in Heaven, that day.

One of the unique ways that Jesus used Catherine to battle the evils of the Renaissance had to be through the Souls, *the Church Suffering* she had helped to enter Heaven, who you can be sure were praying for the redemption of those still on earth being deluged by that deadly influence of the Renaissance. This is one way she combated that deadly era. But another way was her sign, the *living contradiction* she had been to the *shallow values of her day*.

In the life of St. Catherine, we see the Lord fighting the evils of the Renaissance in a completely different, indirect way, through a *suffering servant*. While it's true that her mysticism, her ecstasies and her stigmata attracted the attention of many, she was basically *a cloistered nun*. She didn't go out into the world and spread the good news of Jesus. She *suffered* for the redemption of the world, as her Spouse before her. The power of God was manifested through this ailing daughter. Through Catherine, the Lord showed another way of life, another set of values, an option to the debasement being offered by the Renaissance. Was the Lord telling these people, and us,today, "*There is another way. You don't have to buy into this lifestyle. Come to Me. I have proven to you, through My people, that you can live a wholesome life, a life close to Me, and be happy. Where your treasure lies, there is your God. Make Me your God!*"

St. Mary Magdalen de Pazzi

and her visions of Purgatory

It is the Sixteenth Century. We are again at a time of struggle and crisis in the world and in the Church. A priest[1] will cause many innocent lambs, not aware of his disobedience and betrayal to the Church, to stray. As always, when the Church is under attack and things look hopeless, God raises up a powerful Saint to save His Church. St. Mary Magdalen de Pazzi was one of those Saints. She was born in Florence, Italy, into a very prominent and most influential family; both sides of her parents' families were close friends of the ruling Medici family. They would be responsible for contributing, down through the history of Florence, many highly acclaimed statesmen, but none whose mark would be so profoundly and everlastingly felt on the Church and the world, as a Carmelite Nun from their ranks who would far surpass their fleeting fame.

She was baptized Catherine after *St. Catherine of Siena*. From her earliest years, she showed an affinity for the religious life. When her father was appointed Governor of Cortona, Catherine was placed in a convent school there and learned to love the prayerful and holy life, she saw so authentically lived out each day. When she made her decision to enter the Carmelite Order, at first her family objected; they had plans to marry her off to another leading family, uniting the two families into one *major* entity, a dynasty more powerful than either had been before.

But when her family saw that none of the suitors who asked for her hand in marriage, could dissuade her from her intended plans to become a *"Bride of Christ,"* Catherine was finally allowed to enter the Convent of St. Mary on the Feast of the Assumption. On January 30, 1583, she received her habit and Catherine received the name *Sister Mary Magdalen.*

---

[1]Martin Luther

At the vesting ceremony, the priest placed a crucifix in her hands, with the words: "*God forbid that I should glory save in the Cross of Our Lord Jesus Christ.*"

As he pronounced these words, her face became radiant, the overwhelming desire to suffer for Christ filling her heart and mind. This yearning never left her, nor did the pain that accompanied it. When her physical pain became evident to one of the other sisters, she asked Sister Mary Magdalen how she could bear so much suffering without crying out. Pointing to the crucifix, she exclaimed:

"See what the infinite love of God suffered for my salvation. That same love sees my weakness and gives me courage. Those who call to mind the sufferings of Christ and who offer up their own to God through His Passion find their pains sweet and pleasant."

After this, the sisters helped her to the infirmary, and Sister Mary Magdalen went into an ecstasy lasting an hour. But with the ecstasy came the agony. She not only suffered physically, but she experienced great spiritual dryness. The devil attacked her, every way imaginable. Although she fasted on bread and water alone (except on holidays and Sundays), she had to fight the sometimes almost overpowering craving she would have for food, and it took all the strength she could summon, to resist devouring everything in sight. No sooner did she conquer this temptation, the enemy hit her with impure thoughts that drained her as she battled to wipe them from her mind. She turned to the Blessed Mother and Our Lord Jesus.

One battle fought and won, the enemy of God never sleeps; he is ready with another attack more brutal than the last. Sister Mary Magdalen found herself in a state of intense darkness, where she saw herself as a terrible sinner, without hope, beyond help, alone and forsaken. She was to go through this desolation for *five long years*. When her time in the desert[2] was at an end, it was as if God had released her from exile and she went into ecstasy. When she came to, after an hour's time, she turned to the prioress and the novice-mistress and said: "*Rejoice with me, for my winter is at an end! Help me to thank and glorify my good Creator.*"

Finally, this trial over, another one began. Sister Mary Magdalen felt empty, forsaken; she couldn't feel anything. *Didn't He love her anymore?* But through all the pleading with no response, she remained true to her Spouse, often giving Him 100% and receiving nothing, no emotions, no comfort, not even the smallest awareness of His Presence. But because of her faithfulness and unconditional love for Him, Our Lord began pouring out His Graces upon her.

From that time on, she was endowed with many Heavenly gifts. She was able to *foretell* the future. She told Alexander de Medici that he would be Pope but that he would have a short reign. His papacy lasted twenty-six days!

Sometimes a gift and other times a cross, Mary Magdalen was granted the Grace to *read men's hearts*.

Many witnesses attested she *bi-located*, appearing to different people in different places at the very same moment.

The Lord made her an instrument of *healing* and many were healed through her prayers and intercessions.

Her ecstasies came more and more frequently. There were those times, when she was experiencing heavenly rapture, when her body would become taut and remain stiff, almost lifeless like rigor mortis had set in. Then there were those other times when the sisters were completely unaware *anything* was happening. How could they know, she was communicating with Jesus and possibly one of His Heavenly Court; as Sister Mary Magdalen went about her daily duties.

There were occasions when they could tell she was sharing in the Passion of Our Lord Jesus, the agony plainly

---

[2]spiritual

revealed on her face and body. She looked like one of the women of Jerusalem who followed Jesus and wept. At other times, Sister Mary Magdalen could have been Veronica boldly going past the centurions and wiping her Lord's bleeding Face. Then there were those times when she evidenced excruciating pain, her face and eyes filled with horror and unbearable grief. *Was she standing beneath the Cross beside Mother Mary as her Son took His Last Breath; was she crying out for Mary, who dared not weaken that those around her would be strong? Was she like her namesake, Mary Magdalen who had wiped His Feet with her tears and now was prostrate at those same Precious Feet?* Whatever part she may have been reenacting in the Passion, it was obvious she was there with her Lord and His Pain.

And then there were those times, when they thought they would lose her; only the weight of her body kept her from soaring up to Heaven. She looked as if she did not want to come back. She later shared with the sisters (under obedience to her Superior) that she was ecstatically engaged in conversation with her Spouse Jesus, at other times with Mother Mary, and then those joyful times with Jesus' Heavenly Army of Angels. *Was she seeing Our Lord, the Lord of Easter Sunday, He Who had risen? Was He standing at the gates of Heaven and she wanted in?* All they knew, she was not with them, and they did not know if it was the kindest thing to do to pray she not leave them.

The closer St. Mary Magdalen got to her Divine Lover, the more she grieved, as He did over Jerusalem,[3] shedding tears over the stony hearts of heretics, the deaf ears of unbelievers and the blind eyes of pagans. She prayed relentlessly for their conversion. The more she embraced

---

[3]*"Jerusalem, Jerusalem, you who kill the prophets and stone those sent to you, how many times I yearned to gather your children together, as a hen gathers her young under her wings, but you were unwilling!"*(Mt 23:27)

the Cross, the more she begged for forgiveness of sinners, as her Spouse had during His last moments on the Cross.

Jesus told Mary Magdalen that what pleases His Eternal Father most, moving His Heart to pity, is the offering of His Son's *Blood*. As Jesus softened His Father's Heart and opened the curtain that separated us from eternal life, with His Blood on the Cross, now He is once again pleading with the Father through such as Mary Magdalen. She offered Our Lord's Blood fifty times a day. In ecstasy, she saw many sinners repent and convert to the Lord, as well as a multitude of souls being released from Purgatory.

Jesus added, if this offering which *commemorates* His Passion can soften His Father's Heart, how much more the *actual* renewal of the Sacrifice of the Cross during the Sacrifice of the Mass where we are present at the Passion of Jesus! Attend Mass daily if you can.

The deliverance of a Poor Soul from Purgatory

The Lord raised her to the heights of Mount Tabor. She had been as close as one can be on earth to the Beatific Vision; now she was to walk the Way of the Cross to Calvary with her Lord. It was time for Him to share with her those Poor Souls in Purgatory whom He dearly loves.

One day, while praying before the Blessed Sacrament, St. Mary Magdalen saw the tortured soul of one of the sisters, who had passed on recently. She saw her rising painfully from the earth, encircled by leaping flames wrapping themselves around her body. The only thing that kept them from scorching the sister's body was a sparkling white robe covering her, shielding her from the blazing fire. She had been faithful to the Rule. She had led a pious life. Then why was she coming to Sister Mary Magdalen like this? This sister explained that she had *grudgingly* spent time before the Blessed Sacrament while she was alive. And now, she was being denied her Spouse's Beatific Vision. She went

Left:

The closer St. Mary Magdalen de Pazzi got to her Divine Lover, the more she grieved, as He did over Jerusalem, shedding tears over the stony hearts of heretics, the deaf ears of unbelievers and the blind eyes of pagans. She prayed relentlessly for their conversion. The more she embraced the Cross, the more she begged for forgiveness of sinners, as her Spouse had during His last moments on the Cross.

Right:

One day, while St. Mary Magdalen de Pazzi was praying in the garden of the Convent with the other religious, she became enraptured in ecstasy and saw before her the pits of Purgatory opening. She later shared that she heard a voice, beckoning her to follow and witness the pain, the Poor Souls in Purgatory had to endure. The voice explained this was so that when she prayed for them, she would pray relentlessly and compassionately. The sisters heard her say, "Yes, I will go."

over to where the Blessed Sacrament was exposed and remained kneeling at the foot of the altar, oblivious to the flames about her, adoring her Lord so very preciously present in His Body, Blood, Soul and Divinity. Oh how she had longed to see Him, once more! Worse than the furnace, which enveloped her in Purgatory, was the loss of the vision of her Lord. She remained motionless, her eyes transfixed on her Savior. At the end of her hour with her Lord in this Garden of Gethsemane, her penance ended, St. Mary Magdalen saw the sister rise to Heaven.[4]

St. Mary Magdalen glimpses the various levels of Purgatory

One day, while praying in the garden of the Convent with the other religious, she became enraptured in ecstasy and saw before her the pits of Purgatory opening. She later shared that she heard a voice, beckoning her to follow and witness the pain, the Poor Souls in Purgatory had to endure. The voice explained this was so that when she prayed for them, she would pray relentlessly and compassionately. The sisters heard her say: *"Yes, I will go."*

She began to pace in circles round and round the spacious garden, for two hours, hesitating at times, as if in great pain. She later confided that these were times when she contemplated the suffering of the Poor Souls before her in Purgatory. Her back bent, as if carrying the sorrow of the world, her tiredness increased and her strength seemed to be ebbing away. As she saw the intense agony of the Poor Souls, the blood drained from her face; she rung her hands helplessly, tears streaming from her eyes. She wept:

"Mercy, my God, mercy! Descend, O Precious Blood, and deliver these souls from their prison. Poor souls! you suffer so cruelly, and yet you are content and cheerful. The dungeons of martyrs in comparison with these were gardens of delight. Nevertheless there are those still deeper.

---

[4]Father Francis Cepari S.J.

How happy should I esteem myself were I not obliged to go down into them."[5]

She descended deeper into the pits of Purgatory. She thought she had suffered all she could until she came upon *Religious* in a level filled with greater terror and suffering! What could they have done to deserve this act of Justice! She never shared the cause of their punishment or the type of sufferings they had to endure, but the sisters could hear her sighing deeply and weeping helplessly, with each step.

Souls making retribution for sinning out of ignorance

Then God, in His mercy had the voice lead her into a more merciful level of Purgatory. It was the place reserved for *simple souls* and those of *children* who had sinned more out of ignorance than out of malice and forethought. Their suffering appeared to be less painful than that of the other Poor Souls she had viewed before. Mary Magdalen saw their Guardian Angels beside them strengthening and sustaining them with their presence. Although Purgatory is a place of hope and anticipation of all the Poor Souls, these were the closest to realizing the end of their journey and of being with the Holy Trinity, Mary and our entire Heavenly Family of Angels and Saints in Heaven.

The Pain of Souls who were guilty of hypocrisy on earth

Anxious to leave, but obedient to the voice who was her guide in Purgatory, Sister Mary Magdalen continued a few more steps to a place more painful than any she had encountered in Purgatory. What could these souls have done to deserve this intense purging? She was told, these were those who were guilty of *hypocrisy*. Oh how much damage is done by those who pretend to be and do good, who gain the confidence of innocent lambs, only to lead

---

[5]*"Purgatory"* by Fr. F.X. Shouppe, S.J. - Tan Publications

them astray and oftentimes into Hell. Our Lord spoke plainly to such as these when He said:

"Whoever causes one of these little ones, who believe in Me, to sin, it would be better for him to have a great millstone come around his neck, and to be drowned in the depths of the sea."[6]

The dungeon of those who had lacked charity toward others

Going a little further, she came upon a large group of souls who looked as if they had been pinned under a huge cement pillar. She was told that these were the souls of those who had shown little patience and charity toward those less fortunate and of those who willfully resorted to disobedience toward their superiors and instilled acts of disobedience in others. As she went deeper into this dungeon and looked at the suffering of these Poor Souls, her face became more and more filled with pity and dismay for these souls who had lost all their earthly smugness and self-assuredness. They looked so helpless. They remind us of the rich man who asked for a drop of water from Lazarus.[7]

Sister Mary Magdalen enters a Purgatory much like Hell

[Author's Note: People ask us why there is a level so much like Hell. The best way we can explain is by giving an example. Suppose Adolf Hitler made a perfect Act of Contrition just before he died. He would be saved; but he would have a great debt to pay in Purgatory for the inhumane atrocities he had committed. We believe he would be at the very bottom pit of Purgatory until the end of the world!]

Shortly thereafter, the sisters saw St. Mary Magdalen become greatly agitated. She let out an anguished cry. The voice had led her into one of the deepest levels of Purgatory, most resembling the region of Hell. As she approached what appeared to be a bottomless pit, she saw souls writhing in

[6]Matt 18:6
[7]cf Luke 16:19-31

pain; their suffering beyond description. She had entered the level of *Purgatory* reserved for "*Liars.*" She sobbed.

When we bear false witness against someone, the harm is irrevocable; the uncurable effects much like that of a terminal illness. As with cancer, the poison of lies cannot be self-contained; it spreads and destroys the good along with the bad, everything and everyone with which it comes in contact. The damage to one's name and very self can never be totally erased, mankind preferring to think the worst. There are wounds of many kinds that can be healed, but the wound to one's reputation is a wound which attacks the very personhood of a human being. The punishment in Purgatory, much like that of Hell, is that severe because although these sins have been confessed and absolution has been granted, the damage is so far-reaching, oftentimes affecting whole families, churches, communities, countries, the world. It is as the English poet, John Donne wrote:

> "*No man is an island entire of itself;*
> *Every man is a piece of the continent,*
> *a part of the main;*
> *If a clod be washed away by the sea, Europe is the less,*
> *As well as if a promontory were,*
> *As well as if a Manor of thy friends,*
> *or of thine own were;*
> *Any man's death diminishes me,*
> *Because I am involved in mankind;*
> *And therefore never send to know*
> *for whom the bell tolls;*
> *It tolls for thee.*"

So it is with a lie; it is like a pebble thrown into a body of water; the small ripple spreads and spreads covering the entire area, affecting the river which spills into the ocean, covering the universe. There is no such thing as a *small* lie, just as there is no such thing as a small cancer that is *malignant*. Although with cancer, sometimes it can be all cut out, but still you do not know when it can resurface. We can admit we have lied, a paper can retract a false statement but as we have so often seen, the lie can come back to haunt us nonetheless. Is this book on *Heaven, Hell and Purgatory* written to frighten you? No, not at all. But if we did not report authentically what the Saints saw and experienced, we are as bad as liars who falsify or withhold the truth, often telling you what you *want* to hear, rather than what you *have* to hear.

Souls who sinned through weakness

When Sister Mary Magdalen approached this next dungeon, she was told these were souls who sinned through *weakness*. She was surprised to see them in a separate dungeon from those (in Purgatory) who were paying for the damage done by sinning through *ignorance*. All about her, she saw frantic flames licking at the already scorched souls. The fire was more furious than had been in the dungeon of ignorance. *Why?* What is the difference of the one sin from the other? With those who sinned out of ignorance, a debt had to be paid for the harm done, but their sin was done unwittingly; they knew no better. With the souls in this dungeon, they knew full well while on earth, the seriousness of the sin and its repercussions, but whether bending to self-interest, self-preservation, fear of rejection or just plain peer pressure, they chose to do it nonetheless. They pay not only for the damage done to their own souls but for the harm done to other souls.

Souls who had chosen the false gods of materialism

Someone once said that if an announcement were made that *Jesus was coming* that very moment, there would be people rushing off to the mall; there would be those who had to finish decorating their new home, others buying that new model car, and then those getting their hair styled. A priest at a retreat, asked us all to put down on paper the most important areas of our lives. Then he said to put next to those listed, the time spent on each. Try it! It really blew us away! Naturally, Jesus was on the top of the list as the most important. But how much time do we spend on Him versus the items lower down right to the bottom of the list? Do we give Jesus a five minute call, dropping in on Him waiting for us in the Tabernacle? Is going to Mass on Sunday, a *"let's get it over"* thing, *"I've done my obligation"* thing in our life? Do we realize that it is Jesus Himself Who is coming to us under the appearance of a Host? Or are we impatiently waiting for the Mass to be over so we can spend the rest of our Sunday enjoying ourselves or doing good things but not holy things?

What St. Mary Magdalen saw were those souls of whom our Pope John Paul II speaks, those for whom no amount of money and possessions is enough; they lived each day to protect what they had and to get more and more of that which they did not need but instead desired. Their possessions became the keepers and they the slaves. She saw all the blindness of avarice[8] in those here who had spent every waking moment seeking and trying to hold onto possessions that would most assuredly *perish*, instead of striving to attain those which would most assuredly *guarantee* everlasting life.

She saw all these souls being thrown into the fire, like raw crude metal which needs to have all earthly impurities burned away so that only precious gold remains. Was all these souls had strived for and accumulated worth this? Thank God, they only knew that *one time*[9] when standing before Our Lord, they saw the times they had hurt Our Lord,

---

[8]*One of the capital sins - the overindulgent love of temporal or earthly things, in particular riches. It need not be the direct possession of money or wealth, but it is excessive when one is not guided by reason, or by need, or when one goes to any means to attain, or is selfish and lacks charity in giving.* (Cf. Catholic Encyclopedia by Broderick)
[9]See chapter on Catherine of Genoa

and seeing, condemned themselves to Purgatory, understanding that *one time why* they needed to spend this time here. Once there, they only wait for that time when they will be released and be able to see the Beatific Vision of God.

How many can look down on these Poor Souls? How many of us can look forward to time there? Choose God, before it is too late. Remember what Jesus said:

"As was in the days of Noah, so will it be when the Son of Man comes. For in those days before the Flood, people were eating and drinking, taking wives, taking husbands, right up to the day Noah went into the ark, and they suspected nothing till the great Flood came and swept all away. It will be like this when the Son of Man comes. Then of two men in the fields, one is taken and one is left; of two women at the millstone grinding, one is taken and one left.

"So stay awake, because you do not know the day when your Master is coming. You may be quite sure of this that if the householder had known at what time of night the burglar would come, he would have stayed awake and would not have allowed anyone to break through the wall of the house. Therefore you too must stand ready because the Son of Man is coming at an hour you do not expect."[10]

Souls who had been soiled by impure thoughts and actions

A young man came up to us one day, and said that his confessor had told him, it was alright to think about other women, but not to act on the thought - that the sin was in the doing not the thinking. Well, we told the young man that he probably misunderstood the priest because sin begins in

---

[10]Matt 24:37-44

the mind.[11] *Thoughts* that are not fought become *actions*. Surely, thoughts can be temptations by the demons and we are not responsible for those thoughts.   But should we entertain and persist willingly in these thoughts, they will most assuredly lead us to act upon these impure thoughts and sin.   Impure and unholy thoughts begin in the mind and then travel to the other members of the body.

Her next stop was a dungeon that was filled with an unbearable stench, infested by filth and mire, diseased souls bearing the marks of such highly fatal, infectious and contagious diseases, such as the Bubonic Plague (the social ills of our time - Syphilis, Aids and etc).   She was almost overcome by waves of nausea, the sight and smell was so offensive.   She was told that this was the place reserved for those who souls had been tainted by *impure actions*.

A special place for the proud and ambitious

The sisters saw her rushing to another place in the garden. She later shared that, not able to view the disgusting spectacle any longer, the presence of so much decay and pestilence almost choking her, smothering her so she could barely breath, she had to flee to the next place no matter how horrible it might be; anything had to be better than this.

The next area of Purgatory was dedicated to those souls whose focus in life had been to be *popular*, to be *admired*, to be looked up to. Their aims were ambitious, to the exclusion of any and all human feeling for others; their philosophy being, the end justifying the means, *What ever it takes to succeed, go for it*. Well, they went for it, and now they were in this dungeon of obscurity, with no one to console them. These souls sought the elusive treasures of this world, and the world and its lies betrayed them. They chose the respect

---

[11]*"You have heard the commandment, 'You shall not commit adultery.' What I say to you is: anyone who looks lustfully at a woman has already committed adultery with her in his thoughts."* Matt 5:27-28

of men over the Divine Respect of God and as always the father of lies,[12] who leads us to this folly, betrayed them and here they were. The respect of humans died with them, and now much of their suffering, like that of others in Purgatory, was the longing to behold the Divine Image of that God to Whom they gave second place on earth.

Souls who had not thanked Our Lord for His plentiful Gifts

Coming toward the end of her journey into Purgatory, her next to last stop was reserved for those who prayed when they needed help from the Lord but, like the nine lepers, never thanked Him. They lit the candles in petition, but forgot Him in thanksgiving. When their petitions were granted, they soon forgot it was the work of the Lord and began to believe Satan's lie that it was *their* doing and not the Lord's, or that it was due to circumstances not miracles that the course of their lives had changed for the better.

These souls were immersed in a pool of boiling, bubbling, molten lead, many of them barely able to stay afloat. It seemed as if their cries would penetrate past the walls of Purgatory. Oh, she thought, If only those on earth could hear and see these poor souls, how they would pray!

The Last Stop

The last stop was a place of the least pain and suffering. It was filled with those souls who had not committed any grave wrongdoing, but out of lack of prudence had been guilty of lesser faults, venial sins. The problem with these sins is that they could have led to more serious mortal sins. They'd had a Guardian Angel (as all of us have), who warned them when they were doing something that could lead them astray and they, through pride or lack of wisdom, or just plain desire, chose to ignore the messenger of God and commit these minor infractions; then it is God's Justice

---

[12]Lucifer is referred to as "The father of lies."

that they be cleansed of these imperfections by sharing to a lesser degree the suffering of the other Poor Souls in Purgatory.

At last, peace!

St. Mary Magdalen left the garden hurriedly. She was heard pleading with the Lord to spare her this suffering in the future. She implored the Lord not to subject her to this again as she did not believe that her spirit could survive it. She shared she did not know why He had chosen her to share in these heartbreaking scenes, if not to make her aware of the hurt He suffers when we are party to the smallest sin, and to encourage her to avoid any stain of sin which would separate her from Him, not only in this world but in the next.

St. Mary Magdalen sees her brother in Purgatory

Mary Magdalen saw her brother when she was visiting the different dungeons of Purgatory. He had led a truly Christian life, but he had received the many Graces to enable him to do so; therefore his responsibilities were great and he had failed to fulfill them as he should. There were faults that he had not atoned for, while still alive. Many times, Mary Magdalen had tried to warn him, but to no avail; he knew what he was doing. He shared that although he whole-heartedly accepted the suffering necessary to make him presentable to God, he longed to be in His presence. He pleaded with her to receive 107 Holy Communions, to help him make restitution for the times he had not put the Lord first in his life. Good and holy sister, she did as he had requested, all the while pleading with the Lord on his behalf.

The Sister who did not correspond to God's Grace

There is another serious imperfection which requires God's Justice and must be satisfied. It is the violation of God's Grace. Grace is God's Gift to us, and to not cooperate with it, is to throw it back in God's Face. It is a precious Gift, a Gift to help us on our pilgrimage on earth.

The Sister whom St. Mary Magdalen saw in Purgatory was guilty of not having appreciated God's Grace on three different occasions. When we speak of this Sister's offense against God, we must understand:

"Much will be required of the person entrusted with much, and still more will be demanded of the person entrusted with more."[13]

Religious are granted special Graces to practice their vocations faithfully and fully. Heavenly Graces, as with earthly gifts, are to be appreciated to the extent they are given: the size of the gift, the importance of the Giver, and the thought behind the gift. With Religious, these Graces are imparted by the *Perfect* Spouse Who provides them with all His Heart. He bestows these Graces upon them, knowing His beloved *brides*; and knowing them, He knows their needs. He carefully fashioned them for Himself, in His Mind and Heart before the world began. Because He loves them, He desires to protect them for His very own. Imagine the Wounds on Jesus' Heart when His religious, His brides refuse His Gifts. Such is what happened with this Sister who was in Purgatory.

St. Mary Magdalen begins with the sister's *"rejection of an infusion of Grace"* she received on one of the Church's Feast Days. Although she was supposed to dedicate this day to the Lord, this sister chose to do some embroidery, instead. She heard that inner voice tell her, she was to observe this Holy and Solemn Feast in prayer and meditation. Although it was not urgent and could have waited, she chose to disobey the Rule and follow the dictates of the world with its shallow compensations.

---

[13]Luke 12:48

Another time, knowing that there was a problem in the Community and she should tell her Superior, she chose to be silent. Knowing that sharing this would ultimately benefit the other Sisters, she elected to be still. Knowing how they would initially react, she traded God's Divine Respect for that of the human respect of the Sisters. If she had realized the consequences of putting *their* acceptance or rejection before *God*'s, would she have done so?

The third fault is one that most of us have to fight, our *inordinate attachment to our loved ones on earth*. When this sister became the Bride of Christ, she pledged to Him her undying love, placing Him before all others. This was the covenant she made with the Lord. Her Spouse gave her His all, showering her with His Love. She, on the other hand, found herself becoming more and more involved with the concerns and ongoing demands of her family. Knowing this displeased her Lord, having the presence of His Grace there to advise and admonish her, she ignored it believing she could make it up to the Lord, and He would understand. She had forgotten Jesus' words:

"Whoever loves father or mother more than Me is not worthy of Me, and whoever loves son or daughter more than Me is not worthy of Me."[14]

Well, as we said before, you never know when the Lord is coming. Remember the story of the bridesmaids awaiting the Bridegroom? Five fell asleep without preparing oil for their lamps and five were prudent and were prepared when He unexpectedly arrived. When He came, the five who were unprepared asked for oil from the five who had prepared; they refused. When the five unprepared asked the Lord to *"open the door"* for them, He replied:

---

[14]Matt 10:37

"'I tell you solemnly, I do not know you.' So stay awake, because you do not know the day or the hour."[15]

Needless to say, the Sister did not have time to make it up to the Lord, for she died soon after she had betrayed her commitment to the Lord.

St. Mary Magdalen began to pray for her soul. Sixteen days after her death, the Sister appeared to Mary Magdalen and announced her deliverance from Purgatory. It shocked St. Mary Magdalen that this Sister, who was known for her piety, had suffered this long in Purgatory. When St. Mary Magdalen asked *Why?* the Sister shared that she had to make atonement for those times that she had ignored God's Grace and put the world before Him. She said her period of suffering would have been much longer, had the Lord not taken into consideration her fidelity to Him (most of the time), and her faithful following of the Rule, as well as her good will in handling countless situations, and her love toward her other Sisters.

Visions of Heaven

Then there is the vision of a professed Religious[16] who suffered greatly toward the end of her life. The Community prepared the Sister's body and it was laid out in the church, as was the custom. Having gotten very attached to the Sister, as she had cared for her in her final days, St. Mary Magdalen desired to see her one more time. No sooner had she pressed her face against the grill, separating the cloister from the main church, than she went into ecstasy and beheld the Sister ascending to Heaven. She was beautiful, no signs of the ravages of illness that had finally taken her life! As the Sister was soaring up to her Spouse, Mary Magdalen was heard exclaiming:

---

[15]Matt 25:12-13
[16]*"The Life of St. Mary Magdalen"* by Father Cepari

"Adieu, dear Sister; adieu, blessed soul! Like a pure dove, you fly to your celestial home, and leave us in this abode of misery. Oh, how beautiful and glorious you are! Who can describe the glory with which God has crowned your virtues? What a short time you have passed in Purgatory! Your body has not been consigned to the tomb, and behold! your soul is already received into the sacred mansions. You now know the truth of those words I so lately addressed to you: That all of the sufferings of this life are nothing in comparison with their reward which God has reserved for His friends."

While she was having this vision of the Sister, Our Lord told Mary Magdalen that the soul of the Sister had only spent fifteen hours in Purgatory. He said this was because she had atoned for her transgressions during her life with her suffering on earth and because of the plenary indulgences[17] she had received.

Mary Magdalen and her vision of a Sister in glory

In St. Mary Magdalen's convent there was a Sister called Sister Benedicta. Father Cepari said that she was so pious, she often accused herself, out of humility, of all types of faults. She did not want people to admire her or look up to her as a Saint. She tried to convince every one that she was totally lacking in prudence and discernment. She practiced obedience to her Superiors, with the trusting innocence of a child, trusting in their wisdom, obeying without need of explanation. They said it; that was enough for her to respond promptly, without question. At the end, Our Lord did not share His suffering with her, the agony

---

[17]The remission of the temporal punishment due for sins and hence, the satisfaction owed to God for one's sins is called an *indulgence*. The Church grants such indulgences after the guilt of sin and its eternal punishment have been remitted by sacramental absolution (by the Sacrament of Penance) or by perfect contrition. (Catholic Encyclopedia by Broderick)

that so many of the Saints had, before going to Him and His Father. She had a very short illness when she was called *Home*.

The morning following her death, the Sisters were attending Mass when St. Mary Magdalen lapsed into ecstasy. At the moment the good Sisters sang the Sanctus (Holy, Holy, Holy), God gave St. Mary Magdalen the gift of seeing the good and holy Sister's glorified *body*, as it will be after the Last Judgment. She was clothed in glory, with a star as a reward for her kindness and generosity in dealing with all situations. She had rings of precious stones on all her fingers. The Lord told Mary Magdalen these rings were for her faithfulness to her vocation and for her uncompromising obedience to the Rule. Then, for her love of Jesus crucified, He placed a golden crown on her head.

St. Mary Magdalen goes Home

In 1604, at 38 years of age, our Saint became hopelessly ill, she couldn't move her legs; she experienced a very painful numbness, similar to the sensation you feel when a part of your body has gone to sleep. But when the other sisters tried to alleviate the pain, she was filled with such excruciating spasms, they had to stop. She remained bid-ridden, suffering not only unbearable agony *physically*, but *spiritually*, as she once again experienced the "*Dark night of the Soul.*" Feeling nothing but pain and loneliness, her Lord withholding Himself from her, she begged her Lord for more suffering, as she knew it was helping Poor Souls in Purgatory. But if her pain ceased, she praised the Lord, as well, because she accepted this as His Divine Will.

This went on for *three years*! Finally, the time came for St. Mary Magdalen came to say good by to her Community. She knew she was going Home. She said:

"Reverend Mother, and dear sisters, I am about to leave you. My final request is that you love Jesus alone,

*that you trust in Him completely and that you encourage
each other to willingly suffer out of love for Him."*

On May the 25th, 1607, at age 41, St. Mary Magdalen
went *Home* to her Spouse and to all her friends, the Saints in
Heaven. She had had such love and compassion for the
Poor Souls in Purgatory, they had prayed for her when they
were admitted into Heaven. These Souls now Saints, had
been waiting to escort their friend to her Celestial reward.

As a visible sign of His special favor, the Lord left her
body incorrupt, that all could see His precious and faithful
Bride. It can be viewed till today, in the Carmelite Convent
in Careggi (Florence). St. Mary Magdalen de Pazzi was
added to the Calendar of Saints in 1669, sixty-two years after
her death to this world and new life in *the world*, we all look
forward to living in some day.

†

We have spoken in this chapter of a most extraordinary
Saint, a role model for all time. In this dire time, when we do
not know what to believe and whom to follow, we pray that
the messages from the souls who came to St. Mary Magdalen
de Pazzi help you in your walk toward holiness, your road to
Sainthood, your goal - eternal life with the Father, Son and
Holy Spirit in Heaven.

†

Visions of St. Margaret Mary

Friend to the Souls in Purgatory

St. Margaret Mary Alacoque is one of Jesus' most powerful workers in the vineyard.[1] She is best known for the Apparitions of Our Lord Jesus and His Sacred Heart. Through the work of St. Margaret Mary, in obedience to Jesus' mandate, devotion to His Sacred Heart became a strong movement throughout the world.

Because she is best known as the spearhead of this movement, many of us are not aware that she also had a great compassion for, and did much work to alleviate the suffering of the Poor Souls in Purgatory. But if we read a quote she wrote about her early days, we become aware of her great repugnance for sin:

"O my only love! How indebted I am to You for having predisposed[2] me from my earliest childhood, by becoming the Master and Possessor of my heart, although You well knew how it (my heart) *would resist You! As soon as I could know myself, You made my soul see the ugliness of sin, and impressed such horror of sin upon my heart, that the slightest stain caused me unbearable torment; and to put a stop to my childish impetuousness one needed only to tell me it was offending God. This stopped me short, and kept me from doing whatever I was eager to do."*

From her earliest years as a child, the Lord prepared this Mystic and future Saint for her mission, by molding her into the vessel necessary to carry out His commands. Come with us to Paray-le-Monial, a quiet little town in the Burgundy section of France, with a great message. As we walk through the narrow streets of this quaint village, we can still hear Our Savior's most passionate cries. Here, Our

---

[1]For more on St. Margaret Mary, read Bob and Penny's book: *"Visionaries, Mystics, and Stigmatists."*

[2]to make receptive beforehand

Jesus showed His wounded Sacred Heart to St. Margaret Mary, revealing the pain He feels because of the neglect and apathy of His children, for whom He suffered and died. He commissioned her to tell us that His Heart, pierced on the Cross, still bleeds out of love for us, His ungrateful children. "My enemies placed a Crown of Thorns on My Head, My friends on My Heart."

Chapel inside Monastery of the Visitation at Paray-le-Monial

Lord spoke to a little nun, in the Seventeenth Century, over a period of seventeen years. In a small Chapel, Our Lord shared His Sacred Heart, wounded and bleeding, because of His Love, unreturned.

He showed His wounded Sacred Heart to Margaret Mary, revealing the pain He feels because of the neglect and apathy of His children, for whom He suffered and died. He commissioned her to tell us that His Heart, pierced on the Cross, still bleeds out of love for us, His ungrateful children. *"My enemies placed a Crown of Thorns on My Head, My friends on My Heart."*

Sacred Heart Devotion had existed in the Church for many years before Our Lord appeared to St. Margaret Mary. But as we said, our hearts had grown cold. Other things had taken importance over Our Lord in this devotion, and so He gave her the mandate to spread fervor to His Sacred Heart all over the world. He knew when He gave her the job that she could do it, and she did.

Margaret Mary was a unique person, a special Saint, very open to the Lord, completely open to what she believed was His Will and His desire, and so He was able to share with her other gifts and visions. He allowed her to witness the plight of the Souls in Purgatory, and come to their aid.

†

We want to share with you some insights the Lord has given us about sin and Purgatory. He has put people and situations together for us in this book in a way we could not have possibly considered. In researching this book on *Heaven, Hell and Purgatory,* we have learned things we never knew before. For instance, there are certain sins which are regarded more serious than others, and require greater Purgatory time than others because they are against Jesus' great Commandment, *"Love one another as I have loved you."*[3]

---

[3]John 15:12

Sins against charity are big offenses in the eyes of Our Lord Jesus and our Heavenly Family, such as lack of charity towards our neighbors, gossip, defaming someone's character and other sins, such as calumny[4] and slander, ruining the reputations of people.

We knew sins of the mouth required heavy penance. St. James talks about this in Chapter 3 of his letter:

"Think of ships; no matter how big they are, even if a gale is driving them, the man at the helm can steer them anywhere he likes by controlling a tiny rudder. So is the tongue only a tiny part of the body, but it can proudly claim that it does great things. Think how small a flame can set fire to a huge forest; the tongue is a flame like that. Among all the parts of the body, the tongue is a whole wicked world in itself; it infects the whole body; catching fire itself from Hell, it sets fire to the whole wheel of creation. Wild animals and birds, reptiles and fish can all be tamed by man, and often are; but nobody can tame the tongue - it is a pest that will not keep still, full of deadly poison. We use it to bless the Lord and Father, but we also use it to curse men who are made in God's image; the blessing and the curse come out of the same mouth. My brothers, this must be wrong - does any water supply give a flow of fresh water and salt water out of the same pipe? Can a fig tree give you olives, my brothers, or a vine give figs? No more can sea water give you fresh water."[5]

There is a story of a woman who went to Confession to her local priest. She confessed to having gossiped about some of the people in the parish. The priest told her that for her penance, she should take a feather pillow up to the bell-tower of the church, and shake out all the feathers in the pillow. She did as he instructed, and went back to the priest

---

[4]False and malicious statement meant to hurt someone's reputation
[5]James 3:4-12

for absolution. He said to her, "*Before I can absolve you of your sins, you must now go out into the village and pick up all the feathers which you scattered.*" She said to him, "*But father, that's impossible.*" He replied, "*That's true, as impossible as trying to undo the damage you have done by slandering your neighbor.*"

†

We heard that story years ago, but never connected it with Purgatory. It never occurred to us that certain sins require special penance and retribution in Purgatory. A vision of St. Margaret Mary Alacoque confirms this.

One night, she was praying for two people of high standing in the secular world who had recently died, when she had a vision of Purgatory. She saw these two women of the nobility, there, two women of the same station in life, but their periods of purging were completely different.

The one, a noble, had been guilty of ruining the reputations of many of her subjects. She was sentenced to *many years* in Purgatory. How many is many? We don't know for sure, but considering the serious *repercussions* resulting from her sins, you can be sure they were beyond any suffering she could have done on earth. And that's understandable. However, the thing that really surprised us was that all the *Masses* offered for this lady first had to go to the souls of members of the families who had been ruined by the gossip and slander, which this person had spread about her subjects. After all the prayers and indulgences and Masses were used for the families, they would then be credited to her until she served her *full* time in Purgatory.

On the other hand, the other lady was a completely different story. She was sentenced to as many *days* as she had lived *years* on the earth, because of the way she treated *her* subjects. She had put up with the shortcomings and faults of her neighbors with great love and charity. She may have actually been a role model for them, where charity was concerned. In addition, she took great pains to overcome any animosity she may have had toward them. So, in the one instance, sins against charity caused one soul to suffer *longer* in Purgatory, while in the other instance, giving charity to a brother and sister reduced the amount of time the other soul spent in Purgatory.

St. Margaret Mary was given many visions of Souls in Purgatory. One day, she was praying for two deceased nuns, when she had a vision of them in Purgatory. They were each in cells of suffering. However, one suffered much more than the other. This nun now regretted greatly, how she had lacked charity toward the other nuns in her community, but she could not undo the harm she had done. Her eyes had been opened and she grieved because she had not only deprived them of her friendship, but herself of their friendship. Not only had she missed the love and fellowship of her sisters in religion that she could have been sharing while on earth, but because she had refused to love her sisters, she could not benefit from the prayers being offered for her by them.

We really have to think about the consequences of our actions. Our Lord is telling us here that we are not only responsible for how we treat others, but in addition to the time we spend in Purgatory for the pain we cause them, we will suffer for the effect we had on those with whom the injured came in contact. In other words, if because of our behavior to Sally B, she lives a miserable life, and passes on that misery to others, that's our fault as well, and we will suffer for that. In addition, the prayers and Masses for our speedy release from Purgatory will first have to be used for those lives which have been affected adversely because of us. It goes back to a phrase we coined some years ago. It was with regard to anger. *"Anger does not effect only one person. It buckshots, and hits whoever is in its path. Anger begets* anger." The same would apply to our sins against one another.

We don't mean for this to become a lesson on how we are to act with, and react to, our brothers and sisters, although it can be found in St. John's Gospel, and in his letters. It is Scriptural, and now we find that the way we love (or do not love) one another will have a far-reaching effect on our time in Purgatory.

The Lord also allowed souls to come to St. Margaret Mary whom she had known in life. On the Feast of Corpus Christi one year, she was praying before the Blessed Sacrament, when suddenly she had a vision of a person completely enveloped in flames. She was taken aback at first, from the shock of this apparition coming to her at this time, while she was deep in prayer before Jesus in the Blessed Sacrament on His special Feast Day.

But she realized it must be important, and that it would not have happened if the Lord hadn't allowed it. So she took a close look at the person before her, suffering terribly. The heat from his suffering was almost too much for her to bear. She thought she would go on fire, any moment. She realized, all at once, that she had known him! He was a Benedictine monk from the Convent in Cluny, some twenty miles from Paray-le-Monial, where she was stationed. She only knew him from having gone to Confession to him once. It was an important time, however, in her life. This monk, filled with the Holy Spirit, convinced her she was worthy to receive Communion, and actually ordered her to do so. This had been a breakthrough for St. Margaret Mary, who had always had a great inner struggle between her ongoing desire to receive Jesus in the Eucharist, and her constant doubts about her worthiness.

The Lord rewarded this Benedictine monk by allowing him to appear to St. Margaret Mary. The condition in which she found him, suffering dreadfully, gave her a strong urge to help him. He was very humble in his request, considering the agony he was enduring. He simply asked her to offer up for his release from Purgatory, all the trials which she would undergo for the next three months. Well, he had to know to whom he was talking. Margaret Mary not only did what he asked, but went far beyond his expectations in offering her Masses, her Rosaries, fasting, and just about everything she did for that period of time.

The monk told her *why* he was suffering so badly. It all had to do with human nature, putting his *humanness* before the Lord. He put his own concerns above glorifying the Lord and doing His Divine Will; his good reputation and what people thought of him became his primary concern. He also *lacked charity*. That is such a big offense, my brothers and sisters! [We had no perception how serious an offense against God, this is. And strangely enough, this is one infraction of which many of us are guilty. Very often, it is committed by people in authority, in headship over the well-being of other souls.] The monk said that he had had no problem giving a good tongue-lashing to someone under him, to whom he may have been giving spiritual direction. For some reason, he hadn't considered it a sin to whip someone with his tongue. [Remember the words of St. James earlier in this chapter, regarding the tongue. He either didn't pay attention to the writings of St. James, or felt they didn't apply to him. Those who, like this Poor Soul, have lacked charity, on the day of Judgment, will have to pay the price for this ill treatment of their fellow men.]

The other fault for which he was suffering was a natural affection towards others. Now, realize, we're not talking about an unnatural or abnormal affection, but a natural attachment to others. You might say, *"Well, what's wrong with that?"* We must remember that for those to whom much is given, much is required. In this monk's relationship with Jesus, that of a religious priest, he was to live, and to say to

Jesus, like St. Thomas Aquinas before him, "*Your Grace is enough for me.*" Not only he, but we too, must love the Lord with all our hearts, putting no one's affections and respect ahead of that One Lord Who died for us.

There is no way to really describe the degree of suffering St. Margaret Mary experienced, those three months. The deceased priest never left her side. She was in excruciating pain. But at the end of that time, the priest was released from Purgatory, and St. Margaret Mary was relieved of the suffering.

St. Margaret Mary would immediately begin praying for a particular soul, as soon as she learned of his (or her) death. She knew the value of praying for the Souls in Purgatory, and offering Masses for their release. On one particular New Year's day, she began praying for three souls, two religious and one lay person, who had died recently, when Our Lord came to her. He was so full of love for her, especially for her concern for the Poor Souls in Purgatory. He offered her a gift. "*My daughter,*" he said to her, "*as a New Year's gift, I give you the deliverance from Purgatory of one of these three souls, and I leave the choice to you. Which shall I release?*"

St. Margaret Mary, taken back and somewhat breathless by this gift from the Lord, replied, "*Who am I Lord to say who deserves the preference? Deign Yourself to make the choice.*" Our Lord Jesus released the lay person from Purgatory, because the laity did not have at their disposal during their lifetime, all the means of making atonement for their sins as the Religious.

Margaret Mary was also chosen by the Lord to suffer for souls who were still alive, but who were in danger of losing their souls, and risking eternal damnation. In one instance, the Lord showed her a nun who was alive. She heard the words "*Behold this nun who is one only in name; I am on the point of rejecting her from My Heart and abandoning her to herself."*   Margaret Mary felt an overpowering trembling fear for the nun, inside her. She fell to the ground, prostrate, and stayed that way for a long time. When she recovered, she offered to suffer for the Divine Justice which had to be appeased, in order that this nun not lose her soul, that it not be abandoned to itself.

Margaret Mary was immediately struck by tremendous suffering, as if God was venting all the anger on her that He had for the fallen nun. A crushing weight pressed down on her shoulders. Her soul was in a state of rebellion and perplexity. She experienced a great interior anguish, which tended to confuse her, *Why was the Lord angry with her?*

Then the Lord gave her the gift of physical illness, from which she found it difficult to recover. In this way, she could feel in a real way the chastisement He was about to inflict on some souls who had hurt Margaret Mary. She begged for the gift to atone for their wrongdoings, and pleaded with Him to use her suffering to blot out their sins, rather than permit them to go down to everlasting punishment.

He said to her, *"But they don't love thee, and cease not to afflict thee."* She replied: *"That doesn't matter, Lord, provided they love Thee, and stop afflicting Thee. I will not cease entreating Thee to pardon them."* He responded, *"Let Me do as I will; I can bear them no longer."* She persisted: *"No Lord, I will not leave Thee till Thou has pardoned them."* He relented, *"I will do so, if thou wilt be surety for them."* She excitedly agreed: *"Yes, my God, but I will pay Thee only with Thy own goods, which are the treasures of Thy Sacred Heart."* Content with her answer, He relented of the punishment He had meant to give them.

Margaret Mary was a special worker for the Lord. She not only prayed for and ministered to the Souls in Purgatory, she also prayed for and suffered for sinners on earth. We can just imagine the welcome she received from the Souls whose Paradise she paid for with her own suffering.

Visions of the Curé of Ars
St. John Vianney, Patron Saint of Parish Priests

In doing research for this book and our television series, we've found Saints who've had a relationship with the souls in Purgatory, or had visions of Hell, also had a great urgency to convert sinners. This *Roll Call of Saints* which include: Saints Catherine de' Ricci, Mary Magdalen de Pazzi, Margaret Mary Alacoque, Catherine of Siena, Teresa of Avila, Jean Vianney, and many other Saints were given a special mandate from on High, to do everything in their power to insure there be as few as possible (with the ultimate goal of no souls), going to Purgatory or Hell.

St. Jean Vianney dedicated a great part of his life, close to eighteen hours a day, to hearing confessions, to head off souls racing toward Hell. When he entered Ars, there were four dance halls in the town, but not enough room or desire for one church. Through his priesthood, swearing turned to praying, people in the fields worked with a rosary in their hands and stopped to pray the Angelus at noon, dance halls emptied, the church filled, conversion came about!

It was believed that he *"enjoyed the sight of Our Lord's presence in the Eucharist."* One time, after the Consecration of the Mass, he said, *"As soon as we pray for sinners, when Our Lord is on the altar during Mass, He casts towards them (sinners) rays of light, in order to make them see their misery, and so to convert them."*

A humble priest, in his humility and desire for anonymity, Curé John Vianney *never discussed* the visions he received. [Most of the knowledge we have, came from *other* sources who lived during his time and testified at the Cause for Beatification and Canonization of St. Jean Vianney.] It was typical of the Curé, when the faithful tried to give him credit for favors and miracles received, to insist that all praise and tribute go to either Jesus, His Mother Mary or

Left:
***St. John Vianney
the Curé of Ars***

Above: ***The Curé of Ars spent up
to 18 hours a day hearing
Confessions. He is the "Patron
Saint of Parish Priests."***

Above: ***The Burnt Bed
The Devil was furious with the
Curé and made visits in the night,
making strange noises, and once
set his bed on fire leaving a
charred remains.***

Above:
***The parish Church at Ars where
the Curé spent his life as a Priest
serving the needs of the faithful.***

the intercession of Saint Philomena. He always kept the spotlight off himself, emphasizing, he, of his own power could do nothing, of himself he was nothing.

It was fitting that he be made Patron Saint of Parish Priests. The priesthood was his life! The Sacraments were his life! We mentioned above that he spent as many as eighteen hours a day in the confessional. When he celebrated Mass, it was said that he looked almost transformed; an aura enveloped him, as if his eyes were seeing beyond, cutting through the curtain which separates Heaven and earth. There were those who reported he looked as if he were in ecstasy. He once said that, after holding the Lord in his hands, he was oblivious to all that happened around him; there was only the Lord Present before him. When asked what he did during these times of ecstasy, he replied very simply, "*I look at Him, and He looks at me.*"

He truly believed in the Real Presence of Jesus in the Eucharist. One time, during a moment of great passion, he exclaimed he had seen God! When questioned on whether he had ever *really* seen God, he modestly replied that it was not through the eyes of the body; instead that it was that he had received great *Graces* during the Mass when the Lord became present on the Altar. Did he see Jesus? There are many who claimed, although never saying it in so many words, it was he to whom he was referring, when he said:

"*There are priests who see Him (God) daily during the Holy Sacrifice of the Mass.[1]*"

He admitted to someone close to him that at times, he needed only the Eucharist to sustain him. As he barely took a few minutes a day to eat a boiled potato, we can believe this was so. One day, he told his housekeeper he had been

---

[1]from the chapter in Bob and Penny Lord's book: "*Saints and Other Powerful Men in the Church*"

famished during Mass until he received Communion. When he had consecrated the Host, he had cried out to the Lord *"My God, feed my body as well as my soul."*[2] And then, after receiving His Lord, his former hunger was gone; he was full.

The Curé and his Visions

He avoided responding to the question whether he had ever had visions. There were times, when some one would overhear him talking in his bedroom and a female voice responding. But when they peered inside his bedroom to see with *whom* he was conversing, they would see a Lady in white, and at other times in blue. Awaiting her exit, they only saw him leave the room. Then anyone who might have doubted, knew it had to have been the Blessed Mother.

There were times of great joy, when his spirit soared like an eagle; and then at other times he suffered the depths of Hell, when the devil would attack him, interrupting his little sleep; and when that did not shake the little Curé, the devil knocked his bed from one side of the room to the other, and then finally set it on fire.

Our little Curé is allowed to see the world to come.

A countess once stated that she was sure that the Curé was communicating with the dead. One of her sons had gone to war and lost his life. A few days after his death, they received word he had given his life for his country; they went to the Curé, and he told them not to despair. He consoled: *"...he is in Purgatory, but for a short time."* Although she wanted to believe the Curé, the countess could not help *grieving* over the possibility, her son had not had the opportunity to confess to a priest before he died. Then, six months after receiving the sad news, a second letter came, this time advising the parents that their son had gone to confession shortly after having been wounded and that he

---

[2]The Curé of Ars - Abbé Francis Trochu - Tan Publishers

had died with the benefit of the Sacraments. When the count came to the Curé and told him the good news, St. John Vianney shared he was happy for their sakes, but *he had already known that their son was saved.*

†

Then, there was the wife who confessed that her husband worked on Sunday. The Curé cautioned the wife to tell her spouse to stop working on the Sabbath, and that he would be grateful someday for following his advice. He proceeded, telling her something that only she and her husband knew. Convinced the Lord was speaking through the Curé, the husband ceased working on Sunday. One year later, while returning from church on Trinity Sunday, her husband fell off his horse and died immediately, without the benefit of any of the Sacraments.

Now, in those days, there was a dark screen between the priest and the person confessing. There was no way that the Curé could have seen the grieving widow. But before she could begin her confession, he said: *"You are afraid that the person for whom you are praying is doomed to spend all eternity in Hell, but I do not believe he is."*

Relieved that her husband was not in Hell, she then asked if the person she was praying for would have to spend a long time in Purgatory. The Curé excused himself and sat back deep into the confessional. She could hear him speaking softly, as if to someone, for about five minutes. The Curé returned to the widow and said that although her husband had not handled his affairs wisely, and had left them penniless, he was asking her to have a few Masses said for him so that he could be released from Purgatory and enter Heaven. The Curé assured her, he would be in Heaven in three years, and she would learn about it from one of her children.

Three years passed; one of the widow's children was at the home of an aunt when the child suddenly died. The mother (widow) shared, she had previously had a dream of the child going up to Heaven with her father beside her. As the child was in the best of health, the mother paid no attention to the dream, until she later learned of the child's death. Then she remembered the Curé's prophetic words. In spite of the devastating sorrow she felt, she had peace knowing that not only was her child in Heaven, but her husband as well.

†

How many spouses have had to suffer the pain and fear connected with the fate of a spouse who was an unbeliever? This is about a woman who had prayed for her husband's conversion for years, but to no avail. She would lovingly dress the statue of Mother Mary with fresh flowers each day. Her husband, although he insisted he wanted no part of religion, would pick the flowers for her. In spite of his obstinacy in refusing to attend church, he had always been good to her and had never stopped her from attending Mass or participating in other Church devotions.

The time came when he suffered a heart attack and died without the benefit of the Sacraments. She feared the worst for him. She could not stand the thought of her husband lost in the furnaces of Hell. She became distraught; then she became ill and did not eat; her friends feared she would lose her mind. Finally, she went to the Curé. Before she could speak, the Curé reminded her of her husband's generosity, in helping her to honor Our Lady. He consoled, *"Did she think that the Lord did not hear her cries and would not show mercy on her husband who knew no better?"* These words of comfort brought color back to the woman's cheeks and hope to her heart.

†

There is only one case known, where the Curé spoke firmly of the possibility of eternal damnation. When a woman asked him the fate of a dead relative, he simply replied: "*He refused the Sacraments and would not see a priest.*" It was all true and since the Curé did not know the woman nor the person in question, he could not have known this ahead of time. The grieving woman knew what that meant!: Our Lord stands at the threshold of our hearts, ready to forgive us through His priests. It is in our hands to say yes to Him and the hope of everlasting joy, or to the enemy of God and suffer the fires of Hell. It reminds us of the painting of Our Lord standing at the other side of a door. There is only one door knob, and it is on our side. We see Him knocking; it is up to us to let Him in. The Lord had knocked on the dead man's heart through His priest. He had that moment when he would decide for all eternity; sadly, he made a choice he would have to live with *ad infinitum.*[3]

†

There were times when the Curé would bring the good news that a loved one was in Heaven. A girl came to him, deeply grieving the loss of her dear mother. Her mother had had a hard life, one of sacrifice and suffering. The girl appeared to be inconsolable. The Curé approached her with the words: "*Oh, Mademoiselle, so you have lost your mother?...She is in Heaven!*" The girl cried: "*Oh, I pray for that with all my heart.*" "*Well,*" he answered, "*she is in Heaven!*"

†

Another time, when someone asked for a Mass to be said for a lady who had been most charitable, who led a truly pious life, and yet suffered the worst painful illnesses and afflictions before she died, he answered: "*Have them said for some Poor Soul in Purgatory. She has no need for your prayers or for Masses to be said for her; she is in Heaven!*"

†

---

[3]eternally

The Curé had the gift of tears. He could not speak of sinners and sins without bursting into tears. The wounds suffered by God the Father, in company with the Son and the Holy Spirit because of the rejection of man plunged deep into his heart, and he cried so very much, his eyes would almost close shut in sorrow. As he prayed, processing before the fourteen Stations of the Cross, he was truly walking beside His Savior, and he shed the endless tears of the women of Jerusalem, as he relived the Passion with His Lord.

When he spoke of the Eucharist, of the Lord Who had thought of him that *Last Supper*, as He left Himself under the appearance of a humble Host to be consumed for our salvation, and that this Lord had chosen him, a poor instrument, to be a vessel of that Love, he would be moved to endless tears.

When he offered the Sacrifice of the Mass, the thought of this being the ongoing *Sacrifice of the Cross* would grieve him so overwhelmingly, he would cry such uncontrollable tears, he could barely continue the Mass.

†

St. John Vianney had great confidence in the power of the intercession of the Poor Souls in Purgatory. He once said to a fellow priest, "*Oh! if it were but known how great is the power of the good Souls in Purgatory with the Heart of God, and if we knew all the Graces we can obtain through their intercession, they would not be so much forgotten. We must, therefore, pray much for them, that **they may pray much for us**.*"

†

The devil knew the great impact he had on the faithful and the powerful comfort he was to the souls in Purgatory.

"*The Devil's nightly visits usually occurred when there were sinners, eager to return to the Sacraments of the Church. The Curé, through his hours in the confessional, was calling many to new life, and the Devil was furious!*

"Some priests, staying in the rectory, heard strange noises coming from his room, one night. When they inquired, he answered simply, "It's the devil. He is furious about the good that is being accomplished here."

"The priests snapped, "It's all in your head!"

"The next night, there was such a racket outside the rectory, the priests shot up from bed. They all panicked. There was a battle ensuing, coming from the Curé's room; they were positive he was being killed. They charged into the room. The Curé was sound asleep but his bed had been dragged into the center of the room! When they wakened and questioned him, he apologized, 'The devil dragged out the bed. I'm sorry. I should have warned you. But it's a good sign: we'll catch a big fish tomorrow.'

"Imagine the fun his fellow priests had with him when tomorrow came and nothing unusual happened! But the day was not over; when evening came, there was a knock at the door. Monsieur des Murs, a nobleman, who like the rest of his class had long ceased receiving the Sacraments, had come to have the Curé hear his confession. There was no more kidding. Now it was, 'The Curé is a Saint!'"[4]

†

The Curé was the servant who had received ten thousand talents. He had invested them all wisely in his faithful observance of his vocation. He had served the living and the dead, and the Lord was truly pleased with Him. And to show how very much the Lord loves His priests, He gave them as Patron Saint the most holy of heroes for their very own, one of whom they could be proud and challenged to emulate. Saint John Vianney is how the Lord sees you, our dear priests. How do you see yourselves?

---

[4]excerpt from the chapter in our book, *"Saints and Other Powerful Men in the Church"*

Left:
St. John Bosco
Below:
***Painting above altar in the
Church of the Sacred Heart***

Below: ***St. John Bosco celebrated Mass at this altar in
the Church of the Sacred Heart in Rome.***

Visions of St. John Bosco

Pied-piper to the young, Founder, Visionary and Prophet

"St. John Bosco, better known as Don Bosco, is one of the great apostles of the Nineteenth Century. His ministry was to the children of Turin, in Northern Italy, victims of the Industrial Revolution in that country at that time. Don Bosco was God's gift to the Church of that century. The magnetism of Don Bosco reached out and touched souls all over the world. He was one of the most multi-faceted diamonds, the Lord has ever given us. In addition to being a pied-piper to the young, attracting them, embracing them, protecting them, guiding them, he founded a Religious Order, was an author, a super church-builder, as well as a visionary and prophet." [1]

While there are so many cuts in the diamond we call St. John Bosco, so many aspects of the life and ministry of St. John Bosco that we could write about, we want to limit ourselves in this book to his visions and dreams, his prophecies of *Heaven, Hell and Purgatory.* Most of these were connected with his ministry to the children of his oratory; but we can all take lessons from these messages he received from the Lord. We're going to paraphrase the dream, because there is just so much to cover, but we do recommend you read more about him.

"At first I was hesitant about giving these Dreams the importance they deserved. I often regarded them as mere flights of fancy. As I was narrating these dreams and predicting deaths and other future events, several times I wondered if I had rightly understood things, and I became fearful that what I said might actually be untrue. Occasionally, after narrating a dream, I could no longer remember what I had said. Therefore, in confessing to

---

[1] excerpt from chapter on Don Bosco in *"Saints and other Powerful Men in the Church"* - Bob and Penny Lord

Father Cafasso,[2] I sometimes accused myself of having spoken perhaps rashly. The saintly priest would listen to me, think the matter over, and then say: 'Since your predictions come true, you need not worry. You may continue to make them.'"[3]

Don Bosco had a monumental task in governing, teaching and spiritually directing hundreds of boys at any time, plus running a religious order, and directing his brothers and priests. Therefore, we believe that most of the Dreams, Visions and Prophecies given to Don Bosco were in the form of teachings from the Lord, which he could pass on to his children and his Community. For that reason, we're not going to limit our writing to his dreams of *Heaven, Hell and Purgatory,* but also to his dreams of *Judgment,* which contained a great many teachings for his young charges.

One thing we have to understand about the Dreams, Visions and Prophecies of Don Bosco is that most of them were for *his people* of *his time.* As he progressed in his life and ministry, Dreams, Visions and Prophecies of his younger years became part of the history of the Community, and new Dreams, Visions and Prophecies were eagerly anticipated. They were very much a part of the Community at the time when they took place.

A great example was a dream he had of *Judgment* on April 25, 1876. It was during a very special retreat he was giving the boys in preparation for the month of May, Our Lady's month. Don Bosco was not to tell the boys the content of the dream until May 4, some nine days later.

May 4, he finally told them the dream. He shared that, in his dream he had found himself in a valley, with great hills on either side of him. At the end of one side, there was a brilliant light, while on the other end, it was dark, not pitch

---

[2]a comrade of St. John Bosco's, who was very close to him during his lifetime, and was subsequently canonized a Saint of the Church

[3]*"Dreams, Visions and Prophecies of Don Bosco"*

black, but dusky and murky. Two of Don Bosco's colleagues, who were with him, talked him into mounting a tall, strong horse, which brought him after a long ride, into what seemed like his room. All the priests and clerics of the Community were there and were concerned about something they couldn't describe. Don Bosco asked the doorkeeper what was wrong. He answered him, saying things which didn't make sense, talking about people coming and going.

Someone handed Don Bosco a trumpet, and he heard the command, "*Blow the trumpet.*" He blew it and then heard, "*We are in the land of trial!*" With that, Don Bosco saw huge masses of boys coming down one side of the hill. There were more than a *hundred thousand*, he thought. As they raced down the hill into the valley, he could recognize many of the boys from the Oratory, or who had gone through the Oratory at one time or another. They were carrying weapons, pitchforks. An amazing thing he noticed, as they furiously worked their way down the mountain, there was complete silence. It didn't seem possible.

Then from the other side of the hill, came thousands upon thousands of evil, black, slimy, very ugly creatures, deformed, misshapen, obviously in the camp of Satan. They had the shapes of beasts. Their bodies were unusually big and strong, but their heads were very small. They came down the hill at breakneck speed and proceeded to attack the boys who stood their grounds and fought off the enemy with their pitchforks.

Now here's a very interesting part. The pitchforks the boys used were different. Some had two prongs with a rusty, broken handle. These boys were wounded by the enemy. Others had only one prong and a new handle. These also fell in the battle. There were those who had two prong pitchforks and new handles. They were victorious over the enemy. They were not hurt. Then there were those who had no weapons at all. Many of these were killed. But the boys fought valiantly, all of them. Even those who were killed fought courageously and valiantly. The boys were able to fight off the first line of attack of the enemy.

During the entire attack, Don Bosco was aware of filthy, slithering serpents crawling all over his horse, who proceeded to jump up and down, first his front legs kicking wildly in the air and then his rear legs rearing up and down, stomping, moving around in circles, crushing the serpents beneath his hoofs. And as he struck, he became bigger and bigger. Then Don Bosco cried out: "*What do the two pronged forks represent?*" He was handed one. He looked at it. On each prong was written a word. On one it read "*Confession*", and on the other "*Communion*".

"*But what does it mean?*" he cried out.

Again he was ordered to blow the trumpet. He did and he heard the words "*Good confession and Good Communions.*" Once more he sounded the trumpet. He heard the words "*Broken handle: sacrilegious confessions and Communions.*" "*Worm-eaten handle: Faulty confessions.*"

Then Don Bosco rode over the battlefield and looked at the dead strewn over the fields. The boys who were dead looked ghastly, not a sign of any of their former innocence. They had died from two causes: the strangled ones represented those who had sinned as young boys, *but had never repented or confessed their sins*. Others died of starvation, although there was food right near them. They represented those who had confessed their sins, but had never followed their confessors' advice. Next to the pitchfork with the worm-eaten handle, used by each of the boys who had been killed, was a word. For each boy it was different. Some were *Pride, Sloth, Immodesty*.

The sky darkened again, and an even greater horde of evil, ugly-looking enemies descended the valley to attack and kill everyone in sight. Now Don Bosco found himself also surrounded by the foul-smelling enemy. He twisted and

Left:
St. John Bosco is better known as St. Don Bosco. His ministry was to the Children of Turin, Italy, victims of the Industrial Revolution in that country at that time. He was God's gift to the Church of the 19th Century. He had a series of dreams in which he was led by a Heavenly guide through areas (like Heaven and Hell) and experiences which could be used as teachings for his boys.

Right:
Bob and Penny Lord with Fr. Don Vito Fabian at the Church of the Sacred Heart in Rome. Fr. Vito shared with Bob and Penny about St. Don Bosco who had visited this Church, stayed there for periods of time and celebrated Masses there.

whirled on his horse, jabbing at the enemy with his pitchfork with a frenzy, as did all the boys who had the good pitchforks. The force of the good army beat the evil army, and they scattered to escape annihilation.

He blew the trumpet and heard the words "*Victory! Victory!*" He couldn't understand how victory had been accomplished with all the dead bodies strewn over the battlefield. He blew the trumpet again. He heard the words "*Truce for the vanquished.*" With that, the skies opened and a beautiful rainbow appeared. He looked around him. All the boys who had been victorious wore brilliant gold crowns. At the far end of the valley, where the great light emanated, a beautiful Lady spoke to them. "*Come, my children, and take shelter under my mantle.*" At that moment, a huge mantle spread out and began floating to the ground. All the boys ran to take cover under the mantle. Some actually flew. These had the word *Innocence* on their foreheads.

A few days later, Don Bosco explained to his priests and his children the meaning of the symbols:
† *The valley, the land of trial, is the world.*
† *The semi-darkness is the place of perdition.*
† *The two hills are the commandments of God and the Church.*
† *The serpents are the devils.*
† *The monsters are evil temptations.*
† *The horse is trust in God.*

Don Bosco's Vision of Hell

Don Bosco had a series of dreams in which he was led by a Heavenly guide[4] through areas and experiences to be used as teachings for his boys. On April 17, 1868, the guide

---

[4]Could it have been his Guardian Angel? Throughout Don Bosco's life, there have been accounts of Angelic intercession, even in the form of an ugly grey dog, called Il Grigio.

said to him, *"Why don't you tell them?"*[5]   Don Bosco asked, *"What should I tell them?"*   The guide replied, *"What you have seen and heard in your last dreams and what you have wanted to know and shall have revealed to you tomorrow night!"*

The following evening, the guide brought Don Bosco on a journey to Hell. They began by walking a fairly level path. Don Bosco would have complained had it been steep, because his legs had been bothering him. Actually, it would have been his excuse not to go. As much as he wanted to know these things, his humanity made him hesitate. They walked along a desolate plain, a sun-parched desert. Finally, however, it opened onto a road where there were green hedges covered with roses and other flowers.

As they were walking, Don Bosco became aware that his boys from the Oratory were following him, as well as others whom he didn't know. He noticed that as they were walking, some would fall to the ground, and be immediately dragged by an invisible magnetism towards an empty hole which fed into a sloping furnace. Then they would disappear. Disturbed, Don Bosco asked the guide why that was happening. He was told to look closely at the ground. Don Bosco saw what looked like just some filmy fiber. He questioned the guide, again. The guide replied, *"A mere nothing; just plain human respect."* The guide was telling Don Bosco these boys were being pulled into Hell because of the compromises they made, out of desire for human respect.

Don Bosco said, *"Why do so many get caught? Who pulls them down?"* The guide instructed him to look closer.

Don Bosco wrote: *"I picked up one of the traps and tugged. I immediately felt some resistance. I pulled harder, only to feel that, instead of drawing the thread closer, I was being pulled down myself. I did not resist and soon found myself at the mouth of a frightful cave. I*

---

[5]referring to his boys

halted, unwilling to venture into that deep cavern, and again started pulling the thread towards me. It gave a little, but only through great effort on my part. I kept tugging, and after a long while a huge, hideous monster emerged, clutching a rope, to which all those traps were tied together. He was the one who instantly dragged down anyone who got caught in them....Then I went back to my guide. 'Now you know who he is,' he said to me. I responded, 'That's the devil himself.'"

Then Don Bosco examined the traps. Each of them bore an inscription: *Pride, Disobedience, Envy, Sixth Commandment, Theft, Gluttony, Sloth, Anger* and on and on. The most dangerous of all were *impurity, disobedience and pride.* Don Bosco noticed that the boys were almost jumping headfirst into these traps. He couldn't understand it. "*Why*", he asked the guide, "*Why such haste?*" The guide smiled, "*Because they are dragged down by the snare of human respect.*"

In Don Bosco's dream, he saw, as he continued down the steep road, knives along the road, put there to help the boys cut themselves loose from the traps. These knives represented *Meditation, The Blessed Sacrament, frequent Communion, and devotion to Our Lady.* A hammer represented *Confession*, and other knives included *St. Joseph's intercession* as well as other *Saints.*

The hedges began to dry and wither through the rays of the blazing sun. The roses were gone. The road became steeper and steeper. Don Bosco complained, he feared he might not be able to get back to the Oratory, the hill was becoming so steep. The guide said, "*Now that we have come so far, do you want me to leave you here?*" Apprehensive, Don Bosco replied, "*How can I survive without your help?*" The response was "*Then follow me.*"

Don Bosco enters the gates of Hell

"We continued our descent, the road now becoming so frightfully steep that it was almost impossible to stand erect. And then, at the bottom of the precipice, at the entrance of a dark valley, an enormous building loomed into sight, its towering portal, tightly locked, facing our road. When I finally got to the bottom, I became smothered by a suffocating heat, while a greasy, green-tinted smoke lit by flashes of scarlet flames rose from behind those enormous walls which loomed higher than mountains.

"'Where are we? What is this?' I asked my guide.

"'Read the inscription on that portal and you will know.'

"I looked up and read these words, 'The place of no reprieve.' I realized that we were at the gates of Hell. The guide led me all around this horrible place. At regular distances, bronze portals like the first, overlooked precipitous descents; on each was an inscription, such as:

'Out of my sight, you condemned, into that everlasting fire prepared for the devil and his angels.'[6] *'Every tree that does not bear good fruit is cut down and thrown into the fire.'"*[7]

As Don Bosco and his guide trudged along, they came to the edge of a precipice facing the first opening to Hell. All of a sudden, Don Bosco saw a young man running at breakneck speed down the hill, his eyes glazed with fear. He kept looking back as if someone were following him. He lost control, and began rolling down the hill until he smashed into the huge bronze door leading to Hell. His speed had so accelerated, and he hit with such an impact, it caused the door to fling open, and swallow him up inside. It caused a chain reaction and what seemed to be thousands of doors

---

[6]Matt 25:41
[7]Matt 7:19

behind the main door opened briefly, to show billowing furnaces inside.

Don Bosco recognized the young man as one of his boys. He turned to the guide who said to him:

"Don't you know how terrible God's vengeance is? Do you think you can restrain one who is fleeing from His just wrath?"   Don Bosco asked: *"Why was he looking backward in terror?"*   The guide answered, *"Because God's wrath will pierce Hell's gates to reach and torment him even in the midst of fire!"*

Don Bosco heard screaming behind him. He turned and saw three more of his boys careening down the hill towards the bronze gate. They were like bowling balls, which had been pitched at lightning speed. They hit with such force, it would seem like all their bones would break. Don Bosco tried to call out to them, but they didn't listen. He saw more and more of his boys being sucked into that portal of Hell. He saw *bad boys*[8] pushing some of his boys down the hill. He saw others going by themselves. On each of their heads, their sin was imprinted.

Don Bosco turned back to his Heavenly guide, pleading with him. *"If so many of our boys end up this way, we are working in vain. How can we prevent such tragedies?"*

His guide answered, *"This is their present state, and that is where they would go if they were to die now."*

The guide continued to bring Don Bosco deeper and deeper into the bowels of Hell. They passed prophetic inscriptions on the walls, and then came to a courtyard.

The guide said to him, *"From here on, no one may have a helpful companion, a comforting friend, a loving heart, a compassionate glance, or a benevolent word. All this is gone forever."*[9]

---

[8]Don Bosco's words

[9]This is the judgment of the God of Justice. At this point, the God of Mercy leaves off, and the God of Justice gives out punishment.

The two entered into a huge cave. They stood on a platform, sort of an observation deck. Don Bosco felt fear in every part of his being. For as far as the eye could see were mountains and abysses of white-hot flames. If it were possible to measure the temperature, it would have to have been *thousands of degrees.* He could not begin to describe the horror before him. He could see boys plummeting down into the center of the white-hot cave, crying out ghastly, shrill, ear-piercing screams as they fell to the bottom. One after the other, more and more of his boys were falling into the pits of Hell.

He looked at a group of them. They were striking each other. They were clawing the skin off their own bodies. At given points, the ceiling of Hell would open, and show these boys their companions who had saved themselves and were sitting in Heaven in the bosom of the Lord. This made these boys (in Hell) even angrier, causing them more pain. There was another group of boys, all covered with worms and vermin, who were biting at their vital parts, their hearts, eyes, hands, legs, every part of their bodies. He tried to speak to them but they were being bitten so ferociously, and were in such agony, they could not hear him.

After walking Don Bosco through all the corners of Hell, and his guide showing him which sins merited each type of eternal punishment, Don Bosco asked him what he could say to his boys to insure that they never come to this place.

The guide told him, "*Keep telling them that by obeying God, the Church, their parents, and their superiors, even in little things, they will be saved.*"

Don Bosco asked, "*Anything else?*" "*Warn them against idleness. Because of idleness David fell into sin. Tell them to keep busy at all times, because the devil will not then have a chance to tempt them.*"

Then the guide began to lead him out of Hell. As they passed the last gateway, he told Don Bosco he would have to touch the wall to experience a little of what eternal suffering felt like. Don Bosco shrunk back. He wanted none of that.

The guide convinced him that it was necessary. *"Only one touch, so that you may say you have both seen and touched the walls of eternal suffering and that you may understand what the last wall must be like if the first is so unendurable. Look at this wall."*

He showed him an extremely thick wall.

"There are a thousand walls between this and the real fire of Hell. A thousand walls encompass it, each a thousand measures thick and equally distant from the next one. Each measure is a thousand miles. This wall therefore is millions and millions of miles from Hell's real fire. It is just a remote rim of Hell itself."

At that, the guide pressed Don Bosco's hand against the wall. The pain was so excruciating, it awakened him. His hand was burning. Even the next day, as he was telling the boys of his dream, his hand was still red and swollen and blistered. And that was from touching the *outer* wall, *millions of miles* from the fire of Hell.

Don Bosco not only taught the children, but groups of all ages, including his priests and seminarians of the Salesian Order,[10] from this dream. It was as if the Lord had wanted Don Bosco to pass through this, to impress on everyone the seriousness of sin and the righteous punishment of Hell.

Don Bosco's Vision of Heaven

Because Don Bosco's work was with young people, his Dreams, Visions and Prophecies would naturally have to do with his ministry. This *vision* or dream of *Heaven* involved a large group of his young people. The dream took place over a period of three nights. Each night, it continued where it had left off the night before. Because of his frame of

---

[10]Don Bosco founded the Salesian Order as an offshoot of his ministry to the young.

reference, being from the country rather than the city, most of his dreams took place in open fields. In addition, since this was usually the only place he could fit the huge number of boys who were part of his life and his community in real life, it only stands to reason, this is where his dreams would take place. After each dream, he would recount it to the young people.

His next dream began in a huge field. In answer to the question, "*What should we do?*" the boys in his dream all responded in unison, "*Let's hike to Heaven.*" An enormous mountain loomed in front of them. All along the mountain, people were climbing, trying to reach the top. The boys and Don Bosco could see that some people, who had attained higher levels of the mountain, came back down to help others who were struggling to climb the great incline. At the top, they could make out the figure of God, Who was welcoming them into Heaven. So they all knew that Heaven was at the top of the mountain.

As only the young can do, they attacked the project with the attitude of "*It's a piece of cake.*" They forged ahead toward the great ascent, and then they came to their first valley! They had to go down into a great valley and cross a lake to the other side; then they would be allowed to begin the climb up the mountain. Some of the boys ran so quickly, Don Bosco was not able to keep up with them. When they approached the end of the valley, they saw a horrendous sight. The lake separating them from the mountain was filled with blood, and there were dead bodies with legs and arms broken, strewn over the lake. The boys wanted no part of this, and ran to Don Bosco, pleading to leave this place.

As Don Bosco approached the edge of the lake, he saw a sign which read, "*Through Blood.*" He asked a person, who was standing there, what this meant. He was told that the blood was the blood of the Martyrs who had already reached the top of the mountain. They had shed their blood for the

Faith. He added, in this lake, too, flowed the Blood of the Lamb - Jesus. Don Bosco was then told, this lake spilled into a much deeper valley, which would also be filled with the blood of future Martyrs.

[Remember, this is 1861 we're talking about. So many things have not yet happened. The carnage of the Twentieth Century, brought about by man's inhumanity to man, the American Civil War, the Russian Revolution, the First and Second World Wars, religious purgings in Africa, slaughter of the innocents,[11] so many atrocities, were still long in coming. We could very easily fill that other valley up by the end of the Twentieth Century, if not before. We read somewhere that there have been more Martyrs in the Twentieth Century than in the previous nineteen centuries combined.]

The person who spoke to Don Bosco further explained that the dead bodies strewn on the banks of the lake were those who tried to destroy the Church. Their bones were scattered over the shores of the lake. Don Bosco and the boys ran along the edge of the lake in search of a path which lead them to the other side. They had run quite a distance, when they came to the end of the lake. There was another lake filled with dismembered limbs. They were told that these mutilated limbs belonged to those who had recently attacked the Church.

A sign read, "*Through water!*" They were told this was the water which flowed from the Side of Christ, and through which all men must be baptized before they can enter into the Kingdom; this is the baptismal water that washed and purified those who climbed the mountain; all who want to go to Heaven must be cleansed in this water; and there is no other way to Paradise than through penance or innocence.

---

[11]abortions

They continued along the path, until
another lake, as large as the first. This was more
and more torn parts of bodies. The inscription on this lake
was "*Through fire!*" This was explained in this way: This is the
Fire of Charity of God and His Saints. These are the flames
of love and desire through which all must pass who have not
gone through the blood or water. They were told that this
was also the fire used by tyrants and torturers to persecute
many of the Martyrs. The torn limbs were those who had
fought the Church.

Don Bosco did not consider himself worthy to cross any
of these lakes, and the boys considered themselves less
worthy than Don Bosco. So they continued to try to find a
path which would go around the lakes and bring them to the
other side where they could ascend the mountain. Finally,
they saw a large plaza. At the end it narrowed into a path
between two tight boulders, through which many people
were squeezing, in order to climb the mountain to Heaven.
There was not much room to get through. As a matter of
fact, those crossing had to strip themselves of everything they
had that was not absolutely necessary, to get through the
boulder.

At first, Don Bosco and the boys stood on the line.
Then their curiosity got the best of them. They saw other
valleys beyond the main plaza. They walked in various
directions trying to find out what people were doing in those
other valleys. These valleys turned out to be distractions
from going to Heaven, such things as laziness, stubbornness,
concupiscence, gluttony of things of man's lower nature. At
first, the boys were sort of swept along with all these things,
not noticing that the road was going down ever so slightly,
until they got to a point where the road took them to a steep
bank. Before them was a beautiful garden filled with roses,
but they were only beautiful on the outside. They were
rotting on the inside, and the smell was horrible. They ran

from this, into another garden with fruit that looked so appetizing; it was rotten on the inside. The boys kept asking what all this meant. They were told this was the world, and all it had to offer.

They saw large groups of people heading down the road, being led by very handsome men and women. But they were leading them into Hell! As soon as Don Bosco and the boys realized where they were going, they immediately turned around and went back in search of the boulders and the mountain to Heaven. Finally, they found the right road, went through the boulders and came upon a dangerous bridge which would bring them to the foot of the mountain. The boys would not proceed, until Don Bosco led them. Together, they found their way across, and began the long ascent up the mountain.

It took a while, before the grade became easier to climb. On their way up, they encountered many obstacles. At one point, they passed many people in great pain. They saw people taking different paths up the mountain, not just the path they had chosen. As Don Bosco quickened his pace, he got closer and closer to the summit. He could see those who had reached it, being welcomed by others and brought into the Kingdom. But as he turned around to share this with the boys, he realized that almost all of them were still somewhere down around the middle of the mountain. He looked down at them. They were doing silly things, chasing butterflies, resting on the ground. He yelled down to them to follow him, but they didn't hear, or chose not to listen. He grabbed as many as he could and told them to continue up the mountain.

He went down after the rest, like the Shepherd Who went after the one lost sheep. He kept grabbing them, and pushing them until they started up the mountain again. By the time he had gotten all of them headed in the right direction, he found that he was almost at the bottom of the mountain again, where he had begun the strenuous climb. As he began his ascent back up the mountain, he tripped on a stone and woke up. That was the end of the dream.

There are many symbols in this dream, which Don Bosco later explained to his Salesian priests and brothers:

† The three great lakes are the *Church*.

† The mountain is the Oratory, the ongoing struggle to bring all his young men up the mountain to Heaven.

† The people in pain are those in *Purgatory*.

† The boys lollygagging on the side of the mountain are those of us who allow unimportant things to take up their time, when they should be concentrating on reaching the Kingdom.

St. John Bosco had many Dreams, Visions and Prophecies. We have chosen to bring you these because they are important to the book we are writing. But we recommend you read more about this powerful Saint in the autobiography of Don Bosco, "*Memoirs of the Oratory*," and the book from which we took these passages, "*Dreams, Visions and Prophecies of Don Bosco.*"[12]

What we have brought you in this chapter are just some of the many *Dreams, Visions and Prophecies* of St. John Bosco. St. John Bosco began having dreams at age nine, and continued until the end of his days. Most of his prophecies have been fulfilled, except for the ones dealing with the end times, of which there are many; whereas the prophecies dealing with his own century, all have come to pass.

Most importantly, St. Don Bosco is also a powerful intercessor. In these troubled times, where so many of our children are being led astray, keep in touch with the Pied Piper of the young. He will intercede for them.

---

[12]Bob and Penny Lord have written a chapter on Don Bosco in their book: "*Saints and other Powerful Men in the Church.*"

Above:
St. Bernadette of Lourdes

Above:
During the fourth Apparition of Lourdes, St. Bernadette heard the sounds of Hell coming from the Gave river.

Above: ***The grotto at Lourdes where the Apparitions took place.***

St. Bernadette and Sounds of Hell

One of the most powerful Marian Apparitions we have researched, occurred in Lourdes, France in 1858. The visionary, a girl who grew up to become St. Bernadette, was basically a no-nonsense person. She was very down to earth, without any outward ethereal qualities, not at all the type you would envision as being a Mystic or Visionary. And yet she was the one whom Our Lady chose to visit, and affirm the doctrine of the Immaculate Conception, proclaimed by Pope Pius IX just four years before.

"We once wrote that Bernadette was a simple girl, an illiterate at the time that Our Lady appeared to her, but never did we consider her a stupid girl. Her behavior throughout the period of the Apparitions, her inner strength to hold up against great powers in the government and the Church, are a strong indicator of this. Her life after the Apparitions, and in the Convent of St. Gildard in Nevers, is proof of her strength.

"She really underestimated her role in the Apparitions at the grotto of Massabiele in the little hamlet of Lourdes. Our Lady needed one such as she knew Bernadette could be. This was a very important message she was bringing the people of the world. She could not take a chance on trusting a weak person, who could be reduced to tears or shot down at the first sign of adversity. She needed someone who would have the strength to stand up before the powers of Hell, and Bernadette was that person."[1]

St. Bernadette never actually had a vision of Hell, as much as she experienced the *Sounds of Hell* during one of the times when Our Lady appeared to her. This occurred during the fourth apparition, which took place on Friday, February 19, 1858. Our Lady had no sooner appeared to

---

[1]Excerpt from chapter on St. Bernadette in *"Saints and Other Powerful Women in the Church"* - Bob and Penny Lord

Bernadette, when the child heard the most horrible roaring sounds, much like screaming and raving, very low and guttural at first, very angry. The sounds seemed to come from the River Gave, which was in front of the Grotto of Massabiele. They started off with a low rumble, and graduated to loud yells. In his book on St. Bernadette, Abbe François Trochu describes the experience as follows:

"At a certain time, the apparition seemed different from before. Suddenly loud yells, belched from the Gave (River), had rent the sacred silence of Massabiele. They 'challenged, crossed, collided with one another, like the clamor of a brawling crowd'. One voice, more furious than the rest, dominated them all and roared out: 'Get out of here!...Get out of here!' Bernadette guessed rightly that the threatening curse was by no means addressed merely to her humble self, but was an attack directed beyond her to the Vision of Light standing above the child.

"The Vision merely glanced in the direction of the rushing stream. This single look, one of sovereign authority, reduced the invisible mob to silence: the enemy of all good would not drive her from the grotto where she gave her audiences."

In his best-selling book, *Song of Bernadette,* Franz Werfel described the incident as follows:

"Bernadette seemed to hear nothing. A quite other noise sounded in her ears. Once more the Gave (River) seemed in rebellious spate. Once more a rout in panic terror seemed to race across the river, comparable to the echo of galloping horses and rattling vehicles; once more the piercing cries arose: Flee, flee...Avaunt from here! Fearfully Bernadette raised her arms toward the Lady whose countenance for the first time was stern and proud, as though her pilgrimage also was not at an end, as though she too had still to wage battles and vanquish her enemies. With wrinkled brow she looked attentively at the river, as

though to tame it with her eyes' radiant blue. The uproar
yielded at once. The hoarse voices crashed into silence.
The immemorial rumbling and foaming of the Gave came
to the Lady's heel like a daunted wolf."[2]

I must share here, I love when we see the power of
God, Our Lady and the Angels manifested. All the powers
of Hell were roaring, using the Gave River as their vehicle,
to disrupt and even stop the Apparitions. We don't know
for sure what they were thinking. Did they believe they
could scare Bernadette from the place? That was possible.
But they were not after Bernadette; they were after Our
Lady. And all it took was a glance from her, and they took
off like frightened goats.

We know that the power is in the hands of the Lord; we
know it takes but a look or a gesture and Satan with his
cohorts are propelled into the pits of Hell. So why, we often
ask, does it seem as if Satan and his band of misfits are
taking over? The world truly seems to be going to Hell in a
handbasket.   Abortion, pornography, murder for drug
money, permissive judicial systems, blatant wholesale evil in
governments of nations, liberal elements in the Church
hellbent on destroying its people, all of this would seem to
indicate that we're losing the battle badly. But yesterday was
Sunday, and the Gospel was about the wheat and the chaff.

"Jesus proposed to the crowd this parable: 'The reign of
God may be likened to a man who sowed good seed in his
field. While everyone was asleep, his enemy came and
sowed weeds through his wheat, and then made off. When
the crop began to mature and yield grain, the weeds made
their appearance as well. The owner's slaves came to him
and said, 'Sir, did you not sow good seed in your field?
Where are the weeds coming from?' He answered, 'I see
an enemy's hand in this.' His slaves said to him, 'Do you

---

[2]The Song of Bernadette - Franz Werfel

want us to go out and pull them up?' 'No,' he replied,
'pull up the weeds and you might take the wheat along
with them. Let them grow together until harvest; then at
harvest time I will order the harvesters to first collect the
weeds and bundle them up to burn; then gather the wheat
into my barn."[3]

In his homily, the priest said that the owner was *Jesus*;
the enemy was Satan; the good people are the *wheat*; the
bad people are the *weeds*; harvest time is the Last Judgment;
the harvesters are the Angels who will enforce the orders
given to them by Jesus at the Last Judgment, and I don't
think we have to spell out where the burning place is. We
need to be praying desperately for the conversion of sinners,
like little Jacinta,[4] who did so, because *she saw Hell.*

At Massabiele, the future was to prove that the spirit of
evil, in this burst of fury, had been vanquished. By leaving at
the glance of the Mother of God, he had admitted his defeat
in the Grotto; he was not able to extinguish the great
radiance that would issue from this dark, peaceful nook,
where so many sinners would renounce sin.

But the evil one had by no means given up at Lourdes.
He had submitted to a direct command from Our Lady to
leave the Grotto of Massabiele and stop making hellish
noises there. But that was all he did. He still continued with
his devilish plan to discredit the Apparitions. He knew too
well what the value of the Apparitions would be to the world
in the upcoming years.

"For several months in the Lourdes area, there raged a
regular epidemic of visionaries, some of them obviously
manipulated by occult forces, others, the sport of their own
temperament, whose weaknesses could be exploited by
Satan for his perverse ends. There were fanatics,

---

[3]Matt 13:24-30
[4]One of the visionaries of Fatima

exhibitionists, lying maniacs, hysterics, half-wits, with a few tricksters thrown in. And there were exhibitions of contortions, fits of hysteria, grotesque and even indecent posturings, fainting attacks...To disentangle human trickery from the devil's deceits in all this, would be more than a little difficult.

"In every case a point of utmost importance stands out clearly: 'The suspect apparitions never showed themselves in the niche where Bernadette customarily saw Mary Immaculate,' nor on the exact spot 'where Our Lady sometimes came to continue her conversations with the visionary'."[5]

They knew their boundaries and their limitations. But they were determined to disgrace the Apparitions of Our Lady to Bernadette. If they couldn't go to the Grotto and disrupt the proceedings there, the praying of the Rosary, the sick coming to wash in the spring, then they would create such confusion, the people would wonder if anybody, except the devil ever came to Lourdes.

And doesn't that sound familiar? Don't we have the same situation with us today? There are so very many people today, who claim to see the Blessed Mother. We can't turn the corner without running into an alleged visionary or mystic. That was the reason we wrote the book, *"Visionaries, Mystics and Sigmatists"* in 1995. The best and most prudent course of action is to wait upon Mother Church.

Now it is possible that one of them, or maybe even more than one are receiving authentic messages from Our lady, or have the true Stigmata, or are seeing Our Lord Jesus. Perhaps they're trying to warn us about apocalyptic times, and we can't hear them because we're being distracted by

---

[5]St. Bernadette Soubirous - Abbe François Trochu

the many clanging bells of false visionaries.[6] We know that
Our Lord Jesus and Our Mother are trying to reach us,
today. But Their message might be drowned out by the same
noises of Hell that the evil one used to try to deter Our Lady
and Bernadette at the Grotto of Massabiele in 1858.

But Bernadette was strong; she turned, her arms
outstretched and reached out to the Mother of God for help.
Our Lady looked distastefully at the offenders and they
withered away. There is a great message for us here from
Our Lady and Bernadette. Look to the Mother of God for
help. Don't let the noises of the clanging gongs deceive you.
Mary is speaking to you; Jesus is speaking to you. Don't
allow the distractions to keep you away from them. It is just
at that *moment*, when you are tempted to run to this
visionary or that mystic that you need to *keep your mind and
your heart open* to our Heavenly Family. They have a truly
important message for you. ***Listen to it!***

---

[6]1 Cor 13:1

Padre Pio and the Poor Souls

Padre Pio had a profound, lifelong relationship with the Poor Souls in Purgatory. He had a great devotion to them, and offered his Masses and *his* suffering for the merciful release of these anguishing Souls. They pleaded with him to help them; so he walked with many of them, alongside their Guardian Angels, supporting them through their seemingly endless time in Purgatory. Their agony was eased somewhat, knowing he was available, and they were in the forefront, in his mind and heart. They were always with him. At one time, he said, *"More souls of the dead than the living climb this mountain to attend my Mass and seek my prayers."* That is quite a statement, considering the hundreds of thousands who came and continue to come up the mountain to San Giovanni Rotondo to appeal to Padre Pio for help.

From an early age, Padre Pio spoke to the Souls in Purgatory. Padre Pio was sensitive to their call; he heard and answered them. And the word got out in Purgatory. The more souls he helped, the more implored his help.

One of the first recorded times, a soul in Purgatory implored Padre Pio's help, took place in his home town of Pietrelcina shortly after his ordination. Because of his fragile health, he had been allowed to study for the priesthood, there. The Capuchin superiors originally tried to have him go to various friaries, but he would no sooner arrive than he would become deathly ill and was sent home. The day after he returned home, he was better. His condition remained that way until they felt he was well enough to be sent to another friary. The same thing would happen again. He would become deathly ill, and be sent home. Eventually, the superiors got the message: The Lord wanted Francis Forgione to stay in Pietrelcina, and he did. Even after his ordination, he was allowed to stay there, for a short time.

Above: ***Padre Pio celebrating Mass***
Right:
Padre Pio praying in the choir
where he had received the Stigmata
Below:
Padre Pio's cell in San Giovanni
Rotondo, Italy

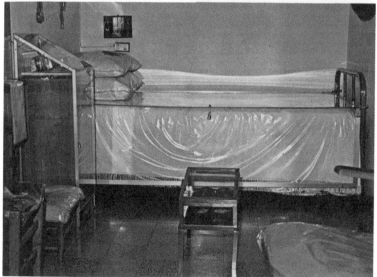

His parish priest, Don Salvatore Pannullo, whom he affectionately referred to as Zi' Tore,[1] had been Padre Pio's theology instructor during his time in Pietrelcina. This was a small parish church, and there was no sacristy at the time. Zi' Tore prepared the altar for his prize student to celebrate Mass every day. When Zi' Tore celebrated Mass, he always vested up *behind* the main altar; but he had Padre Pio vest at the side altar. Although obedient; Padre Pio wondered why he had asked him to do this. He didn't say anything for a few days. When he asked why he had done this, Zi' Tore explained that the previous pastor had died many years before. But when Padre Pio began celebrating Mass at the Church, the old priest appeared in back of the main altar and stayed there praying, during Padre Pio's entire Mass. Then, when the Mass was over, he disappeared.

Zi' Tore wanted to leave the area behind the altar free, so he could watch the old priest. He knew there had to be a reason for his coming back to this church, now and at this time, when Padre Pio was celebrating Mass. This went on for about a month.

At the end of a month, the dead priest went up to Don Salvatore,[2] *"Salvatore! I'm leaving now, and I won't come again. How terrible it was and how dearly it costs me to have taken part in the 'procession' after Mass, without first making my thanksgiving."* He disappeared, and never returned.

Don Salvatore explained to Padre Pio that the priest had been a good man, but that he would rush off to join his *paisanos*[3] after Mass. Instead of taking time to thank Our Lord Jesus for His Sacrifice and the privilege of celebrating the Mass, he spent this precious time in the local cafe savoring friends, coffee and sweet rolls. For this, he was accorded quite a time in Purgatory. The Lord allowed this

---

[1]Uncle Tore (nickname for Salvatore, which means Savior)
[2]the name of Zi' Tore as priest of the parish
[3]friends and acquaintances

priest to return to the Church, the scene of his ingratitude, to pray for forgiveness at Padre Pio's Masses, because he always included the Souls in Purgatory.

Another instance of how Padre Pio was constantly in touch with souls in Purgatory, took place just a few years after he had received the Stigmata (September 20, 1918). He was praying in the choir loft where he had received the Stigmata, when his prayers were interrupted by the sound of candlesticks falling from the main altar. He called down, inquiring who was there. There was no answer. He shouted now and looked over to the Altar. He saw what appeared to be a young friar standing next to a broken candle.

After shouting at the young man one more time, the friar answered that he was dead, and had to serve his Purgatory in the church of Our Lady of Grace in San Giovanni Rotondo. His great sin was that he had lacked diligence in doing his duty in that church. He had been dead sixty years, and he was still in Purgatory.

He told the young man, he would remember him in his Mass the following morning. Padre Pio left the church and went back to his cell. He spoke to some of the friars, and had them return with him to the church. When they did, they saw the broken candlesticks, which was proof to Padre Pio that he had truly seen what he thought he had. The next day, he celebrated Mass especially for that young man.

Padre Pio made a moral from this story, *"For lack of diligence in doing his duty, that friar was still in Purgatory sixty years after his death! Imagine, then, how much longer and how much more difficult Purgatory will be for those who commit sins which are more serious."* We believe there's another moral to that story. This young friar was dead for sixty years, and was still in Purgatory. Who did he know that many years later, whom he could ask to pray for his release? Most everyone he had known was probably dead by this time.

Who prays for those who have been in Purgatory for more years than a lifetime?

The last example, we will give about doing their Purgatory at the place where they have offended God, has to do with Padre Pio's early days in San Giovanni Rotondo. The year was February, 1920. He had already received the Stigmata, and so people had a tendency to listen to him. He shared with the friars that some nights before, he had gone to warm himself by the fireplace. It had been an extremely cold day, and it was next to impossible to warm the friary. This room was like a haven to all the friars. Strangely enough however, there were only four friars in the room, all around the fireplace. Their heads were covered with their cowls, and they were not speaking. He greeted them; they did not reply. He looked at them. He was not comfortable. Once again, he greeted them; they remained silent.

He went upstairs to the father superior's cell and asked if any new friars had come that day. The answer was no. Padre Pio shared about the four friars, downstairs. The father superior immediately went down with Padre Pio. The room was empty. *"I finally realized"* he told his brother friars, *"that they were four dead religious, who were doing their Purgatory in the place where they had offended God."*

Souls in Purgatory are sometimes allowed to return to the places where they had offended God. Were they allowed to return to these places because of the power of the Saint's intercession for them, as in the case of Padre Pio, or to do reparation there for past offenses? In many of the visions in this book, Souls have come to Saints who are known for their sympathy toward the Souls in Purgatory. Let us pray for the Poor Souls; one of them may be just the future Saint we need to intercede for us in Purgatory.

†

An intimate way of following the life of Padre Pio, and especially getting into the tenderness he felt for the members of the *Church Suffering* is through his letters. These are as close to an autobiography of this saintly priest as anything you will ever read. While there are many good biographies on the life of Padre Pio,[4] very often we like to just take time out and read through some of the two volumes of letters of Padre Pio which have been translated into English.

As an example, there are a series of letters he wrote to his spiritual director, Padre Benedetto, who was a saint of a man. He had to go through some of the most difficult times with Padre Pio. But in the early days, at the time of these letters, in 1910, shortly after his ordination, Padre Pio made a special request to his spiritual director. The newly ordained priest had made a decision, no doubt after much prayer and affirmation by the Holy Spirit, that he was to be *victim-soul* for Poor Souls in Purgatory. And so he wrote,

"Now, my dear father, I want to ask your permission for something. For some time past I have felt the need to offer myself to the Lord as a victim for poor sinners and for the souls in Purgatory.

"This desire has been growing continually in my heart so that it has now become what I would call a strong passion. I have in fact made this offering to the Lord several times, beseeching him to pour out upon me the punishment prepared for sinners and for the souls in a state of purgation, even increasing them a hundredfold for me, as long as He converts and saves sinners and quickly admits to Paradise the souls in Purgatory, but I should now like to make this offering to the Lord in obedience to you. It seems to me that Jesus really wants this. I am sure that you will have no difficulty in granting me this permission."[5]

This letter was dated 29 November, 1910. His superior sent him an answer on 1 December, 1910, just two days later,

---

[4]Bob and Penny wrote about Padre Pio in their book, *"Saints and Other Powerful Men in the Church."*
[5]Letter 23

"Make the offering of which you speak and it will be most acceptable to the Lord. Extend your own arms also on your cross and by offering to the Father the sacrifice of yourself in union with our most loving Savior, suffer, groan and pray for the wicked ones of the earth and for the Poor Souls in the next life who are so deserving of our compassion in their patient and unspeakable sufferings."[6]

There are some very important points in this little discourse from one to the other. The first is that Padre Pio, only a priest for six months at this time, understood the importance of *prayer*, deep prayer for the Souls in Purgatory. He was only twenty-three years old, and he wanted to devote all the sufferings he was to endure for the next fifty-eight years for his brothers and sisters, the Poor Souls in Purgatory. He knew what powerful intercessors they would be once they entered into the Kingdom. However, that was not his motive. Padre Pio was an instrument of love. He offered himself out of pure love for the suffering.

But there's another point in the exchange which we have to address. In Padre Pio's letter, he also says *"as long as He converts and saves sinners,"* and in Padre Benedetto's letter, he says *"groan and pray for the wicked ones of the earth."* They both make reference not only to the Suffering Souls, but to those on earth, who may wind up either in Purgatory, or worse, in Hell.

In the same decade, 1917 to be exact, Jacinta Martos, one of the visionaries at Fatima,[7] offered her whole life as *victim-soul* for the Church Suffering. She had a vision of Hell, and was never the same. For the last few years of her life (she died in 1920 at age 10), she spoke almost exclusively about praying for the conversion of sinners. She constantly prayed the prayer our Lady had given the children,

---

[6]Letter 24

[7]Read our chapter on the Visions of hell of the Children of Fatima and the chapter on Fatima in *The Many Faces of Mary, a love story*

*"Oh my Jesus, forgive us our sins; save us from the fires
of Hell. Lead all souls into Heaven, especially those in
most need of Thy Mercy."*

In this same time period, Padre Pio, newly-ordained
priest and his spiritual director, Padre Benedetto, saw the
great need for praying for the conversion of sinners. What
was going on in the world at that time? In Yugoslavia,
where the First World War started, trouble was brewing. All
Europe was having problems. In Russia, Satan was rearing
his ugly head, planting poison in the hearts of certain people
there, agitating the people into the beginnings of the Russian
Revolution, which would wreak havoc on the entire world
for the next seventy some-odd years. *Who is praying for the
conversion of sinners today?*

Padre Pio had communications with the Souls in
Purgatory. He knew the intensity of the pains of Purgatory.
Many of our most well-respected Saints have agreed with
this. St. Thomas Aquinas wrote that the pains of Purgatory
were as furious as those of Hell. Padre Pio once said in the
presence of a friar:

*"If the Lord were to give permission to the Soul to pass
from the fires of Purgatory to the greatest fire on earth, it
would be like passing from hot water to cool water."*

On another occasion, when asked what Purgatory was
like, he said:

*"...the souls in Purgatory would like to throw themselves
into a well of our earthly fire, because for them it would be
like a well of cool water."*

It was not an unusual occurrence for Padre Pio to be
called from the refectory[8] to speak to Souls in Purgatory.
One instance occurred in the following way:

*"The friars, as was customary, had come together to
partake of their frugal meal, and Padre Pio, too, was*

---

[8]Dining Room

nibbling on something. The lively chattering was abruptly cut off by a brusque movement on the part of Padre Pio. He suddenly darted to the door of the friary and started up a lively conversation with some people who, however, remained invisible to the other friars who had followed him. As they watched Padre Pio talking to what seemed to them to be nobody, the friars remarked to one another, 'He has gone crazy!' However, they asked him whom he was talking to. Understanding their chagrin, he smiled and answered, 'Oh, don't worry. I was talking to some souls who were on their way from Purgatory to Heaven. They stopped here to thank me because I remembered them in my Mass this morning.' With that, he returned to his place in the refectory as if nothing out of the ordinary had happened."[9]

Padre Pio's Vision of Demons and his lifelong Battle

Padre Pio also had a lifelong relationship with the demons, only not in the same way as with the Souls in Purgatory. He began battling demons when he was five years old, but with the Divine balance of being strengthened by apparitions and inner locutions of Our Lord Jesus, our Mother Mary and our Heavenly Family of Angels and Saints. For many years, he thought that everyone had visits from our Heavenly Family.

There's an elm tree on the *Piana Romana*[10] where he would graze his herd of cows (two), and where he studied as a youth.[11] Francesco used to sit under that tree to take advantage of its shade during the hot summer days. But he went through harsh battles with demons there. Friends and neighbors testified, they could see him fighting some invisible

---

[9]The Holy Souls - Fr. Alessio Parente OFM Cap

[10]Roman Plain

[11]The bark has since been picked clean by over-enthusiastic pilgrims who wanted these relics because that was where Padre Pio received the Invisible Stigmata in 1911.

force. It looked like he was defending himself against a swarm of bees. These battles with the enemies of God would continue on and off until his final days.

One of his most frightening experiences with the fallen angels came at about the time he was to enter the seminary.

"Finally, he received permission to enter the Capuchin friary at Morcone in January 1903. The few days before his entry into the seminary, were days of visions from the Lord, to prepare him for the battle that lay ahead for him. Jesus was allowing Francesco[12] to see the battle plan, the treacherous enemy, the obstacles, the impossible odds. It was as if He had laid out the conflicts Padre Pio would experience all his life, and how, with the help of his Guardian Angels, and Jesus at his side, he would overcome the enemy.

"In this vision, Jesus acted as Francesco's guide. He led him onto an immense battlefield. On one side were radiant looking men dressed in white. On the other, hideous creatures dressed in somber, dark, gloomy colors. Jesus pointed to a towering monster, bigger than anything Francesco had ever seen. It was a terrifying sight. Jesus told the young Francesco, he had to do battle with the creature. Francesco's knees began to shake. He pleaded with the Lord not to ask him do it. There was no way he could be victorious over such a grotesque beast.

"Jesus repeated His request to Francesco, but said He would be at his side. Francesco did as he was told. He went into a ferocious combat. The pain inflicted on him was excruciating. But he was triumphant. The monster fled, as did all his repulsive followers, screaming at the tops of their voices, making inhuman sounds.

"Jesus told Francesco, he would have to do battle with this demon again, and throughout his life. But Jesus

---

[12]Francesco Forgione, Padre Pio's name before becoming a friar

would always be with him, to protect him, and help him. 'Fear not, I will be with you always, until the end of the world.'[13]

"This particular vision petrified Padre Pio for the next twenty years. In reflecting on it, the thirty-five year old Padre Pio shuddered as he spoke of the experience. Just think of how the fifteen-year old Francesco felt after he went through it. Jesus was giving Francesco a physical sign of the enemies that all of us have to battle, all our lives."[14]

Throughout his life, he battled the demons, as Jesus said he would. He was thrown from wall to wall from his earliest days. When he was studying in Pietrelcina in a little loft which was loaned to him by relatives, neighbors complained to his parents that he was having wild parties up there. They claimed to hear loud noises all throughout the night. In truth, he was being beaten by the demons.

In San Giovanni Rotondo, he always had to have a friar assigned to him to help him during the night when he was attacked by devils. Once when he was being fiercely beaten, Our Lady came to him. Naturally, the demons fled when she came. She gave him a blue pillow, which she placed under his head. That pillow is still there in his cell to this day. Even on the weekend he died in September 1968, he was under attack by the envious fallen angels. He called the friars to his cell many times to protect him. While they could never see the demons, they could see how badly Padre Pio was beaten, and would give him first aid.

Could Padre Pio see into the future? Was he aware of what the world was becoming during his lifetime, and would deteriorate into, after his death? Did he sacrifice his eighty-one years of life, being physically as well as spiritually tortured by the fallen angels of Satan, so that the common

---

[13]Mt 28:20

[14]Chapter in Bob and Penny Lord's book, *"Saints and Other Powerful Men in the Church"*

man, the simple believer, would have something to hold onto? Did he allow himself to be a crucified Christ to give us strength?

We'll probably never know the full extent of sacrifice that Padre Pio made for us, during our lifetime. We may not even understand it in what time is left of this world of ours. Perhaps he was a modern-day Don Quixote, the Man of La Mancha, who wanted nothing more than to save the world, and was willing to sacrifice himself in the process. Doesn't that sound a lot like Jesus? We believe the Lord gave Padre Pio the *impossible* dream, that Padre Pio *held onto* that dream, *fought* for that dream, and *died* for that dream. Did he live in vain? Were his eighty-one years of agony for nothing? *That, my brothers and sisters, depends entirely on us.*

†

Prayer before the Crucifix where Padre Pio received the Stigmata

You call Me the Way	but you don't follow Me.
You call Me the Light	but you don't see Me.
You call Me the Teacher	but you don't listen to Me.
You call Me the Lord	but you don't serve Me.
You call Me the Truth	but you don't believe in Me.

Don't be surprised if one day, I don't know you!

†

Visions of the Children of Fatima

The precious children of Fatima, Lucia, Jacinta and Francisco, have captured our hearts, as the brave trio who fought against all secular odds to keep a promise to Our Lady. She asked them to come to her on the 13th of each month for six months, in the year 1917; and against overwhelming odds, they said *Yes!*

Our Lady gave them important messages during that period of time, many of which they couldn't begin to understand. Some of the profound things she said to them were for them alone; others were for the world. But the drama of the *Miracle of the Sun* on October 13, 1917, witnessed by more than 70,000 people in the *Cova da Iria*, and as far off as the Azores mountains, overshadowed for a time many of the messages she gave these little people.

Over the years, we have had an opportunity to go through all the occurrences of that six month period which would change the world forever. Everything was important to them, but some things burned an impression on their hearts and minds, more than others. One of these events was a vision, rather than a message from our Lady.

We have to preface this with some things, the children shared with one another. Most of this came to the world, years later from Lucia, when, under obedience to her bishop, she wrote on those early years. The messages connected with Hell played an important part in the Apparitions of Our Lady in 1917, as well as in those of the Archangel Michael in 1916. Just think about some of the things which were said to the children. One of the most forceful references to Hell was when Our Lady said to the children, *"Many souls go to Hell because no one prays for them."*

This was the beginning of her plea to us to pray for the conversion of sinners. Much of the thrust of the Fatima

Above left: ***The Children of Fatima, Jacinta, Francisco, and Lucia***
Above right: ***Our Lady of Fatima***
Below: ***The vision of Hell that the three children witnessed***

message had to do with praying for sinners in an attempt to keep them from plunging into the eternal flames of Hell.

This accounts for the prayer, Mary gave to the children and to us through them, which we say at the end of each decade of the Rosary,

"Oh my Jesus, forgive us our sins; **save us from the fires of hell.** *Lead all souls into Heaven, especially those in most need of Thy Mercy."*

After this, Mary opened her hands and pointed down to the earth. The brilliant light opened the earth, burrowing deep into the bowels of the Underworld. The children were given a vision of Hell. In Lucia's third memoir, she describes it as follows:

"Our Lady showed us a great sea of fire which seemed to be under the earth. Plunged in this fire were demons and souls in human form, like transparent burning embers, all blackened or burnished bronze, floating about in the conflagration,[1] now raised into the air by the flames that issued from within themselves together with great clouds of smoke, now falling back on every side like sparks in a huge fire, without weight or equilibrium, and amid shrieks and groans of pain and despair, which horrified us and made us tremble with fear. The demons could be distinguished by their terrifying and repellent likeness to frightful and unknown animals, all black and transparent. This vision lasted but an instant."[2]

They spoke about a sea of fire, filled with devils and the souls of people, black or bronzed, burning fiercely, ghastly screams of indescribable pain coming out of them, being sucked into a river of fire, like molten lava, embers of burnt skin flying off their charred bodies. The demons could be distinguished from the people in that they looked like

---

[1]fire, blaze

[2]*"Fatima in Lucia's own Words"*, Third Memoir, the Vision of Hell

ghoulish, deformed animals. The grotesque vision would have bristled the hair on the necks of the strongest adults. These innocent little children were petrified. Mary spoke to Lucia.

"You have seen Hell where the souls of poor sinners go. To save them, God wishes to establish in the world devotion to my Immaculate Heart. If you do what I tell you, many souls will be saved and there will be peace. The war will end, but if men do not cease to offend God, another worse one will begin.

"When you see a night illumined by an unknown light,[3] *know that it is the great sign given you by God that He is about to punish the world for its crimes by means of war, famine and persecutions of the Church and of the Holy Father."*

This vision of Hell, and Our Lady's words, had a devastating effect on the children, especially Jacinta, who was extremely sensitive and only seven years old. Actually, these were all little people, Lucia *ten*, Francisco *eight*, and Jacinta *seven* years old. Jacinta was upset by the vision of Hell. Really, she was disturbed by the whole idea of Hell.

When the apparitions first began, she would ponder on Hell. She was happy that the Lady had said she would go to Heaven. However, she was concerned about all those who would *not* go to Heaven, but to Hell. She stopped playing; she sat and prayed and meditated. This was *before* they had the vision of Hell. Lucia asked her once what was wrong.

"That Lady said that many souls go to Hell. What is Hell, then?"

Lucia answered,

"It's like a big deep pit of wild beasts, with an enormous fire in it - that's how my mother used to explain it to me -

---

[3]This prophecy by Our Lady was fulfilled on the nights of January 25 & 26, 1938, when a great light, which was attributed by science to an Aurora Borealis, was seen by most of the world.

and that's where people go who commit sins and don't confess them. They stay there and burn for ever!"

"And they never get out of there again?"

"No!"

"Not even after many many years?"

"No! Hell never ends!"

Jacinta had a problem coming to terms with the *forever* perspective of eternity. She would go for days, saying nothing and then all of a sudden, while they were playing, she would ask:

"But listen! Doesn't Hell end after many, many years then?"

Or she would ask:

"These people burning in Hell, don't they ever die? And don't they turn into ashes? And if people pray very much for sinners, won't our Lord get them out of there? And if they make sacrifices as well? Poor sinners! We have to pray and make many sacrifices for them!"

Then she would smile and say,

"How good that Lady is! She has already promised to take us to Heaven."

This was partly the cause for Jacinta's great sacrifices for the conversion of sinners. She believed and rightly so, that if they didn't sin, they wouldn't go to hell. If she gave up lunch, and gave her portion to the sheep, souls would be converted. If she gave up drinking water in the sweltering Portuguese afternoons, and gave her ration to the sheep, she would be helping a soul from going to Hell.

Some years after the death of Jacinta, actually in 1941, Lucia was asked by her bishop to write yet another account of the apparitions of Our Lady and to a great degree, her relationship with Jacinta and Francisco. One of the areas they wanted her to reflect on was why Jacinta took on this role of sacrificing so intensely, for the conversion of sinners. It had become a commitment for her, or so some thought.

Lucia explained it in many ways, all of which were true. But bottom line, the overpowering reason was: *She had seen a vision of Hell!* Our Lady had touched her little heart, and she would do anything to save sinners from Hell. She would give up her very life, if necessary, so that sinners would convert.

She would sit on a rock and ponder about Hell. Then she'd burst out,

"Oh Hell! Hell! How sorry I am for the souls who go to Hell. And the people down there, burning alive, like wood in the fire!"

Then, having conjured up that vision which was implanted in her brain and her heart, she would break into serious prayer.

"O my Jesus! Forgive us, save us from the fires of Hell. Lead all souls to Heaven, especially those who are most in need."

She would repeat the prayer for hours on end, on her knees, rocking like a mother rocks a baby. She was in ecstasy. She would come out of it long enough to look at Lucia or Francisco or both, and chide them,

"Francisco! Francisco! Are you praying with me? We must pray very much to save souls from Hell! So many go there! So many!"

Then at other times,

"Why doesn't Our Lady show Hell to sinners? If they saw it, they would not sin, so as to avoid going there! You must tell Our Lady to show Hell to all the people (those who went to the Cova da Iria for the apparitions). You'll see how they will be converted."[4]

She would ask Lucia,*"What are the sins people commit, for which they go to Hell?"*

---

[4]Jacinta told Lucia what to tell the Lady because she never spoke to the Lady. Only Lucia had any conversation with the Lady.

Lucia would answer: *"I don't know. Perhaps the sin of not going to Mass on Sunday, of stealing, of saying ugly words, of cursing and of swearing."*

Jacinta asked *"So for just one word then, people can go to Hell?"*

And Lucia answered *"Well, if it's a sin."*

Then Jacinta cried: *"It wouldn't be hard for them to keep quiet, and go to Mass. I'm so sorry for sinners! If only I could show them Hell!"*

Then she would think for a moment, and grab her cousin.

"I'm going to Heaven. But you are staying here. If Our Lady lets you, tell everybody what Hell is like, so that they won't commit any more sins and won't go to Hell."

When we wrote about the Apparitions of Our Lady in Fatima,[5] we glanced over the vision of Hell as many others had. There were too many other things: The Miracle of the Sun, the prophesy of World War II, the promise from Our Lady that *"in the end, my Immaculate Heart will triumph."* But in researching the vision and the effect it had on the children, in particular Jacinta, we realize that Our Lady was trying desperately to warn us, through these children, of the horrors that await those who break relationship with Jesus. Jacinta had to be projecting what the Lady feared for us. She became a sacrificial lamb, offering up a tortuously painful illness and death for the conversion of sinners.

My brothers and sisters, we tell you about this terror that the vision of Hell put into the heart of this little girl, so that you can have a small idea what Hell is like. And hopefully, as this touches your heart, you, like Jacinta will not stand by while our brothers and sisters are suckered into Hell. Remember, her panic was not because she feared Hell for herself. She knew she would be in the Kingdom. It was

---

[5]*"The Many Faces of Mary, a love story"* - Bob and Penny Lord

for us, those who have not seen Hell, who do not have a tiny concept of the torture of Hell. She was so concerned about us that she was willing to suffer and give up her life to save souls, so that they would not have to experience what she had seen with her own eyes.

It gives you pause to think. Hell is not a popular subject these days. We don't hear anything about Hell, especially from the pulpit. The truth, the teachings that have come down through the centuries that there is a devil and there is a Hell, has been replaced by *psychobabble* that there is no devil, just psychosis; there is no place called Hell, its a state of mind; this is all there is; there is no punishment for sin, there is no nothing. We've said somewhere else in this book that Satan's greatest accomplishment in the Twentieth Century would be for us to deny his very existence. And here we have some of our own priests, professors of theology in Catholic Universities, playing right into his hands, doing just that, denying his existence. Of course, it may be easier, on earth, taking that route, going with the flow, not making waves, afraid perhaps that their fragile canoe will capsize. We'll pray for their immortal souls. After all, there is a time when we all have to face the Lord; and they, having been given the *responsibility* for the guidance of our souls into Heaven, will have also serious *accountability* before His throne. Pray they not be lost. But most of all, pray that they not lead any of the Lord's little ones, you and us to Hell. Listen to the word of the Lord, as taught to us from the ancients right to our Pope John Paul II. Don't let Satan fool you; don't let him drag you down the primrose path to the pits of Hell. Listen to Jacinta and the other Mystics who have seen Hell. Take their advice. ***They've seen Hell!***

The Promise of Divine Mercy

Blessed Sr. Faustina's Visions of Divine Mercy

One of the greatest gifts the Catholic Church has been given in the Twentieth Century has been the messages given to us by Our Lord Jesus through Blessed Sr. Mary Faustina Kowalska, of Cracow, Poland.

The Messages of Divine Mercy, and the Devotion to Divine Mercy have given us strength to persevere in the battle, and courage to endure the struggles and sufferings of our lives. But one of the greatest gifts of the Messages given us by the Lord was that regarding the Feast of Divine Mercy. We quote from Sr. Faustina's diary:

"My daughter, tell the whole world about My inconceivable mercy. I desire that the Feast of Mercy be a refuge and shelter for all souls, and especially for poor sinners. On that day the very depths of My tender mercy are open. I pour out a whole ocean of Graces upon those souls who approach the fount of My mercy. The soul that will go to Confession and receive Holy Communion shall obtain complete forgiveness of sins and punishment. On that day all the Divine floodgates through which Grace flow are opened. Let no soul fear to draw near to Me, even though its sins be as scarlet. My mercy is so great that no mind, be it of man or of Angel, will be able to fathom it throughout all eternity. Everything that exists has come forth from the very depths of My most tender mercy. Every soul in its relation to Me will contemplate My love and mercy throughout eternity. The Feast of Mercy emerged from My very depths of tenderness. It is My desire that it be solemnly celebrated on the first Sunday after Easter. Mankind will not have peace until it turns to the Fount of My Mercy." (#699)

The Lord gave her this message towards the end of September, 1936. During the course of her lifetime, He repeated it to her *fourteen times* that we know of. From this we can believe without doubt that it was an extremely

Above:
Bl. Sister Faustina had a vision of Hell. *"I, by the order of God, have visited the abysses of Hell so that I might tell souls about it and testify to its existence. I cannot speak about it now, but I have received a command to leave it in writing. ... I noticed one thing; that most of the souls there are those that disbelieved that there is a Hell. ...How terribly souls suffer there."*

Above right:
The location at the Convent in Plock, Poland where our Lord appeared to Sr. Faustina.

Right:
Image of Divine Mercy

important devotion to the Lord. And it makes so much sense. Are we aware what the Lord was saying to us in this one passage about the Feast of Divine Mercy?

"The soul that will go to Confession and receive Holy Communion shall obtain complete forgiveness of sins and punishment."

"...all the Divine floodgates through which Grace flow are opened."

"Let no soul fear to draw near to Me, even though its sins be as scarlet."

"My mercy is so great that no mind, be it of man or of Angel, will be able to fathom it throughout all eternity."

These are some extremely powerful commitments from a faithful God to an unfaithful people. This statement is so compelling that the satanic attacks began almost immediately. Sr. Faustina felt the presence of Satan in her room. She had to carry her crucifix with her and make the Sign of the Cross until the presence left her.

Sr. Faustina has a Vision of Hell

A month later, Sr. Faustina went on an eight day retreat, during which she had a vision of Hell. She wrote about it in her Diary (#741):

"Today I was led by an Angel to the chasms of Hell. It is a place of great torture; how awesomely large and extensive it is! The kinds of tortures I saw: the *first torture* that constitutes Hell is the loss of God; the *second* is perpetual remorse of conscience; the *third* is that one's condition will never change; the *fourth* is the fire that will penetrate the soul without destroying it - a terrible suffering, as it is a purely spiritual fire, lit *by God's anger*; the *fifth torture* is a continual darkness and a terrible suffocating smell, and despite the darkness, the devils and the souls of the damned see each other and all the evil, both of others and their own; the *sixth torture* is the constant company of

Satan; the <u>*seventh torture*</u> is horrible despair, hatred of God, vile words, curses and blasphemies. These are the tortures suffered by all the damned together, but that is not the end of the sufferings. There are special tortures destined for particular souls. These are the torments of the senses. Each soul undergoes terrible and indescribable sufferings, related to the manner in which it has sinned. There are caverns and pits of torture where one form of agony differs from another. I would have died at the very sight of these tortures if the omnipotence of God had not supported me. Let the sinner know that he will be tortured throughout all eternity, in those senses which he made use of to sin. *I am writing this at the command of God, so that no soul may find an excuse by saying there is no Hell, or that nobody has ever been there, and so no one can say what it is like.*

"I, Sister Faustina, by the order of God, have visited the abysses of Hell so that I might tell souls about it and testify to its existence. I cannot speak about it now; but I have received a command from God to leave it in writing. The devils were full of hatred for me, but they had to obey me at the command of God. What I have written is but a pale shadow of the things I saw. *But I noticed one thing; that most of the souls there are those who disbelieved that there is a Hell.* When I came to, I could hardly recover from the fright. How terribly souls suffer there. Consequently, I pray even more fervently for the *conversion of sinners*. I incessantly plead God's Mercy upon them. O my Jesus, I would rather be in agony until the end of the world, amidst the greatest sufferings, than offend You by the least sin."

There are so many incidents and teachings in the life of Sr. Faustina which we would like to include in this book. We've tried to keep them down to the subject at hand, which is *Heaven, Hell and Purgatory*, but there is one visit from the Lord which we found so touching, we have to share it with

you here. Excuse us for getting off the track a smidgen. But
we think you'll agree it was worth veering off the course.

*"Jesus came to the main entrance today, under the guise of
a poor young man. This young man, emaciated, barefoot and
bareheaded, and with his clothes in tatters, was frozen because
the day was cold and rainy. He asked for something hot to eat.
So I went to the kitchen, but found nothing there for the poor.
But, after searching around for some time, I succeeded in
finding some soup, which I reheated and into which I crumbled
some bread, and I gave it to the poor young man, who ate it.
As I was taking the bowl from him, he gave me to know that He
was the Lord of Heaven and earth. When I saw Him as He
was, He vanished from my sight." (#1312)*

Family, we say we need help, and we do need help. The
world is all around us, trying to crush us, to destroy us. The
Lord holds His Hand out, the Hand of Divine Mercy, and
offers us tools to get through this pilgrimage on earth, and
prepare for the journey to Heaven. Take them; they're
yours. They've been brought to earth for you, for your
salvation. Don't pass Jesus by. *He's standing at the door; let
Him in!*

St. Maximilian Kolbe

Above:
**Statue of Our Lady of Mount Carmel
on Mount Carmel in the Holy Land**

St. Frances Cabrini

Left:
**St. Teresa of
Avila
and St. John
of the Cross,
Co-Founders
of the
Discalced
Carmelites**

The Miracles of the Scapular

One of the most powerful *Sacramentals* is the Brown Scapular. On July 16, 1251, Our Lady appeared to St. Simon Stock, accompanied by her Heavenly Army of Angels and made the following promise:

"Whoever dies wearing this Scapular shall not suffer eternal fire."

Now, it was not our Lady's intention that the Scapular should replace the living out of a holy and virtuous Christian life. Instead, she meant it to remind us of the life she led, one of *obedience* to the Will of the Father, *of humility, of fidelity*, a *willing vessel* bringing the Savior to us.

Then in 1332, Our Lady made a second promise called the Sabbatine Privilege (or Saturday Privilege) when she appeared to **Pope John XXII**:

"I, the Mother of Grace, shall descend the Saturday after their death, and whomsoever I shall find in Purgatory, I shall free."

The Pope declared, in his Bull *"Sacratissimo uti culmine"*, that the Blessed Virgin appeared to him and asked that the indulgences which Her Son had already granted in Heaven, be sanctioned by him as Vicar of Christ on earth and therefore conferred upon the Carmelites and all other wearers of the Scapular. These indulgences were:

(a) A *plenary indulgence*, at death for members of the Carmelite Order.

(b) A *partial indulgence*, remitting one third of the temporal punishment due to sin for the Confraternity members.

The Pope said that the Mother of God further told him that she would descend into Purgatory on the Saturday following their death and bring those enrolled in the Scapular up to Heaven. Of course, this was according to the following three conditions:

(1) The wearing of the Scapular

(2) Living a chaste life according to one's station in life. For example, a married couple would live a chaste and holy life in keeping with their Sacrament of Matrimony; whereas, the single person would choose to lead a chaste and holy life as a celibate (one leading a life of abstinence).

(3) The daily recitation of the Holy office of the Blessed Virgin Mary.

For those who could not recite the Holy Office of the Blessed Virgin Mary, they could instead fast Wednesdays and Fridays. *[Now, this was originally instituted for the pious Lay groups and Confraternities that were an off-shoot from the Carmelites. They would gather together, pray the Office and fast on Wednesdays and Fridays.]* Should the saying of the Office and fasting be impossible, a priest possessing the proper faculties could replace these conditions with the praying of the Holy Rosary.

Considering the great Graces received from the Sabbatine Privilege, the Carmelite Order has recommended that number (3) not be replaced by the recitation of anything less than seven each of the Our Father, the Hail Mary, and the Glory be to the Father, to the Son and to the Holy Spirit.

†

Pope John XXII ratified the Bull from his residence in Avignon.

†

Pope Gregory XIII, **Pope Clement VII**, and **Pope St. Pius V** all confirmed the Sabbatine Privilege in the Sixteenth Century.

†

In the Seventeenth Century, during the Roman Inquisition, **Pope Paul V** declared:

"The Carmelite Fathers may preach that those Christians who piously believe in the help which the souls who have departed from this life in charity, have worn

throughout their lives the Scapular, who have led a chaste life, have recited the Little Hours of the Blessed Virgin Mary (or if they cannot read, have observed the fast days of the Church), have abstained from meat on Wednesdays and Saturdays (except when Christmas falls on those days), may derive after death - especially on Saturday, the day consecrated to the Blessed Virgin by the Church, through the unceasing intercession of Mother Mary, her pious petitions, her merits, and her special protection."[1]

What is the Scapular and how did it begin

Our Blessed Mother made three promises to help us with our journey on earth: to protect us from danger, to help us to die peacefully, and to promptly aid us at the time of death. She is consistently interceding for us in life and death, to save us from the pits of Hell, and to bring us to Heaven. The promise of the Scapular, to those who wear it *worthily*, is that they will never suffer the pains of Hell, and with her motherly love will enable them to enter Heaven, as soon as the Lord in His omnipotence ordains it. The Scapular reminds us each day, that we are her children, under her mantle, and she will never allow us to stray from the Shepherd. When St. Simon Stock prayed for a sign that she was the Mother of Carmel, she pointed to his scapular and said: *"This shall be the sign; those who die wearing this shall not suffer eternal damnation."*

The wearing of the Scapular goes back as far as the time of St. Benedict in the Sixth Century, where the Scapular was a standard part of the habit worn by those in monastic orders. It consists of two pieces of cloth, tied at the shoulders that hang down covering the back and the breast. The fact that it hangs from the shoulders has a strong message, for Christ asks us to take up His Cross, the Cross

---

[1]cf book: Brown Scapular of Mount Carmel

He carried for us sinners, on His sinless shoulders. When we wear the Scapular we are saying yes to Jesus' words *of mercy:*

"Come to Me, all you who are weary and find life burdensome, and I will refresh you. Take My yoke upon your shoulders and learn from Me, for I am gentle of Heart. Your souls will find rest, for My yoke is sweet and My burden light."[2]

When the Laity (remaining in their own way of life), wanted to join the monastic communities, to pray with them and follow the different rules observed by the Order, they began to wear the abbreviated version of the Scapular. And that's how the Scapular that you and I wear was begun.

The Sixteenth Century was a time infamous in the history of Christ's Church, because a dissident priest, Martin Luther brought about a revolution which denied all the beautiful Treasures of the Church, including the Scapular. And so, many of our brothers and sisters in Christ who were once Catholic, do not know till today the gift of the Scapular, or any of the other life-giving Sacramentals, rungs on the ladder, which help us to ascend to Our Father in Heaven.

The Saints and the Scapular

St. Teresa of Avila[3] *"La Grande,"* reformer of the Carmelites, Doctor of the Church, and great Mystic, often described herself as a member of *"The Order of Mount Carmel, whose habit I am privileged to wear though I am not worthy of it."*

†

St. John of the Cross,[4] co-reformer with St. Teresa of Avila of the Carmelites, expanded the reform to include not only the Brides of Christ, but the male Carmelite brothers

---

[2]Matt 11:30

[3]You can read more about St. Teresa in Bob and Penny Lord's book: *"Saints and other Powerful Women in the Church."*

[4]For more on St. John of the Cross, read Bob and Penny Lord's book: *"Saints and other Powerful Men in the Church."*

and priests. Famous for his "*Dark Night of the Soul*" and "*Ascent of Mount Carmel,*" renowned as a poet, Doctor of the Church and respected as a great theologian, to us St. John is most special for his *obedience* (saying yes to Teresa, even when he really did not want to), his extraordinary *humility* (accepting unjustified imprisonment and beatings at the hands of his own fellow Carmelites, saying it was for his own good), and his great love for Mother Mary.

Our Lady chose to bear him up to Heaven, the day he died. St. John of the Cross died on *Saturday*, December 14, 1591. Believing deeply in The Sabbatine Privilege, nothing would have pleased St. John more, than dying on a Saturday.

†

St. Robert Bellarmine, S.J., Great Jesuit Cardinal and Doctor of the Church, teacher of St. Aloysius Gonzaga, defended the use of Our Lady's Scapular. He said:

"Anyone dying in Mary's family will receive from her, at the hour of death, either the Grace of perseverance in the state of Grace or the Grace of final contrition."

†

St. Peter Claver, S.J., was a Jesuit Missionary in Africa, with a ministry to the black slaves of Africa. When he could not stop them from being sold into slavery, he ministered to them in the only way he could, teaching them the basic tenets of the Catholic Church, how God the Father created them as well as those who were enslaving them, how His Son Jesus Christ died for them too; and because of Him, they were not slaves but became His brothers when they were baptized. He baptized over 300,000 into the Catholic Faith, investing each of the converts into the Scapular Society of Mount Carmel.

†

St. Claude de la Colombiere, S.J.,[5] confessor to Saint Margaret Mary Alacoque who, with her, had visions of Jesus and His most Sacred Heart, established the Confraternity of the Scapular in Paray-le-Monial, France. He wrote:

"There is no devotion which more assures our salvation than the Scapular. If Our Lady graciously responds to all who practice devotions in her honor, how much more will she do for those who wear her holy uniform."

†

St. Alphonsus de Liguori, founder of the Redemptorist Fathers, was a great exponent of Mother Mary. His book, *"The Glories of Mary"* has been read by countless thousands for the last two hundred years.

St. Alphonsus wore the Scapular. He ardently advocated the wearing of the Scapular. He not only preached on the Scapular, but asked all the other preachers of his Order to promote this Sacramental, as well. His preaching had such an impact in Southern Italy that, should you visit, you will find Our Blessed Mother is most revered under the title of *Our Lady of Mount Carmel.* Her Feast Day, which is still faithfully celebrated till today in this part of Italy, was brought over to the United States by immigrants like my grandparents; and those of us who grew up in Italian American neighborhoods still remember fondly, the *Festas* and the Processions and the push carts with sausage and peppers cooking, and all that was Italian and Catholic.

When they opened his grave, many years after his death, his body had decomposed, but his Scapular was (and still is) completely intact. His words were one of complete trust in that Mother whom Jesus left him and us at the foot of the Cross:

---

[5]More about this Saint in chapter on St. Margaret Mary Alacoque in *"Visionaries, Mystics and Stigmatists."*

"O my Mother, by the love which you bear to God, I beg you to help me at all times, but especially at the last moments of my life. Leave me not, I beg you, until you see me safe in Heaven."[6]

†

St. Vincent Pallotti, *Saint of the modern-day Lay apostle*, has become a favorite of ours because we are in the days of Lay apostles or Lay evangelists. We have always been called, as part of the body of Christ, to *evangelize*; we are required to do so by virtue of our Baptism. But today, beginning with Pope John XXIII up till our present Pope John Paul II, we have been mandated to go out and bring the Good News to the whole world that Jesus is alive and He is in our Church. So, brothers and sisters we have here a great Patron Saint who will intercede for us.

St. Vincent is the Founder of the Society of Catholic Apostolate. The writings of those two great Carmelite Saints, Teresa of Avila and John of the Cross so deeply affected him, he became a Third Order Carmelite.

He was granted the faculty to invest others in the Brown Scapular, and he not only did so, when giving retreats or missions, he commissioned the priests of his Order to do so. The Scapular became such an important part of his life that you can still see his Scapular in the Pallottine Generalate in Rome. Pope John XXIII whose dream was that all Christians return to the one true Church saw fit to canonize him during Vatican Council II, as *Patron Saint of Lay Apostles*.

†

St. Jean Marie Vianney, *The Curé of Ars,*[7] *Patron Saint of Parish Priests*, spent many hours in the confessional.

---

[6]cf paraphrased from book: Brown Scapular of Mount Carmel
[7]Read more about the Curé in this book and in *"Saints and other Powerful Men in the Church"* by Bob and Penny Lord

One of the gifts the Lord endowed him with was the reading of men's souls. One day, a woman came to him. She was about to enter a convent and wanted nothing to be unresolved between herself and the Lord; and so she confessed her sins. When she said she was finished, the Curé asked her if she did not remember the time she went to a dance and there was a very handsome young man who was dancing with everyone but would not have anything to do with her. He reminded her how envious she was of the other girls with whom he had danced. Now, the young woman knew that the Curé had not been at the dance and had no way of knowing about the incident. Lest she not recall the occasion, he described the young man adding *"He had something under his feet that looked like a blue flame."* With this, her mind was opened and she recollected the occurrence. The Curé said,

> *"Although you were hurt and jealous that the young man would not dance with you, the Lord and His Mother were protecting you with the <u>Scapular</u> you were wearing. The young man, in reality was a demon and danced only with those in serious sin. He could not dance with you, and was blocked from approaching you because the <u>Scapular</u> you were wearing kept you safe from him. The devil and his fallen angels fear the <u>Scapular</u>."[8]*

†

St. Conrad, *Saint of the Poor and Doorkeeper of the Shrine of Our Lady of Altotting.*[9]

There is a precious shrine in Bavaria, Germany, one of the oldest shrines to Our Lady in Europe dating back to the Fifth Century. So devoted were the princes of Germany, that they all desired, upon their deaths, their hearts to be

---

[8]cf Curé of Ars - Abbé Trochu - Tan Publications

[9]You can learn more about this shrine by watching the program *"Our Lady of Altotting"* on EWTN or by purchasing the video of the same title.

Left:
St. Conrad - known as the Saint of the Poor. He was the doorkeeper of the Shrine of Our Lady of Altotting, Germany. Before he would give bread to the poor, or pray over someone, he would bring them to his Mother, Our Lady of Altotting, imploring them to first pray to her for her intercession.

Right:
St. Claude Colombiere with St. Margaret Mary Alacoque. He wrote, *"There is no devotion which more assures our salvation than the Scapular. If Our Lady graciously responds to all who practice devotions in her honor, how much more will she do for those who wear her holy uniform."*

placed next to *Our Lady of Altotting*, and so, till today their hearts are entombed in silver urns surrounding the image of Our Lady in her chapel.

Our first encounter with St. Conrad was when, in January, 1993 we first visited *the Shrine of Our Lady of Altotting*. It was a combined trip to Germany, to give a retreat to the American Air Force stationed there and to make documentaries on Miracles of the Eucharist and Shrines of Our Most Blessed Mother. When we were videotaping, the custodian of the Shrine to Our Lady told us about St. Conrad, but time was short and we had a focus. Again, when the Lord wants us to do something, He might wait but He will have His Will, and we believe He wants you to know this Saint and a little more about the Catholics who come from Germany. So, when we began researching material for this book, who would appear but St. Conrad, a powerful Saint!

St. Conrad was a lay brother of the Capuchin Order. As doorkeeper, he became involved with the starving people of Altotting. There was little or nothing to eat. The little children came to the door of the Capuchin's convent and begged for a little food. Now, times were slim for the Capuchins as well, but it seemed the more St. Conrad gave to the poor, the more he had to give away. Miracles came about through the holy and humble doorkeeper - miraculous healings! One day, a mother brought her child to St. Conrad; the little boy's body was covered with ulcerated, festering sores; he was obviously very ill. St. Conrad touched the boy's head, and the lesions dropped off, leaving not even the smallest sign. Word spread and the needy kept coming, not only the poor but nobles and gentry from all parts of Germany. Before he would give bread to the poor, or pray for someone, he would bring them to his Mother, Our Lady of Altotting, imploring them to first pray to *her* for her intercession. They came and they prayed. But that was not all he did.

Even before he joined the Capuchins, he was invested in the Brown Scapular. So committed was he to spreading devotion to Mother Mary, and the wearing of the Scapular, he would, as doorkeeper, hand all the pilgrims visiting the Shrine, as well as the local faithful who came seeking help, a Scapular and asked them to wear it in honor of Our Lady. Hundreds of thousands came and were invested in the Scapular. Devotion to St. Conrad spread and people from all parts of Germany came to him and still pray for his intercession. *He was to wear the Scapular until the day he died.*

†

St. Francis Xavier Cabrini, *Saint of the Italian immigrants*, a naturalized citizen herself, became the first American Saint of the United States.

St. Francis Xavier Cabrini is better known in the United States, especially to those of us of an Italian Heritage, as *Mother Cabrini*. She was born, the evening before the Feast of Our Lady of Mt. Carmel, in the year 1850, just at that period when her countrymen would venture to a new world. Our Saint, too, would leave her native land, but unlike so many of her Italian brothers and sisters, she did not come looking for a better way of life, but to bring to her fellow immigrants *hope* in this new and strange world, often a new world of disappointments, a new world with a new and strange language, filled with new and unfamiliar customs, a Protestant and often prejudiced world. She was sent to feed their minds, their souls and their bodies.

She founded the *Missionary Sisters of the Sacred Heart of Jesus*. She wore the Scapular and turned trustingly to her Lady of Mount Carmel for help with this giant task ahead of her and her sisters. They set out to help the Italian immigrants to know and grow in this land of promise; and they, with the help of Our Lady, would do so well, these uneducated, often illiterate newcomers would become a people respected and a viable part of this melting pot we proudly call the United States of America.

†

St. Maxmilian Kolbe *is best known as a martyr*, but mostly he was a loyal son of Mary, a Knight of the Immaculata.[10]

On August 14, 1941, in the midst of death and destruction, and man's inhumanity to man, a light shone in the darkness, a man gave his life for another, and the world will never be the same. That man was Father Maxmilian Kolbe!

Even if he had not offered his life, that sick day in the prison camp of Auschwitz, he would have been declared a Saint. Our Lady appeared to him when he was a child, and held up two crowns for him to choose from, one white (for purity) and one red (for martyrdom); *he chose both!* His mother shared at his beatification that she knew then that he would die a martyr.

His life was one of faithful service to his Lord and his Immaculata. He founded the *Militia of the Immaculata*, and as a Conventual he wore the Scapular and encouraged all his brothers to do the same. Maxmilian Kolbe had as many as 800 friars in his congregation. There is not enough space here to write of the life of this great Saint,[11] but for this segment, we ask you to meditate on: *What do you think gave this dear priest the strength to die as a martyr for Mother Church?* All we know is, he was devoted to Our Lady, he stopped at the Shrine of Our Lady of Loreto and he wore

---

[10]as he fondly called her, naming his congregation and his magazine after her.

[11]for more on St. Maxmilian Kolbe, read Bob and Penny Lord's books: *"Saints and other Powerful Men in the Church"* and *"Martyrs, They died for Christ"*

the Scapular. When they came for his body, there was a serene smile on his face and an aura about him. It was the vigil of the *Feast Day of the Assumption of Our Lady into Heaven*! Had Our Lady come for him? What do you think?

Popes who have had a special devotion to the Scapular

Pope Benedict XIV in his treatise on the *"Feasts of Our Lord Jesus Christ and the Blessed Virgin Mary"* wrote of the Scapular:

"How much good will is required (to obtain) the promise of the Scapular? Eternity alone will answer the question, for we should be careful not to place limits on the mercy of her who is Refuge of sinners[12] and the Mother of Mercy."

Pope Benedict XV spoke to his sons, future priests of our beloved Church; it was the Feast of Our Lady of Mount Carmel. He spoke to these young seminarians of Rome and gave them advice they would carry in their hearts the rest of their lives, counsel that would protect them as they walked *their* Way of the Cross as victim-priests with Our Lord, *the Victim-Priest*. He said:

"Let all of you have a common language and a common armor: the language - the sentences of the Gospel, the common armor - that of the Scapular of the Virgin of Carmel which you ought to wear and which enjoys the singular privilege and protection after death."[13]

St. Pope Pius X, *Defender of the Faith and Advocate of the Eucharist.* It is only *"right and just,"* as we say during Holy Mass that our Saint Pope Pius X would have a devotion to Mother Mary and the Scapular. He was Pope at the beginning of the Twentieth Century, a turbulent time in the Church, when it was feared that *Modernism* would take over. He fought valiantly and put down this deadly heresy for all

---

[12]one of her titles
[13]cf from book: Brown Scapular of Mount Carmel

time (or so he had hoped). In addition, the Holy Spirit inspired him to allow frequent reception of Holy Communion, knowing that we would need the strength of the Eucharist to withstand the new/old onslaughts of the rest of the Twentieth Century.[14]

St. Pope Pius X was a Carmelite Tertiary and as such wore his Scapular with much devotion. When missionaries from tropical countries asked special dispensation to wear a Scapular medal in place of the cloth Scapular, he granted their request with the stipulation that the Medal have the *Sacred Heart of Jesus* on one side and *Our Lady of Carmel* on the other. He also made the following provision:

"We grant the use of the Scapular Medal, but we prefer that the cloth Scapular be used."[15]

Through St. Pope Pius X the miraculous image of Our Lady of Carmel, which is still venerated at the *Pallottine Fathers' Church of Our Lady of Mount Carmel*, received the special privilege of a *"solemn papal coronation."*[16] She and the Baby Jesus in her arms were crowned on July 10, 1904. The crowns were blessed by the Pope, and he donated a precious emerald of his own to adorn the crowns. To our knowledge, this image of *Our Lady of Mount Carmel* is the only one in America that has received a solemn papal crowning. For those of you who live in New York or are planning to visit, you can find her in the *Pallottine Fathers' Church of Our Lady of Mount Carmel* on First and Pleasant Avenues, New York City.

Other images in North America that have had the blessing of a papal crowning are: *Our Lady of Guadalupe* in

---

[14]For more on the heresies that attacked our Church, and the battles fought and won, right up till today, read Bob and Penny Lord's important book: *"Scandal of the Cross and Its Triumph"*

[15]from book: Brown Scapular of Mount Carmel

[16]from book: Brown Scapular of Mount Carmel

Mexico City, *Our Lady of Cap-de-la-Madeleine* in Canada, and *Our Lady of Prompt Succor* in New Orleans, Louisiana.

Pope Pius XI: *Prophet and peacemaker, his dream was to unite the world under God.*

He reigned in the horrendous time following World War I and into the beginnings of another World War (II), seeing his people suffer once again, now with Fascism under Mussolini and Nazism at the hands of the mad Hitler. He devoted seventeen years trying to achieve peace in the post World War I era, only to see war begin again at the end of his life, with the rising of new monsters. He tried to warn his flock that men separated from God could not bring them anything but an alienation from God, and without God there could be no lasting peace but only tyranny.

His greatest focus was to unite all humanity under the One True King, Jesus Christ. He prophesied with this because we know that either the world will follow the One *True Master* or the fallen imitator, the devil. In the Last Days, the line will be *clearly* drawn, and we will have to choose one or the other. Had the Holy Spirit, Who guides all our Popes, given him this insight, in the beginning of the Twentieth Century, into what we may be looking at very seriously, at the end of this century?

For the life of me, I cannot fathom how the whole world cannot see there is no longer (not that there ever was) a wide road that we can travel to our *Final Home*. If we do not choose the narrow path to Heaven, you can be sure we will be guided off our path to a side road leading to Purgatory or an unmarked detour to Hell.

This Pope, in his encyclical on Christian education, "*Divini illius magistri,*" stressed emphatically the need of a strict Christian education, clearly making the distinction between the rights of the state, the Church and the family to determine the education of children!

With his marriage encyclical, *"Casti connubii,"* he cautions the children of God against stop-gap marriages, *"If it doesn't work out, that's what erasers on pencils are for"* kind of marriages, insisting that marriage is a *Sacrament*; and as such has no room for any arrangement other than a lifetime covenant between two people with God.

When he was forced to sign the Lateran Treaties, which took away most of the Papal property in Italy, it almost broke his heart.

Pope Pius XI kept his eyes on Jesus and His Mother Mary. He held on to, and spoke often of, his belief that *"the protection of Mother Mary will protect us from eternal death."*

Pope Pius XII, *Dry Martyr of World War II*

Maligned and misunderstood, he sold Vatican treasures to ransom Jews from the Nazis in an attempt to keep them from going to Concentration Camps and ultimately to the Gas Chamber. He walked the tightrope between trying to protect his flock and save the helpless children of God who were being mercilessly slaughtered. And since he received no praise and appreciation in this world, we know that he received a golden crown, ornamented with the blood red rubies of Christ's Five Wounds in Heaven.

He spoke of Mother Mary and the Scapular:

"There is no one who is not aware how greatly a love for the Blessed Virgin Mother of God contributes to the enlivening of the Catholic Faith....In the first rank of the most favored of these devotions, that of the Holy Carmelite Scapular must be placed.

"Therefore it has pleased Us greatly to learn of the decision of our Carmelite Brethren...to take all pains to pay homage to the Blessed Virgin Mary in as solemn a

manner as possible on the occasion of the 700th centenary[17] of the institution of the Scapular."

The Pope spoke of the Scapular as the *"manner of achieving safely"* our eternal salvation. He then added:

"For the Holy Scapular, which may be called the Habit or Garment of Mary, is a sign and a pledge of protection of the Mother of God."

In the same letter, the Pope added something which is an essential teaching and admonition to all who would use the Scapular incorrectly or imprudently:

"But not for this reason, however, may they who wear the Scapular think that they can gain eternal salvation while remaining sinful and negligent of spirit, for the Apostle warns us: 'In fear and trembling shall you work out your salvation.'"

He also said of the Scapular:

"Finally, may it be to them a sign of their consecration to the Most Sacred Heart of the Immaculate Virgin which in recent times, we have so strongly recommended."

In some of our stories of the Scapular, we have told you of occurrences that you can accept or refuse to believe ever happened. They are not teachings of the Church. But when the Church teaches, and with the Popes that is the authority of the Church, it is no longer private revelations. Even with St. Simon Stock it is not mandatory that you believe. The only caution is be sure you are not guilty of pride, placing yourself above a 700 year tradition.

Pope Paul VI, *implementer of Vatican Council II and Saint of the family with his encyclical Humanae vitae*

So much has been said, pro and con, about Vatican Council II. The big problem was that some misused and misquoted the Council with the focus of reducing devotion

---

[17]referring to the 700 year anniversary of the appearance of Mother Mary to St. Simon Stock

to Mother Mary, discouraging the praying of the Rosary, and abolishing the wearing of the Scapular; and yet the great implementer of the Council had this to say about the Rosary and the Scapular, *during Vatican Council II*:

*"You will make known Our will and Our exhortations which We base upon the Dogmatic Constitution **Lumen Gentium**, of the Ecumenical Council Vatican II, which is in complete conformity with Our thought and indeed upon which Our thought is based:*

"'That one ever hold in great esteem the practices and exercises of the devotion to the most Blessed Virgin which have been recommended for centuries by the teaching authority of the Church.' (Lumen Gentium 67)

"And among them We judge well to recall especially the Marian Rosary and the religious use of the Scapular of Mount Carmel."

Stories about the Scapular

I guess that there are many stories that can be told about the Scapular. One that touched our hearts deeply was concerning a dear friend who died of cancer. He had been born Anglican and would tease us that he was more Catholic than we were. By the time this very healthy, alive man contracted cancer of the lungs and was reduced to a skeleton, he had joined some cult. But he had always been a good friend and a good man. We would go to visit him every night in the Veteran's Hospital. At first, we asked him if he would like to be blessed with some holy water from Lourdes. He said *Yes*. We anointed him and left the bottle in the shape of our Lady of Lourdes on his bedside table. When we asked him if he would like to speak to a priest, he said no! One of our little members of the Junior Legion of Mary made him a rosary of all different color beads she had accumulated and a favorite crucifix her grandmother had given her.

One night, we took off one of our Scapulars. Penny always bullied him, and this was no time for exceptions. She told him he was to wear this Scapular and under no circumstances remove it. Every night after work, when we would visit him, the Scapular was off: *He would insist he did not want it to get wet, when they gave him a sponge bath; it itched him; it choked him; he would go on and on.* Eddie's pain was getting really bad. When he was in excruciating pain, he would try to joke by saying a Jewish expression (although he was not Jewish) which sounded like - "*Oiy vay!*" He began to lapse in and out of consciousness. We began to say the prayers for the dying over Eddie each night; it seemed to give him some peace.

One night before leaving for home, we turned to the nurses and said: "*We know that Eddie is not Catholic but we are and we want him to wear that Scapular at all times.* A hispanic nurse said, "*I used to be Catholic. I understand the importance of the Scapular. I'll see to it.*" The night Eddie died we missed being with him by a couple of minutes, but the nurse said that the statue of Our Lady of Lourdes was turned facing him, the rosary was in his hands and he was wearing the Scapular. Now, there is not one Mass that we do not pray for Eddie's soul, but we have a feeling that God was merciful to Eddie. Anyway, if he does not need our prayers to be released from Purgatory, we always place them into the loving hands of Mother Mary to use for whom she sees fit, those who need them most.

†

We loved teaching the second graders all about Jesus present in the Blessed Sacrament in preparation for First Holy Communion. Monsignor Tom, being a Franciscan and a mission priest,[18] could and did invest them into the Society of the Scapular. To prepare them, we told them of the many

---

[18]California is considered *Mission Country*

miracles connected with the wearing of the Scapular. We often thought of quitting teaching religion as we felt we were not getting to them, but then they would surprise us.

Well, the big day was here and the children were standing on line with their parents, to receive First Holy Communion. Little Johnny's mother called us over and said: *"I'd like to tell you what Johnny did the other day."* She continued, *"Johnny went up to this big bully in the school yard and told him to punch him hard on his chest."* Now, Johnny was anything but built strongly. We held our breaths, as she went on. "Johnny said: *'He hit me hard right here and it did not hurt me. I was wearing my Scapular.'"* Was it his faith that kept him from getting seriously hurt? Was it his wearing of the Scapular? All we know is that happened to a little boy named Johnny.

†

Another personal experience happened to us in a little town in Mississippi. We rented an office there. The day we were negotiating with the owner, she asked if we could sign the papers that day, as she was going into the hospital the next day. When we asked her what the problem was, she said she was going to have a biopsy taken of her breast, as there was a strong indication there might be a malignancy. Now, that is something that makes a woman tremble. We asked her if we could all pray together. We did and then Penny took off her Scapular and said, *"I do not expect you to believe but we do, and I would be so pleased if you would wear my Scapular tomorrow when you go in for your exploratory surgery."* Penny had a relic of St. Peregrine attached to it.

Our landlord said that she believed that God had sent us that day, as she had been so frightened and suddenly she was not afraid. We asked her to call us the next day. Her mother called, and said that her daughter was resting, but she wanted us to be the first to know that *they found nothing!* They took a biopsy to be sure, and days later the news was the same: she was clean, no sign of cancer! Our lease was not for a long term, but we both cried when we left. Penny did not have the heart to ask her to return the Scapular and the landlord did not offer it. By the way, the lady is a strong Baptist. At least, she was. Now, who knows!

Miracles connected with the wearing of the Scapular

There are testimonies upon testimonies of miracles that came to pass through the wearing of the Scapular.

Do you remember when the priest enrolled you in the Scapular, how he pronounced the following words:

"Receive this blessed Scapular and ask the most Holy Virgin that, by her merits, it may be worn with no stain of sin and may protect you from all harm and bring you into everlasting life."

Our Lady has been living up to her promise to us, ever since she gave the Scapular to **St. Simon Stock**. One day, Our Lady had the opportunity of fulfilling her promise, when one of her priests was called to the bedside of a dying man. The man had been away from the Sacraments for many years. He had not called for the priest; for a matter of fact, he did not want anything to do with him or God. The priest asked the sick man to look at the Scapular he was holding in his hand, and then he added: *"Will you agree to wear it? You do not need to believe in it."* Surprisingly, he allowed the priest to place the Scapular around his neck. Scarcely had an hour passed when he asked to confess his sins; he made his peace with God and then died. Does that surprise you? Is not Mary our perfect *Mother*, left to us at the foot of the Cross of Redemption, together with our Lord, imploring His Father to forgive us? She did not stop interceding at Cana,[19] but has continued to help her children. All we have to do is call upon her.

†

---

[19]John 2:1-11

The very day that St. Simon Stock received the Scapular, an opportunity presented itself to use the Scapular. A lord summoned him to come quickly; his brother was dying. As he entered the house, he could smell the enemy of fear. The man struggling on the bed was frightened, no, almost petrified of dying. I remember my mother telling me about people fighting so hard, they had to be held down for fear of hurting themselves. It was plain to see that the lord's brother was in this type of anguish. St. Simon placed his Scapular over the man; he stopped struggling; he let out a deep sigh and died.

That night, the dead man appeared to his brother and told him that he had been *saved* through the intercession of most Blessed Mother Mary and *protected* by the Scapular of the priest[20] who had ministered to him.

†

God works in mysterious ways to make His Will known. There was a large ship out in the middle of the ocean. The sea suddenly got very rough and the ship was being threatened by huge waves whipping across her bow, threatening to capsize her. The sailors were fighting to stand on the deck, no less try to keep her from capsizing.

There was a Protestant minister aboard with his wife and children. Hearing the blast of the siren warning the ship of danger, and feeling the ship pitch dangerously, they fought their way up to the top deck. The end looked eminent; they began to pray and beg the Lord to have pity on them.

Suddenly, one of the sailors opened his shirt and ripped off his Scapular. Making the Sign of the Cross over the waves, he then threw the Scapular into the sea. The turbulent gales quieted, the menacing wind became a peaceful breeze. But that was not till the next and last wave

---

[20]St. Simon Stock

shot the Scapular back onto the ship's deck and came to rest at the sailor's feet.

The minister and his family, witnessing the power of the Scapular, asked the young sailor about the Scapular. He not only told them about the promises of Mother Mary to those who wear the Scapular, he told them about Jesus' Mother and how available she was to all her children in need. The minister and his family said that when they return home, they were going to take classes with the idea of converting to the Catholic Faith. They wanted some of the same protection the sailor had received. Sound impossible? Can God not do great things when we place our faith in Him!

†

This is a favorite of ours, a story much like the one we shared about one of our young students - How the Scapular protects those who wear it . A priest was on Pilgrimage, and stopped at Einsiedeln,[21] Switzerland. He was on his way to celebrate Holy Mass when he remembered that he had forgotten his Scapular. Not wanting to be without this armor, he rushed back to his room to put it on.

Now, this happened before Vatican Council II when our priests faced the tabernacle and had their backs to the people. Our priest was beginning the Liturgy of the Eucharist when suddenly, a crazed man ran up to the altar and shot the priest in the back, point-blank. Everyone gasped! But wait, the priest continued the Mass! They had to have been mistaken; he couldn't have been shot. But when the priest went into the sacristy and removed his vestments, the custodian of the Shrine spotted the bullet. It had become lodged in the Scapular!

†

Our next story brings us to Germany in May, 1957. A fire broke out in the town of Westboden, Germany. The fire

---

[21] We have visited this beautiful shrine.

spread quickly, affecting a row of homes nestled against each other.   As the fire approached a two-family house, the tenants, being Catholic and very pious, took their Scapular and attached it to the front door of their home.

The fire whipped around the house; sparks flew; the wind fanned the fire, threatening to destroy the little dwelling.   It took less than five hours for the devastating flames to destroy twenty-two homes; leaving nothing, homes became piles of ashes and twisted belongings. All the homes in that area were completely destroyed, all but *one*!   The house with the Scapular was untouched, the Armor of Mary protecting it from all harm.   Word spread and hundreds of people came to see the miracle that had come to pass through Our Lady's intercession.   As we said before, when we honor Our Lady, by wearing her Scapular, her Son responds and the impossible becomes the miraculous.

†

"Come back to Me with all your heart....Long have I waited for your coming home to Me and living deeply our new life."[22]   I remember reading that *"the evil that men do lives long after them."*   When a Defender of the Faith, King Henry VIII, turned against the Faith he had so staunchly pledged to defend, the effect, like a tidal wave, covered the face of what was once Catholic Europe and most especially England.   As heretics tried to wipe off the face of the earth, all that bound the faithful to the Chair of Peter, many relics were desecrated or destroyed and those which could be saved, hidden.   Long had the Lord waited for the return of the Relics of the Saints,[23] and in 1951, the Relics of St. Simon Stock came home to England.

The miracle we want to share with you took place in the ancient home of St. Simon Stock.   As soon as word got out

---

[22]cf Hosea
[23]some of the greatest Relics destroyed, had been in England

that the Relics of St. Simon Stock[24] had returned to his home, pilgrims began to come. Thousands of devotees of Mary and the Scapular came to venerate the Scapular left to St. Simon Stock by Mother Mary. A family whose little boy had Leukemia, came in faith, hoping for a miracle. Their son Peter was very seriously ill, the illness having escalated to a critical stage. Little Peter's legs and arms were covered with abscesses and gaping lesions. This was the family's last hope. They had been told he only had a few days to live.

They knelt and prayed before the Relic for Our Lady's intercession, as a Mother who had lost a Son, and then returned home. That evening, the mother prepared to bathe her little boy when she saw that *all* the sores had vanished; there was not a sign of the cancer's dirty work. They brought the child to the doctor the next day. He confirmed that there was not a sign of Leukemia. Like the mother, in Holy Scripture, who pleaded with Jesus to bring her son back to life, this mother's son, too, had been miraculously snatched from death; he was completely cured!

†

Our next story takes place in the Holy Land. The Holy Land - a place of sin and salvation! The dear Lord cried over Jerusalem. Some say that He was prophesying the destruction by the Romans, of this holy city which would happen thirty-seven years after His death. And we do not doubt that this is probably true; but we have to believe He is still crying over the desecration of this Land made holy by His Birth, Death and Resurrection. From the very beginning, with the Fall of Adam and Eve, the people of God have been in turmoil, the Land made holy - a battleground between cousins, all descendants from Father Abraham.

---

[24]His Scapular

The year is 1944, and a Carmelite Missionary to the Holy Land was summoned to give Last Rites to a prisoner in an internment camp. The priest's driver had to leave him four miles from the camp, as he feared the bus would not make it across the roads, made dangerously muddy by the ongoing downpour of rain. The priest began to walk. But after two miles, the mud became too deep. He began to sink deeper and deeper into the sludge. He began sliding. He tried to get a firm footing and he slipped! He fell and began to sink into the muddy pool. He knew this was the end! All alone in this deserted spot, he turned to His Mother Mary and the promise of the Scapular. He looked down at his habit. Mother Mary had made a promise on Mount Carmel. She would never break her promise. He turned and faced toward Mount Carmel. He could see over the horizon, the mountain where Elijah foiled the followers of Baal, and where the original hermits started devotion to Our Lady. The priest cried out to his Mother: *"Holy Mother of Carmel, help me! Save me!"*

It brings tears to our eyes how loving a Mother our Mother Mary is, how ready she is to help us in time of need! The next thing he knew, he was on dry, solid ground as if transported by the Angels. The priest said he knew that it was Mother Mary, through her Brown Scapular, who saved him. He had lost his shoes in the mud, but in spite of this he walked the rest of the way. When he spoke to the dying prisoner, of Heaven and that Mother who was waiting to greet him, you know that the priest spoke with even more authority. He could speak with the memory of the miracle that had just come about in his own life. That prisoner needed to know that we are in the days of hope and miracles, that there is more than this world, that he was not alone, his Heavenly Mother was waiting to introduce him to her Son.

†

The Scapular is not a holy rabbit's foot, and those who would use it as such will have an unpleasant surprise. There was a woman who had gone astray, and rather than convert and change her life, she bragged that she did not have to worry; at the moment of death, Mother Mary would insure she enter Heaven, as she would be wearing the Scapular.

The woman became critically ill. She was about to die. Suddenly, her Scapular began to burn her. She screamed *"Take if off; I'm burning to death."* After they removed the Scapular, she died. She had forgotten the conditions of wearing the Scapular, one of which was living a chaste life.

†

Then there is the powerful story of *conversion*, through the Scapular, of an Air Force officer. He had been away from the Church and the Sacraments for many years. One day, the priest on the base gave him a Scapular to wear. As he was probably going to be transferred to a war zone, he accepted. Then, after several days, he began to notice a change in his life. He began to go to Mass on Sundays, and then *Daily Mass.* He went to confession. He began to receive Holy Communion daily. He changed his reading material, delving more and more into the Word of God instead of the word of man. He went off by himself and prayed, talking to this God he had gotten to know as if for the first time. He marveled at how close he felt to Jesus. Of course! Who knows the *Son* better than the *Mother*, and did she not bring him back to her Son and to His Church! Needless to say, in a society which prides itself for bravery and cool heads, the officer unashamedly credited his conversion to Mother Mary through her Scapular.

†

We want to close with a quote from **St. Alphonsus Liguori**. For those who have ears, hear what this powerful Doctor of the Church has to say:

"Modern heretics make a mockery of wearing the Scapular. They decry it as so much trifling nonsense."

Doctor of the Church, he said this in the *Eighteenth Century.* Nothing changes much, does it? Satan has been doing all in his demonic power to rob us of the holy weapons and armor we have been given to help us make the often arduous journey to eternity. He has been busy using, very often, unsuspecting foils, to try to destroy our belief in the Sacraments and the Sacramentals.[25] Always in the name of enlightenment, not caring (or perhaps forgetting) that the Popes have approved Sacramentals, and that this is part of the accepted teaching of the Church, over the centuries they have led many astray.

†

Vatican Council II stated in reference to Sacramentals:
"Holy Mother Church has, moreover instituted Sacramentals. These are sacred signs which bear a resemblance to the Sacraments; they signify effects, particularly of a spiritual kind, which are obtained through the Church's intercession. By them men are disposed to receive the chief effect of the Sacraments, and various occasions in life are rendered holy."[26]

†

When we are writing our books, it seems that all hell breaks loose. We later find out why the enemy works so hard at trying to prevent their completion. I think that never have we known more attacks than those we have suffered during the writing of this book. Why?

Just as I was meditating on this and quite frankly complaining to the Lord, I came across the story of **Venerable Francis Xpes** who had the following encounter with the devil himself, and it helped me to better understand.

---

[25]The Scapular, Holy Water, the Sign of the Cross, vestments, candles, rosaries and etc.

[26]Catholic Encyclopedia by Broderick

This one day, Venerable Francis was about to go on his appointed tasks when his Scapular fell off him. Seeing it on the floor, he quickly went to retrieve it. The devil attacked him ranting: *"Take it off! Take off the habit which snatches so many souls from us."*

Venerable Francis quickly put on his Scapular. To the devil's consternation, Venerable Francis forced the *"evil one"* to admit that the three things he and his band of fallen angels fear most are: *The Holy Name of Jesus, the Holy Name of Mary, and the Holy Scapular of Carmel.*

†

What are God and His Mother trying to say to us? Are They not reaching out to us, to tell us that They are with us, and the powers of Hell will not touch us, if we take advantage of the Sacraments and the Sacramentals. Believe, and believing, and living that belief, we will be on the right road to eternal life and joy with Our Heavenly Family.

We love you.

The Dispute on the Blessed Sacrament
from the Raphael Stanzas - Vatican Collection

The battle rages on!

If we deny the gift of *Purgatory*, we open the doors to despair, we sin against the Holy Spirit and we allow ourselves to be trapped in a hopeless situation. Eternity consists of *Heaven, Hell and Purgatory*. If we remove *Purgatory* from the equation, all we have left is *Heaven* and *Hell*; and since we all agree that we are sinners, and none of us are worthy of Heaven, then all that is left is *Hell*. With Purgatory out of the equation, we are denying the mercy and love of our compassionate God; we're hopeless and helpless, and we fall into the hands of Satan and his cohorts. This is why Purgatory has been under attack, argued, denied and disavowed from the earliest days of our Church.

This travesty against the innocent lambs of God started centuries before the priest *Luther* betrayed his vows to his Church, to his priestly community and to his Sacrament of Holy Orders. It began with the Gnostics of the *first* centuries who claimed that the soul is purified on earth by going through degrees of purging *solely* before departing this world. In this way, they believed the soul would release itself from what they called *"the dominion of sensualism,"* what they termed, the domineering tentacles of the flesh on earth, the subhuman nature to which we are all subjected.

Part of the lie, these apostates espoused was that when one went through the earthly purging of the body, the soul became free from the body, and the soul returned to God on earth, with the full awareness of God, while everyone else was engulfed in *eternal* darkness. The apostasy they were selling was that under this new awareness, the soul would see and know the Lord *on earth*, as (we will) when we are in the Presence of God *in Heaven*, experiencing the Beatific Vision. It is so ridiculous, we often wonder how anyone could have bought into this strange philosophy. How can some have Heaven in the same place (earth) where the impure dwell in the darkness of Hell? *That was their teaching!* We believe and know that in Heaven, only the pure may enter; there you will find only light, the Light Who is God!

As this sick heresy denied most, if not all of that which Our Lord Jesus left us through the Apostles, it had no problem discarding the Dogma of Purgatory, that which was believed by the Jews before us.[1] With these heretics we see, back to the very beginning of the Church, the enemies of God claiming that man can be a god. [Sounds like the new/old heretics of today who are telling us that the concept of *"we can be gods"* is *new*. However this story from the *"father of lies"* is as old as Lucifer in the Garden of Eden.[2]]

These heresies were condemned, only to have them resurface with a new name but the same old lie. In the fourth century, a follower of Arius and Arianism, whose name was Aerius, condemned the Dogma of Purgatory as immoral. He twisted the teaching of Purgatory to mean that man could commit all sorts of sins and with money buy his way into Heaven, through others' good works and prayers. They had to be ignorant of the Church's teachings about the requirement to have *true remorse and a firm purpose of amendment* for our sins and the sincere promise to sin no more, in order to be forgiven. Without forgiveness, the next stop is Hell, not Purgatory; and no money, no prayers, no good works can release us from this land of eternal darkness and misery.

The attack on Purgatory in the Sixteenth Century

Down through the centuries, one enemy after another, preceding and including Luther, and after Luther, have tried and continue to try to destroy the fabric of what makes up the Church. Luther never told the people they were no longer Catholic and at one point, he said he had tried to do

---

[1]IIMachabees 12:39-46
[2]Genesis 3:1-7

away with one Pope only to find he had created one hundred popes. And so, he had failed! But the enemy of God never sleeps, so up from the mire of Luther came one even worse, Calvin!

One of the most vicious *"reformers"* and instigators of the Sixteenth Century holocaust, Calvin rejected the teaching on Purgatory, though he admitted that it had been a widely-held belief among Christians from the very beginning. The harm done by such as Calvin has been perpetuated for four centuries, causing our brothers and sisters in Christ to be deprived of the consolation of God's Mercy through Purgatory, even though Protestants have admitted that the concepts of purification after death and the custom of praying for the dead were scriptural and universal in the Church for fifteen hundred years.

Venerable Catherine Emmerich said: Among the most heartbreaking visions she had of Purgatory, were those of the Poor Souls who linger and wither more than others, because they have no one to pray for them. She further said that it was revealed to her that Protestants, who have had a sincere and heartfelt remorse for their sins, but have not made restitution for their offenses against God, will have to spend time in Purgatory.[3] They will have the benefit of God's Mercy in Purgatory whether they believe in it or not.

We see Purgatory confirmed by the graffiti in the catacombs. A number of these markings can be seen on tombs of such Saints as St. Peter and St. Paul, St. Priscilla and St. Domitilla, dating back to the First Century, in the various Catacombs of Rome.

You can go as far back as the Council of Carthage[4] which recommended praying for the dead.

---

[3] cf paraphrase of Catherine's visions
[4] Third through Fifth Centuries

Left:
A Suffering Poor Soul
St. Thomas Aquinas wrote,
"The same fire that punishes
the damned in Hell,
chastises the Suffering Souls
in Purgatory; and if you
were to take the greatest pain
we can suffer on earth, it
would not compare to the
smallest pain we will suffer
in Purgatory."

Right:
St. Nicholas of Tolentino
prayed day and night for
the Poor Souls in
Purgatory, sometimes as
much as six to eight
hours a night. It became
one of the greatest goals
of his vocation, to help as
many souls be released
from Purgatory as he
possible could.

Therefore, the belief in Purgatory is affirmed by the Early Church Fathers, inscribed on the tombs in the catacombs and made Dogma by the decrees of the different councils, down through the history of the Church. There is a warning to those who would deny this truth and lead others to do so:

"By rejecting prayer for the dead and the doctrine of temporal punishment of sin, they disrupt one of the most sacred bonds with which faith has encircled mankind, that is the Communion of Saints."[5]

How men could, after so much authentication and fifteen centuries of ongoing tradition, justify robbing the faithful of their due heritage is an abomination that has to cry out to Heaven.

The Church Militant (those who are still alive), *the Church Suffering* (Poor Souls in Purgatory), the *Church Triumphant* (those who are in Heaven) make up the *Mystical Body of Christ* who has for its Head - *Our Lord Jesus Christ*. Therefore, when you attack any part of the Body, you attack the entire body, you attack the Head, and you attack Jesus Christ Himself.

As we know that there are no dead atheists, because when they die, they *know* there is a God; we believe that there are no dead Protestants because when they die, they will know the whole truth and be one with the Truth.

The Saints speak out

There have always been those who have put themselves above the traditions and teachings of the Church and, bitten by the viper of *Pride*, have dared to deny this Dogma of Consolation, the ancient belief of our Judeo-Christian heritage in Purgatory. Sadly, it seems that bad history repeats itself, man making the same mistakes over and over

---

[5] from book: *"Charity for the Suffering Souls"* by Fr. John A. Nageleisen

again, falling prey to the enemy of God. To combat these elements, whose goal is to *destroy* the Church, the Lord raises up powerful men and women to *defend* the Church.

The great Spanish soldier who turned his fire and bravery towards the defense of the Church and the successors of Peter, the Popes, **St. Ignatius of Loyola** said that those arrogant men who put on an air of elitism, an air of all-knowing superiority, and with this convincing deception, challenge and in their challenge, lead many astray, are *"like the fallen angels."* For as they (the angels) were brought low because of their pride and damned because of their failure to be faithful to the great exalted position they had received from God, so these men became enemies of Christ as they, betraying the trust passed along to them from the Apostles, attacked His Church and its Magisterium.[6] He said that by using poor science and unfounded theories, they sunk below *"the most uncultured nations"* where reason was concerned.[7]

St. Thomas Aquinas said that while *real science* shows man as a humble servant, and defines all things except man, great; *false science* worships man and shows all things, small and insignificant by comparison.

He wrote that the good Angels escort the departed to Purgatory to begin their new life which will culminate with their triumphant entry into Heaven. He also said:

"The same fire that punishes the damned in Hell, chastises the Suffering Souls in Purgatory; and if you were to take the greatest pain we can suffer on earth, it would not compare to the smallest pain we will suffer in Purgatory."

---

[6] the Church's accepted teaching
[7] cf St. Ignatius of Loyola from book: *"Charity for the Suffering Souls"* by Fr. John A. Nageleisen

A Poor Soul appeared to **St. Mechtildis**[8] and shared that the greatest pain suffered by the souls in Purgatory, is that they cannot be with God, and if all the desires of mankind could be grouped together, they would not equal the *all-consuming desire* of one soul for God.

But, there is good news in Purgatory! We know that there is the pain of separation from God and family, and a yearning, a hunger for eternal life with the Triune God. But the good news is that God in His Infinite Mercy does not leave those who are being detained in Purgatory, alone to suffer. One theologian[9] wrote that when the soul leaves the body, it is granted all the necessary senses to communicate with *other souls* and the Heavenly Angels that may come to this temporary stopover.

According to **St. Catherine of Genoa**, the Poor Souls can comfort and support one another to the fullness of their own love and charity, to the degree they are empowered by Almighty God.

St. Bridget had a vision during one of her ecstasies of a soul who had received a triple sentence: (1)an inner and outer fire that almost consumed it, (2) extremely bitter cold, accompanied by (3) callous, rapid, repetitious bombardments from the devil.

St. John Chrysostom said in one of his homilies that it was not without solid reasoning that the Apostles passed down the remembrance of the departed during the Sacrifice of the Cross, for it makes sense that, as the priest offers the Victim, Jesus Christ, to the faithful Father, on the Altar of Sacrifice, the Father would be moved to show mercy toward the departed souls who have died in the Faith.

We repeat **St. Monica's** last words to her son, St. Augustine: *"Lay this body anywhere; be not concerned about*

---

[8]a Benedictine who was a contemporary of St. Gertrude the Great
[9]Bautz

that.   *Only this I beg of you, that wherever you may be,
remember me at the Lord's Altar."*

St. Augustine affirmed *St. Paul's* teaching on Purgatory
by writing:

*"Punish me in Thy wrath, that I may be cleansed in this
world, and so transformed that I shall not stand in need of
the purifying flames, like those that are 'saved as if by fire.'
Why this?   Because they built on the foundation (walls
made of) with wood, hay and stubble, here below.   Had
they built (them) with gold, silver and precious stones, they
would be safe from both fires, not only from the everlasting
one[10] that shall torture the wicked forever, but also from
the one[11] that purifies those that are saved by fire."*

St. Augustine based this on St. Paul's dissertation to the
Corinthians[12] where he teaches that there are those who
attain Heaven by fire.[13] He also explains that there are those
who build on the Foundation Who is Jesus Christ Himself,
but they build a house of wood, hay and stubble; that is, they
believe in Christ but soon *temptations* overshadow *good
works*.   The Church Fathers teach that gold, silver and
precious stones stand for *good works*; and wood, hay and
stubble for *venial sins and failings*.

St. Augustine clearly states the Church's position on
Purgatory when he points to St. Paul, for those he
mentioned are not only examined but made to burn, so that
they suffer by *fire*. The fire of which he writes cannot mean
the fire of Hell, because the one that suffers by the fire is
saved after suffering. It can only mean the purification by
fire, after death, called *Purgatory*.

*And so, the battle rages on, but we will all know the truth
when we depart this earth.*

---

[10]Hell
[11]Purgatory
[12]1Cor 3:9-15
[13]Purgatory

Saved by the Blood of the Lamb

"The Ecumenical Council teaches that there is a Purgatory, and that the souls confined therein are assisted by the suffrages[1] of the faithful, and especially by the Holy Sacrifice of the Altar." - **The Council of Trent**

The Sacrifice of the Mass is the most powerful means to obtain mercy for the *Poor Souls in Purgatory*. Because it is the ongoing Sacrifice of the Cross, where *the Victim-Priest* Jesus Christ unites with the victim-priest, His ambassador *"in persona Cristi capitas,"*[2] offering Himself for the redemption of the sins of the world, it is in itself sufficient to move the Father's Heart to forgive us our sins. So great were the hurts of the Father, wounds caused by man's unfaithfulness and lack of caring, the only acceptable sacrifice was the Sacrifice of His only Son on the Cross.

Every time the Mass is offered in memory of Jesus' Passion, Death and Resurrection, the Father cannot resist His Son's plea for the sinners of the world. All Jesus has to do is show Him His pierced Hands; it is enough to move His Heart to pity. The Blood, shed by the Lamb of God redeemed the sins of the world, and during the Sacrifice of the Mass, again and again, sins are being forgiven by the Father. But based on the severity and long-range damage done by sins of the Poor Soul, more than one Mass may be necessary to pay the debt owed. For, although their sins were forgiven, full recompense may not have been exacted for the harm done.

---

[1]Suffrages are additional prayers of the Divine Office for particular intentions, such as the Church. - Catholic Encyclopedia, Broderick

[2]*"In the ecclesial (Church) service of the ordained minister, it is Christ Himself Who is present to His Church as Head of the Body, Shepherd of His flock, High Priest of the Redemptive Sacrifice, Teacher of Truth. This is what the Church means by saying that the priest, by virtue of Holy Orders, acts in persona Christi Capitas."* - The Catholic Catechism

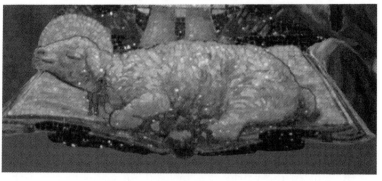

Above:
The Spotless Lamb - Sacrificed for us - Mosaic on the wall of Church of the Transfiguration in the Holy Land
The Blood, shed by the Lamb of God redeemed the sins of the world, and during the Sacrifice of the Mass, again and again, sins are forgiven by the Father.

Above:
Father Jay Voorhies of the Diocese of Lafayette, Louisiana, offering the Holy Sacrifice of the Mass in our Chapel. Fr. Jay is Bob and Penny Lord's spiritual son and has been Spiritual Director on many of our Journeys of Faith Pilgrimages.

Because the Mass is most pleasing to the Father, were it to produce its full power, one Mass could obtain the full release from Purgatory of not only *one* soul but all the souls there.[3] But this is not the Will of Our Lord Jesus Christ. He has willed and ordained that this Sacrifice have a limited amount of atonement, to be determined by Him, so that this Sacrifice will be offered more often and more fervently.[4]

St. Thomas Aquinas wrote:

"Although the power of Christ in the Sacrament of the Holy Eucharist is infinite, yet the effect for which the Sacrament is ordained is limited."

St. John Chrysostom said that every time *"Holy Mass is celebrated, 'the Angels hasten to open the gates of Purgatory.'"*

Then, do not our *own Guardian Angels* rush to open the gates of Heaven to let us in? They have been with us in Purgatory, except for when they have gone to ask for prayers and Masses to be offered for our release from Purgatory.

The Blood of the Lamb of God - the ultimate Sacrifice

As Mass was about to begin in the Church of the Miracle of the Eucharist in Erding, Germany,[5] we saw, at the the side altar, a Lamb on the Cross, His Blood spilling into a chalice, symbolizing the Sacrifice of the Mass, the ongoing Sacrifice of the Cross. Two bastions crossed in front of the Lamb: one with a sponge and the other a spear. The pole with the sponge, dipped in bitter wine[6] represented the world's response to Jesus' cry, *"I thirst."* Jesus refused to drink from *that cup.*

But when the *Father* handed His Son the bitter cup, He drank from it! You remember, Jesus said in the Garden of

---

[3]St. Thomas Aquinas
[4]Teachings of Patritius Sporer, moral theologian of the 17th century
[5]You can learn more about this Miracle from Bob and Penny Lord's video documentary, as well as their book:
"This is My Body, This is My Blood, Miracles of the Eucharist" Book I
[6]wine mixed with gall

Gethsemane, "*If it be Thy will, let this cup pass from Me. But not My Will but Thy Will be done.*"[7] Jesus did not relish the idea of drinking from this cup, but He did, and this perfect act of obedience on the part of the Son was enough to soften the anger of the Father.

And then, when the spear pierced Our Savior's Side, and Our Lord shed His last ounce of Blood, the Church and the Sacraments flowed from His Side, and life began for us.

When Jesus said these last words, "*It is finished*" and gave up His Spirit to the Father, the Father forgave the world its sins and opened the gates of Heaven, the eternal plan was resurrected, and Death was cheated of its sting. The work of the *enemy* had failed, and now creation would once again be with its Creator. And all because of the Blood shed by Jesus, the Lamb of God.

†

It all started in the Garden of Eden, with our first parents. God had created them to be pure and sinless, giving them the "*Free Will*" to love Him.   They had everything, dominion over all God's creation on earth; they were happy; they were content. But the enemy of God was angry; he never wants God's creatures to love God. So, he planted the seeds of discontent and disobedience with the prize being the gift of Pride. He sought out Adam's partner, Eve. He knew her influence over Adam. And so, the woman was used to lure the first man into the sin of disobedience.

Man was created to be free from the inclination to sin, misery, pain, and even death.   But sin destroyed God's original plan for man. And who was the instigator of this sin that had such dire repercussions? The same one who not only disobeyed God, he convinced other angels to do so, as well. And it is said, because of that one final decisive act, one third of the angels were thrown out of Heaven, never to

---

[7]Matt 26:39

return.   The peace that had been God's plan for man appeared to be lost forever.   But even as He was chastising His first creatures, He was planning the salvation of their descendants.   He would send His Son to suffer and die on the Cross for the redemption of their descendants, so that no more would the gates of Heaven be closed to mankind.

Jesus was born, and suffered, and died so that *"The people who walked in darkness have seen a great light; to them that dwelt in the region of the shadow of death, light is risen."*[8] This is our hope.

Souls being released from Purgatory as a result of the Mass.

One Saint said that she saw Sisters from her convent being released from Purgatory after one Mass was said for them.   There were times **St. Mechtildis**[9] said that she could see The Lord, His Mother Mary and a Host of Angels surrounding the Altar, offering up their merits[10] for the Poor Souls for whom the Mass was being celebrated.   She said that she saw some Souls who had been privileged to assist in their own Mass and then soar immediately to Heaven.

†

A daughter of **St. Elizabeth Queen of Portugal**, died, soon after she was married to the King of Castile (Spain). Upon hearing of her daughter's death, St. Elizabeth rushed to her husband's side, to tell him of their loss.   No sooner had she tearfully shared the devastating news, than a hermit arrived at the castle and asked to see the King and Queen.[11] He reported, their daughter had appeared to him and cried that she had been sentenced to a long and painful

---

[8]Isaiah 9:2

[9]Benedictine Nun and close friend of St. Gertrude

[10]The Catholic Encyclopedia by Broderick defines a *"merit as a good work performed for another, which entitles one to a reward."*   Through Jesus we will receive an *"unworldly reward,"* the Father's Mercy which is gained by the Blood of the Lamb.

[11]St. Elizabeth and her husband

punishment in Purgatory; but if her parents would have Masses said each day for one year, she would be released after the year was up. The parents did as the hermit told them and, at the end of the year, their daughter appeared in a vision to St. Elizabeth and told her that because of the Masses that had been celebrated for her, she had been released from Purgatory and was about to join the Savior in Heaven.

†

What do we do when a loved one dies? Mourn! I remember my mother saying: *"Listen, daughter, when your father and I die, first take care of business and then mourn."* My mother, being a very practical woman was referring to the business of the *world*. Now, at this stage of my maturity as a Catholic, I would say to my family, *"Have Masses said for me, and then if you must, mourn. Although I know that you will be in pain, Masses said for my soul will be for my sake, mourning will be for yours. So, first take care of the business at hand and then mourn."*

I still remember, 25 years later, when our most precious son died.[12] First we mourned and then we felt sorry for ourselves, and then we left the Church and Jesus. The contradictory thing about this was that once a year (even when we no longer believed in Jesus, we thought) we would have a Mass said for our boy and attend that Mass. When God had enough of our self-destructive behavior, He took over our lives and *we came back home* to our Church and to Jesus. *But I still mourned.* What time I wasted when we could have been having Masses said for our son! I did not know about the power of having Masses said for the Poor Souls in Purgatory. Besides, our parish priest said our boy was in Heaven, and although that was very kind and

---

[12]Read Bob and Penny's autobiography in their book: *"We Came Back to Jesus."*

consoling of him, how could he be so sure?   We have received signs that would make us believe our boy is in Heaven, but believe me, that has not stopped us from praying for his soul at each Mass we attend daily.

I guess what brought this to my mind, at this time, was when I read about a mother who also lost a son. Like me, she grieved inconsolably, never once thinking of having Masses said for her son's soul. When the Lord in His mercy decided to set *her* straight, He showed her a vision of young people joyously processing up to Heaven. She desperately searched the crowd for her son. Coming slowly from the rear of the procession was a young man who was struggling to keep up with the rest.   His sagging body was being weighed down by a heavy wet cloak which impeded his progress. It was her son! He lamented:

"Dear mother, this garment, which you have made heavy with your tears, hampers me from keeping up with my friends. Please stop crying; and if you really love me, help me by praying for me and my soul, give alms, attend Holy Mass, have Masses said for me and do acts of mercy."

†

Then there was the Saint who, upon hearing of his father's death, began to mourn him terribly, becoming deeply upset and anxious over his father's passing. One day after praying fervently, pleading with the Lord to know his father's fate, he heard a voice say:

"Instead of wasting time and prayer trying to find out the state of your father's soul, why do you not pray for his release from Purgatory, in the event he is there? In that way, your prayers may assist him, or if he is not in need of your prayers, you will be helped by the other Souls in Purgatory to whom the Blessed Mother may assign your prayers and who will pray for you when they enter the Kingdom."

The Saint now began to pray zealously for his father's release from Purgatory. The following night, he saw a vision of his father, suffering, agonizing, tormented. With an anguished cry, he called out to his son for some relief. The Saint redoubled his prayers. Adding Masses and acts of mercy, he petitioned for his father's reprieve. He continued faithfully, until he received word that his father's soul had been released from Purgatory. From that day on, the Saint became an ardent advocate of praying for the Poor Souls in Purgatory, and encouraged everyone, to pray for those who may be languishing in Purgatory.

†

There was a Dominican who not only did *not* pray for the Poor Souls in Purgatory, he discouraged people from doing so, as well, saying:

"Why trouble yourselves about Souls who are in Purgatory. They are in no danger of going to Hell. Their place in Heaven has been assured. I will instead work for those Souls on earth who are in danger of losing their immortal Souls, because of the horrible sins they commit each day. I celebrate all my Masses for their conversion, and I have no doubt that my prayers will be answered and they will not perish."[13]

Although we are sure his intentions were good, and he sincerely meant to do God's Will and not his own, he nevertheless forgot the Church's teachings, the dogma which states that *the faithful can, by prayer and good works, especially the Holy Sacrifice of the Mass, assist the Souls suffering in Purgatory.*

This is one time, when the Lord allowed the Poor Souls to come to earth and attack the instrument that was cheating them of their salvation. As a priest, he was ordained to bring this mercy to the Poor Souls in Purgatory by celebrating the

---

[13]paraphrased by the authors

Holy Sacrifice of the Mass. The Souls were justified in their indignation; they reproached him, following him everywhere, taunting him, showing him the reason for their distress, and then finally explaining that it was God Himself that allowed them to leave their chamber of horror to remind His priest of his duty toward the dead.

Now, the priest was really a holy priest and so he changed his ways. He not only offered Holy Mass frequently for the dead, he encouraged other priests to do so and, in his sermons, reached out to the Laity to pray for the Poor Souls. He confessed his past errors and spent the rest of his days trying to undo the harm he had done. A wonderful theologian once said that the difference between someone who has made an error and a heretic is that one admits he is in error and asks Mother Church for forgiveness and pardon, and the other, mostly out of pride, dies, his heresy still on his lips, the enemy of Pride blocking him from reconciling with the Truth (Mother Church)!

†

Another instance where the Lord allowed a Poor Soul to leave Purgatory: **Blessed Henry Suso** and a brother priest made a pact: whoever died first, the one who remained would celebrate Mass for the departed brother twice a week, for a year. A few years passed and his brother priest died. Father Suso began to pray and fast, but had not had an opportunity to celebrate Mass for him. A short time after his death, the deceased priest appeared to Father Suso and chastised him. He was downcast, upset. He demanded: *"Why have you not kept your promise to say Masses for me? I am suffering horribly!"* Father Suso defended himself with: *"I prayed for you!"* His friend pounded on the table:

"Although your prayers please God, they are not adequate to satisfy the debt I owe to God. Only the Blood of the Lamb, the Sacrifice of the Mass, will begin to put an end to this torment. It is the Blood of Our Lord Jesus

Sacrificed, that is offered up during the Mass, that we suffering Souls in Purgatory are in need of. I would have already been delivered from this chamber of torture if you had kept your promise."

✝

Our beloved Saint Anthony, Defender of the Eucharist and Hammer of Heretics tells this of **Blessed John of Alverna**. One *All Saints' Day*, when Blessed John was offering the Holy Sacrifice of the Mass, a most unusual thing happened. While he was consecrating the Host, saying the words that would change the bread into the Body, Blood, Soul and Divinity of Jesus Christ, he found himself imploring God the Father, through the Blood and suffering of His Only Begotten Son, to release some Souls from Purgatory. To his amazement, what should he see, but *platoons* of Holy Souls having been ransomed by the Mass, departing from a raging furnace in Purgatory, soaring toward their eternal mansion in Heaven.

✝

The Holy Mass is essentially the same Sacrifice as the one offered by Jesus on the Cross, to God the Father, on Calvary that blessed day when the world stood still and we would never be the same. The Council of Trent declares:

"In this Divine Sacrifice of the Mass there is contained the same Christ Who offered Himself on the Cross in a bloody manner, the only difference being that in the Mass He offers Himself in an unbloody manner."

To prove that the Sacrifice of the Mass is virtually the same as the Sacrifice of the Cross, Mother Church further declares:

"For it is the same Victim, and same Minister of Sacrifice through the agency[14] of the priest, Who once

---

[14]the faculties of his priesthood

offered the Sacrifice on the Cross; only the manner of sacrificing is different."

It further states that the Sacrifice of the Mass is not only a Mass of thanksgiving and praise, it is also "*a Sacrifice of Reconciliation for the living and the dead.*"[15]

When we ponder the true meaning of the Holy Mass, that it is the ongoing Sacrifice of the Cross, and recall Jesus reconciled all men to the Father through His Passion and Death on the Cross, we join in the great Mystery of God's infinite love for us, we *the living* and those souls who have departed, *the dead.* Through *this Sacrifice,* the Holy Mass becomes a Mass of thanksgiving and praise to the Lord Who loved us so much, He opened His Arms wide and died on the Cross. *This is the Lord we love; this is the Lord to Whom we offer thanksgiving; this is the Lord Who deserves our praise.*

The Council of Trent mentions *the dead;*   Now, Jesus descended into Hell "*...to free the just who had gone before Him.*" He "*delivered those holy souls, who awaited their Savior in Abraham's bosom.*"[16] - referring to the dead. So, through the Sacrifice of the Mass, Jesus once again offers Himself to the Father, for those who repose in *Purgatory,* reconciling them with the Father, through this Sacrifice wiping away the last remnants of the stain of sin.

On the Cross, Jesus reconciled us, *the living,* to His Father; He asked Him to forgive His persecutors, those who crucified Him, and those today who pierce His Heart with their disobedience and apathy. He pleaded: "*They know not what they do.*" And commending His Spirit to the Father, He drew His last breath, and we were saved, saved by the Blood of the Lamb. And the Poor Souls in Purgatory are saved by the Blood of the Lamb. *Have Masses said for the Poor Souls in Purgatory.*

---

[15]cf The authors have paraphrased for better understanding
[16]Catholic Catechism #633

Epilog

Family, researching and writing this book has been one of the most emotional experiences we've ever had. It has been exciting, inspiring, frightening, uplifting. It has called us to new commitment! We've been brought back to some of the values of our childhood, long forgotten.

We learned most of the teachings on *Heaven, Hell and Purgatory*, sometime in our early Catholic School training, granted, not with as much depth as in this book. But the Souls in Purgatory were always in the recesses of our minds and hearts during our formative years. The good sisters encouraged us to pray for the release of the Poor Souls from Purgatory. And hand in hand, we also prayed very often and fervently for the conversion of sinners, so that there would be fewer Souls in Purgatory, and hopefully none going to Hell. On the *Feast of All Souls,* we wrote on little envelopes, we received in church, all the names of loved ones who had died. During the month of November, our pastor kept those envelopes on the Altar, so that the Poor Souls would be remembered, during the Sacrifice of the Mass.

But what has happened? We're twenty, thirty, forty years older. We've forgotten the devotions to the Poor Souls in Purgatory, which were so important to us when we were young. When we should have been offering Masses and sacrifices for their release from Purgatory, instead we have regressed to the pagan ways of our ancestors, supplanting the life-saving rituals of the Church with the fancy caskets and expensive floral arrangements which will get no one into Heaven. An ironic thing, now that we're older, we know more and more people who have died; yet say fewer prayers, have fewer Masses said, and make fewer sacrifices than we did when we knew fewer people who had died. Brother Joseph's daddy is 82 years old, and he says he's a stranger in his hometown; everyone his age is dead.

Well, they may all be in Purgatory, Willie! Pray for them, so that someday they will be praying for you in Heaven.

We always wonder why the Lord has us do, whatever He assigns us, at a given time in the history of the world. What is there that He knows that we don't know, and should know? Is it *He* Who is bringing this book to us about *Heaven, Hell and Purgatory*? Is He saying, we should be willing, no, anxious to spend our Purgatory on earth? Is He through this book, imploring us to not do the things that will land us in Purgatory, no less Hell? Is He not saying that He and His Most Precious Mother are waiting for us in Heaven?

We said in this book that there have been so many indicators that we're in the *Latter Days*, we should take very seriously the mandates that Our Lord Jesus gave to St. Gertrude the Great, St. Margaret Mary Alacoque, and in our own century, Blessed Sr. Faustina, to pray, pray constantly to His Sacred Heart for His Mercy.

Why did the Lord inspire us to write this book, at this time? Could it be that our deceased relatives, whether they be mothers and fathers, brothers and sisters, aunts and uncles, cousins, grandparents, and descendants going back five and ten generations, are begging us to pray for their release from Purgatory? Are Our Lord and Mother Mary trying to warn of us of something that will happen in the final days of the *Second Millennium?* We are on a crash course of destruction, and our Holy Family doesn't want us to be caught up in the devastation. Our greatest weapons have never changed, the Mass, the Rosary, sacrifices for the Souls in Purgatory and the conversion of sinners. Use them! Take to heart St. Paul's command to the Ephesians:

"Put on the armor of God, that you may be able to stand against the wiles of the devil. For our wrestling is not against flesh and blood, but against the Principalities and the Powers, against the world rulers of this present darkness, against the spiritual forces of wickedness on high.(Eph 6:11-12)

Bibliography

Broderick, Robert C. *The Catholic Encyclopedia*
　　Thomas Nelson Inc. Publishers Nashville 1970
Cathechism of the Catholic Church
　　Libreria Editrice Vaticana - 1994
New Catholic Encyclopedia
　　Catholic University of America - Washington, DC 1967
Companion to the Catechism of the Catholic Church
　　Ignatius Press - Oakland, CA 1994
E. K. Lynch, Fr. O.Carm - *Mary's Gift to Carmel*
　　The Friars - Aylesford, Kent 1950
St. John Bosco - *Dreams, Visions and Prophecies*
　　Don Bosco Multimedia - New Rochelle, NY 1986
Sr. Lucia - *Fatima in Lucia's own words*
　　Postulation Centre - Fatima Portugal 1976
John de Marchi I.M.C. - *The Crusade of Fatima*
　　Missoes Consolata - Fatima, Portugal 1964
Abbe Francois Trochu - *St. Bernadette Soubirous*
　　Tan Publications - Rockford, IL 1975
Butler, Thurston Atwater - *Lives of the Saints*
　　Christian Classics - Westminster, MD 1980
Lord, Bob & Penny
　　Saints and Other Powerful Men in the Church 1990
　　Saints and Other Powerful Women in the Church 1989
　　This Is My Body, This Is My Blood 1986
　　Visionaries, Mystics & Stigmatists - 1995
Fr. Alessio Parente OFM Cap.- *The Holy Souls*
　　Editions of Padre Pio of Pietrelcina
　　San.Giovanni. Rotondo, Italy 1988
Order of Benedictines - *St. Gertrude the Great*
　　Tan Publications - Rockford, IL 1976
F.X. Schouppe, SJ - *Purgatory Explained*
　　Tan Publications - Rockford, IL 1986
John R. Nagielsen Rev - *Charity for the Suffering Souls*
　　Tan Publications - Rockford, IL 1982

Padre Pio of Pietrelcina - *Letters - Vol 1 - Vol 2*
   Voice of Padre Pio - S. G. Rotondo Italy 1980
St. Catherine of Genoa -
   Spiritual Dialogue and Treatise on Hell and Purgatory
   Tan Publications - Rockford, IL 1989
Franz Werfel - *The Song of Bernadette*
   Pocket Books - New York 1940

Journeys of Faith®

To Order: 1-800-633-2484 FAX 916-853-0132 E-mail BPLord23@aol.com

Books

Bob and Penny Lord are authors of best sellers:

This Is My Body, This Is My Blood;
Miracles of the Eucharist Book I $9.95 Paperback only
This Is My Body, This Is My Blood;
Miracles of the Eucharist Book II $13.95 Paperback only
The Many Faces Of Mary, A Love Story $9.95 Paperback $13.95 Hardcover
We Came Back To Jesus $9.95 Paperback $13.95 Hardcover
Saints and Other Powerful Women in the Church $13.95 Paperback only
Saints and Other Powerful Men in the Church $14.95 Paperback only
Heavenly Army of Angels $13.95 Paperback only
Scandal of the Cross and Its Triumph $13.95 Paperback only
The Rosary - The Life of Jesus and Mary $13.95 Hardcover only
Martyrs - They Died for Christ $13.95 Paperback only
Visionaries, Mystics, and Stigmatists $13.95 Paperback only
Visions of Heaven, Hell and Purgatory $13.95 Paperback only

Please add $4.00 S&H for first book: $1.00 each add'l book

Videos and On-site Documentaries

Bob and Penny's Video Series based on their books:
A 13 part series on the Miracles of the Eucharist - filmed on-site
A 15 part series on The Many Faces of Mary - filmed on-site
A 23 part series on Martyrs - They Died for Christ - filmed on-site
A 10 part series on Saints and Other Powerful Women in the Church
A 12 part series on Saints and Other Powerful Men in the Church
A 14 part series on Visionaries, Mystics and Stigmatists
Many other on-site Documentaries based on Miracles of the Eucharist, Mother Mary's Apparitions, and the Heavenly Army of Angels. Request our list.
Our books and videos are available in Spanish also

Pilgrimages

Bob and Penny Lord's ministry take out Pilgrimages to the Shrines of Europe, and Mexico every year. Come and join them on one of these special Retreat Pilgrimages. Call for more information, and ask for the latest pilgrimage brochure.

Lecture Series

Bob and Penny travel to all parts of the world to spread the Good News. They speak on what they have written about in their books. If you would like to have them come to your area, call for information on a lecture series in your area.

Good Newsletter

We are publishers of the Good Newsletter, which is published four times a year. This newsletter will provide timely articles on our Faith, plus keep you informed with the activities of our community. Call 1-800-633-2484 for information.